Religion as Self-Transcendence

Religion as Self-Transcendence

A Study of the Concept of Transcendence in Louis Dupré

Savio D'Souza

CWI

Christian World Imprints™

First Published in 2018 by

Christian World Imprints(TM)
Christian Publishing & Books from India
H-12 Bali Nagar, **New Delhi-110015**
info@christianworldimprints.com
www.ChristianWorldImprints.com
Phone: +91 11 25465925

ISBN: 978-93-5148-306-9

Cataloging in Publication Data--DK
Courtesy: D.K. Agencies (P) Ltd. <docinfo@dkagencies.com>

D'Souza, Savio, 1966- **author.**
Religion as self-transcendence : a study of the concept of transcendence in Louis Dupré / Savio D'Souza.
pages cm
Includes bibliographical references.
ISBN 9789351483069

1. Dupré, Louis K., 1925- 2. Transcendence (Philosophy) 3. Self (Philosophy) 4. Philosophy and religion. 5. Experience (Religion) I. Title.

LCC BR100.D76 2018 | DDC 190 23

Printed in India.

This book is dedicated to my dad, Peter D'Souza,
my mum Phoebe D'Souza, Princelene, Princeton & Neil.

Also to Fr. Ivo Coelho SDB, and Professor Giovanni Magnani SJ

They are people whom I hold in much esteem.

Contents

Chapter 1

Introduction

Nearly all individuals at some point or the other of their lives have had an experience wherein they realize that their existence is part of a greater reality. It could be a beautiful sunset, it could be the sight of a child at play, it could be the soothing sound of a church organ, or it could just be the sense of peace one experiences in the stillness of the desert. All of a sudden one is encompassed by an all embracing feeling of mystery and unity. There could be different reasons or prior experiences which might have led to this particular experience, but they all lead to a feeling, or an awareness of transcendence. Generally, such an experience makes us aware of our radical insufficiency and at the same time points us beyond to a reality that is outside the usual limits of our comprehension. It makes us aware of another dimension in the universe. We become aware of our finitude, but at the same time we are able to see that we are fragments, yet part of a greater reality.

To a certain extent such experiences wherein one confronts one's insufficiency are unavoidable because every human being has an innate need to find the significance and meaning of his or her existence. This search for the meaning of one's existence on one hand brings one face to face with one's limitations, while at the same time it makes one aware of a greater reality, of the other dimension. This awareness usually marks the beginning of a journey that has as its aim the discovery, expression and better understanding of the transcendent reality.

The human being is a rational animal and it is his intelligence that sets man apart from other animals. Other animals too have intelligence to a lesser or a greater degree, but what is significant is that each being has a role to play and hence is a part of the great circle of life. And in this complex formation man as an intelligent animal has a special place because he is also a spiritual being. As a spiritual being he is aware of the place that he holds in the entire universe and especially his relation with the ultimate reality that lies within and yet beyond this physical universe. This 'religious' concern has been seen in human beings since creation as is evidenced in the belief in the afterlife that existed in the earliest of human civilizations. We refer to the innate sense of being religious that each and every man possesses.

1.1 The Essence of Religion

Usually this experience of transcendence has to be described using metaphorical language because we have to speak in 'this worldly' terms about something beyond this world and its impact on us. Use of such language is unavoidable since as 'this worldly' creatures we are unable to speak of transcendence as it is in itself. To describe this ultimate, and our relation with it we use religion. There are different ways of naming and understanding this transcendent some of which are in personal terms, others of which are impersonal. But what is of significance is that each account of looking at and understanding transcendence is significant. We cannot say that because one of them is correct therefore all the others are wrong because each one is a particular response to the transcendence and each one in its own way is the mode in which the ultimate has been experienced and responded to, and hence conceived. This generally happens within the structure of religion. When we speak about religion we realize that since the concept and understanding of religion existed much before the word itself, there are different views and attempts to define religion. Man has constantly grappled with the transcendent, at times affirming it and often denying it. Today, the word 'religion' is applied to most phenomena that are referred to as religious. The problem is, that often the paraphernalia that are usually connected with religion are confused with religion and hence leads to different conclusions about the essence of religion.

In speaking of the essence of religion Giovanni Magnani describes religion as a personal relation with God which is not only an individual relationship, but is also communitarian. Through this relation, the whole person in all its dimensions comes into an integral relation with God. Magnani goes on to describe the religious experience as having an intellectual component, a voluntary or willing component, an affective component and an active component.[1] This explanation by Magnani highlights two important aspects of religion. Firstly, that religion involves the acceptance of an ultimate reality that could involve a trans-empirical realm, and secondly, a relationship with this realm, the experience of which leads to certain emotions, behaviour or attitudes in the person.

Dupré describes religion as being very flexible. He looks at religion not merely as an acceptance of a given sacred reality, but he looks at it as a complex

---

[1] Cf. Giovanni Magnani, *Filosofia della Religione* (Roma: Editrice Pontificia Università Gregoriana, 1993), 114-115.

dialectical relation of the mind to reality, a dialectic that opens up a new dimension in human existence. As Dupré writes in *The Other Dimension*:

> The religious act is not a simple experience, but a complex movement by which the mind discovers a new reality which, although lying beyond the phenomenal and contrasting with it, ultimately integrates all reality in a higher synthesis. This other dimension of consciousness is the same today as it was in the past. Yet on the whole the sacred is no longer directly experienced. Modern man has access to it in the more reflective and deliberate attitude of faith. Yet, in faith, however unemotional, he achieves the same all-comprehensive unity... It is essential to the religious experience to overcome the opposition between subject and object. The religious symbol and its mythical explication bring this subjective-objective unity to expression... the concept of God originates exclusively in, and is developed solely by, the religious act.[2]

We realize that in speaking of religion we refer to the self, to the transcendent and also to the relation between the two. For this reason it is significant that Dupré describes religion as a dynamic association of mind and reality which is enhanced by cultural and personal factors.

This feeling or experience of the boundless, of something out there which is much greater than what we are is what allows for this openness to the infinite and which leads us to think and reflect on transcendence. It is through the concept of transcendence that we are able to look at the possibility of and examine the relationship between the immanent and the transcendent dimension. It is this movement of transcendence that takes place within us that could lead to the awareness of God and this in turn in many instances leads to a commitment to the transcendent. And as human beings who are intelligent and rational, the possibility to go beyond ourselves to that which lies beyond is not just one of the many aspects of our existence, but rather, it is 'the' meaning giving factor of our life. The core of religion and the religious attitude in man is this impulse within himself to go beyond. The core is transcendence.

1.2 The Unfolding of the Concept of Transcendence

When we speak about transcendence it is interesting to briefly note the development of the concept from the earliest understandings of the term. The ancients had the all-comprehensive creative principle of nature or *physis*. Thales was perhaps one of the first to speak about it. Later this principle developed into the term *kosmos* as an ordered totality of being which included the transcendent, human and cosmic dimensions. In order to express nature in its entirety *Kosmos* is always seen in conjunction with *physis*. Nature is one united whole with three dimensions, the

---

[2] Louis Dupré, *The Other Dimension: A Search for the Meaning of Religious Attitudes* (New York: Doubleday and Company, Inc., 1972), 10-11.

cosmic, the human and the transcendent. Gradually, as history developed the transcendent was separated from the cosmic and the human dimensions of reality. This new shift especially in the medieval times broke up the unity of nature and as a consequence the element of transcendence was relegated to a separate realm. So, human beings and nature became subservient to God. One of the factors that contributed to this separation was the causal relation that was considered between God and creation. Christian thinkers of the middle ages, especially Thomas Aquinas, explained the relation between God and creation from the Christian point of view through a synthesis with Aristotelian efficient causality. But, then he had to balance this concept with Platonic participation. Later, the Aristotelian framework was abandoned and the synthesis that recognized God as the cause of creation and human action deteriorated. The nominalist theories of the fourteenth and fifteenth centuries developed the idea of an unrestricted divine power with practically no relation between Creator and creature. God was practically banished from creation and the transcendent which had been separated from nature was moved to a 'supernatural' domain. With God on another realm and separated from nature, the human subject became the sole meaning-giving agent and this signalled the dawn of modernity. Humankind was the sole master of nature. And nature, separated from its transcendent and human elements was reduced to merely the cosmos. The cosmos was only an object while the human subject is the exclusive source of reason imposed upon reality. As a consequence the human subject is reduced to a mere function in the process of objectification. As the real has no meaning of its own, the only encounter with transcendent meaning is in the lived experience of one's own subjectivity.[3]

The journey from the earliest all-comprehensive principle to the modern day loss of transcendence has been a long and yet interesting journey. In this book, we shall examine how Louis Dupré looked at the concept of Transcendence. And we shall also examine whether this lost transcendence can be recovered. The concept of transcendence will be dealt with later in the book but let us have an initial look at the term 'transcendence.'

1.3 The Concept of Transcendence

Transcendence can be looked at from three points of view. It can be looked at from a metaphysical point view, an epistemological point of view, or as is most common from a religious point of view. From a metaphysical point of view, as we have said earlier, every person confronts the feeling of uneasiness that comes from the awareness that there is something lacking within himself or herself. This need for fullness initiates a search for that which is beyond the ontological self and this

[3] Cf. Paul Levesque, "The possibility of encountering God in Postmodernity: A return to Apophatic Theology" in *The Presence of Transcendence: Thinking 'Sacrament' in a Postmodern Age*, ed. Lieven Boeve and John C. Ries (Leuven: Peeters, 2001), 108-109.

is the search for transcendence. Precisely this point of view gives rise to a problem since the human being is on the ontological level while transcendence seems to lead to another level of existence. So the question that arises is, "How can I know this transcendence which lies 'beyond'?" From this point of view it can be studied as an epistemological issue. The third point of view is from that of religion. As we have mentioned earlier, religion deals with the sacred or the trans-empirical, and our relation with it. While we are concerned with that which is beyond, the relation is in-this-world, and so is expressed in symbols, language, art and rituals. Besides these three points of view, from another perspective transcendence can also be spoken of as 'divine' transcendence or also as 'human' transcendence. In our study of the concept of transcendence we are not talking of some 'thing' but we are concerned about the religious attitude in the person that enables him to reach beyond himself and beyond the world to that which belongs to the other dimension. It is for this reason that we have chosen to study the concept as it has been dealt with in the writings of Louis Dupré. More than studying the characteristics of the transcendent we look at transcendence as a quest to discover the beyond. This quest for the other dimension need not lie only in the traditional beyond, but it could be innermost to the self. We strive to examine this movement of transcendence that enables us to discover that other dimension.

1.4 Reasons for the Choice of the Topic

The title of this book is "Religion as Self-Transcendence: A study of the concept of Transcendence in Louis Dupré." There are many reasons for the choice of this topic. I found in Louis Dupré a resonance of my own experience of the crisis that was being witnessed in the culture of modern civilization, especially in the West. The search for answers led to an effort to understand this crisis of culture especially in the West, the reasons for the crisis and also a direction towards a possible solution. My study made me realize that this was not just a crisis of society, but that this crisis was reflected in philosophy too, especially in the strong movement towards the subject. In the writings of Louis Dupré I found that the situation had been well documented and examined and that he also presented the seeds of a possible solution. While I do agree that Dupré does not have the ultimate solution, I do believe in his interpretation of the present situation and the direction that he indicates toward a solution. We all feel the need for transcendence, but there is a wide gap between the eternal truths of our religion and a faith that is historical. Hence, it becomes increasingly difficult to fill this gap between our religious faith and religion as lived in our day-to-day life with its challenges and difficulties. The loss of transcendence should not result in a sense of defeat and desperation but our awareness of transcendence can serve as an impetus to rediscover this transcendence by striving for an interiority of existence. Religion can help us experience this transcendence. The experience and expression of religion and the religious can lead us to transcendence.

1.5 Life Sketch of Louis Dupré

Louis Dupré was born in Veerle, Belgium in the year 1925. In the year 1950, he completed a Licentiate in Philosophy at the Berchmanianum in Nijmegen, Netherlands. A Doctorate in Philosophy followed from the Higher Institute of Philosophy in Louvain in 1952. The topic of his dissertation was *Het Vetrekpunt der Marxistische Wijsbegeerte,* which was published in 1954 and for which he received the J. M. Huyghe prize in 1956. In 1958, Dupré emigrated to the United States of America where he is a naturalized citizen. From 1959 to 1972 he taught philosophy at the Georgetown University and in 1973 he was appointed the T. Lawrason Riggs Professor of Philosophy of Religion at the Yale University. For many years, he taught Phenomenology and Philosophy of Religion laying special emphasis on nineteenth century thought and on Christian Spirituality. During his years at the Yale University he also helped to found the Humanities Programme at the Yale University and since 1985 he has taught a course on Modern Culture in this programme. Louis Dupré has lectured in many countries besides the United States of America. He has lectured in Belgium, the Netherlands, Ireland and Italy. In 1971, he was the President of the American Catholic Philosophical Association and in 1972-73 he was the President of the Hegel Society of America. In recognition of his contribution to philosophy he has received honorary Doctorates from Loyola College in Baltimore, Sacred Heart University in Fairfield and from the Georgetown University. In 1996, he was awarded the Phi Beta Kappa Medal as Teacher of the year at the Yale University and in 1997 he received the Aquinas Medal from the American Catholic Philosophical Association for outstanding work in Philosophy. He has now retired from his teaching obligations but still directs doctoral dissertations and gives lectures occasionally. He has written over a dozen books and has edited a few others. He has also published more than a hundred and fifty original articles in various academic and scholarly journals. Some of his books, especially *The Other Dimension,* have been translated into French, Dutch, Polish, Spanish, Chinese and Korean. In 2010, he moved to Courtrai in Belgium.

Louis Dupré is a striking thinker and writer who has written in different fields such as philosophy, theology, history of ideas, ethics and spirituality. From his writings we can say that he sees a connection between the spiritual, philosophical and theological traditions and works therefore toward uniting God, the world and the human being. He holds that the person today in the modern world has been estranged from his origins and is no longer sensitive to the primordial unity. Hence, Dupré's primary concern is the religious dimension of human life. He believes that we are living through a religious revolution and so the basic question is, "Is modern man's world view still reconcilable with a religious attitude? If so, does such an attitude have anything in common with religion as it has been traditionally conceived?"[4]

1.6 A Brief Summary of Dupré's Theory

A brief summary of Dupré's theory would have to begin from the self because for him the self in its most authentic form is grounded in the transcendent and in a way could even be said to coincide with the transcendent. For this the self is dependent on the use of symbols and their interpretation. It is through the mediation of symbols that we are able to express the coincidence of the self with the transcendent. The mediation of symbols takes place in the exercise of freedom and rationality. Still the situation in the world today is such that in the culture of today man is estranged from his origins and so this interiority that could make us aware of our transcendent groundedness is usually not experienced. Hence religion, and specifically Christianity, struggles to be the mode of interiorization and integration of the self and as a result today man is alienated from himself, from the world and from the transcendent. Indeed, man is alienated from the exercise of religiosity itself. The crisis that this situation has led to demands careful intellectual reflection and deconstruction so that it could lead to a personal reorientation. For this we cannot be content with mere philosophical notions alone and so we have to make use of religion. We do this through a philosophical and phenomenological reflection on religion, specifically reflecting on the religious attitude and on faith.[5]

1.7 Works of Louis Dupré

The works of Louis Dupré are many and could generally be divided into different phases of development. While it is true that there is no single trend of thought that he systematically develops in all of his books, the topics he deals with especially in his philosophical works are mostly connected with his primary concern, namely, the religious dimension of human life. We could broadly divide the works of Dupré into three main phases. The first phase of his writing began with the publication of his doctoral thesis in 1956 and culminated in 1972 with one of his most important works, *The Other Dimension: A Search for the Meaning of Religious Attitudes*. During this period he also wrote *Kierkegaard as Theologian: The Dialectic of Christian Existence*, *Contraception and Catholics: A New Appraisal*, and *The Philosophical Foundations of Marxism.* It was this period that prepared the ground for most of his later works. He examines many authors during this phase of maturation and also explores various themes which would characterize the

---

[4] Louis Dupré, "Secular Man and his Religion," *Proceedings of the American Catholic Philosophical Association* 42 (1968), 78.

[5] Cf. Peter Casarella and George Schner, (ed.) *Christian Spirituality and the Culture of Modernity: The Thought of Louis Dupré* (Grand Rapids: Eerdmans, 1998), 227.

second phase which extended into the mid eighties. This second phase from 1972 till the mid eighties is characterized by a number of books but the most significant were two collections of articles, *Transcendent Selfhood: The Loss and Rediscovery of the Inner Life*, and *A Dubious Heritage: Studies in the Philosophy of Religion after Kant*. During this period it is interesting to note that he also published two books on mysticism. *The Deeper Life: An Introduction to Christian Mysticism*, and *The Common Life: The Origins of Trinitarian Mysticism and its Development by Jan Ruusbroec*. Besides, he also edited *Light from Light: An Anthology on Christian Mysticism*. The third phase which begins in the early nineties is marked by the publication of an important book *Passage to Modernity: An Essay in the Hermeneutics of Nature and Culture*. A lecture published in 1994 *Metaphysics and Culture,* could be seen as an introduction to *Passage to Modernity*, and demonstrates a special emphasis on history. This period sees Dupré making a comprehensive study of the crisis of modernity, especially from the point of view of the religious self in this crisis. He also published some articles he had written earlier as a book, *Religious Mystery and Rational Reflection: Excursions in the Phenomenology and Philosophy of Religion*, in 1997, while in 2000 he published *Symbols of the Sacred* which to an extent is a re-working and repetition of some sections of *The Other Dimension*. This stage in which he makes a study of the crisis of modernity still continues as in 2004 he has just released another book which could be seen as a sequel to *Passage to Modernity* which is entitled *The Enlightenment and the Intellectual Foundation of Modern Culture*. He also wrote *Religion and the Rise of Modern Culture* (2008) and *The Quest of the Absolute: Birth and Decline of European Romanticism* (2013).

While we have mentioned only the books that Louis Dupré has published, it is impossible not to mention the more than a hundred and fifty original articles that he has published in various scholarly journals and periodicals.[6] They indicate a great thinker. Most of these works could be grouped together under a few themes that Dupré has developed which unite all of his writings and cover all the stages in the development of his thought. Dupré often speaks about the 'crisis of culture'. This crisis according to him has come about because of the way in which the relation between the self, God and the world is seen today. There has been a transformation in the understanding of each of these components and consequently there is a transformation in the way in which their relationship with each other is looked at. Another theme is the religious dimension of the self, and this is looked at especially in the context of the present crisis. Since, he speaks of the religious dimension Dupré often examines the forms of mediation that take place in religion especially the religious use of language, the symbol and myths.

[6] A complete bibliography of the works of Louis Dupré until 1997 can be found in Paul J. Levesque, *Symbols of Transcendence: Religious Expression in the thought of Louis Dupré* (Louvain: Peeters Press, W. B. Eerdmans, 1997), 281-328.

He also studies religion and the use of symbols for the religious dimension.[7] Besides, these themes that mostly concern the religious dimension of the human life, a significant part of the thought and writings of Louis Dupré is concerned with the western philosophical tradition and the way in which he understands it, as is evidenced in the *Passage to Modernity*. While many of his works exhibit a special interest in Kierkegaard and Hegel, he has also studied Karl Marx. His leaning toward phenomenology could be put down to his interest in Husserl, but as Schner points out, in Louis Dupré, "an increasing interest in Neoplatonism comes to the fore along with explorations in late medieval nominalism and Renaissance humanism."[8]

1.8 The Aim of the Study

This study is an endeavour to examine the concept of transcendence and how we can achieve this transcendence with special emphasis on the role of religion and religious attitudes as developed by Louis Dupré. While the title of this book is "Religion as Self-Transcendence: A study of the Concept of Transcendence in Louis Dupré", the study is not restricted to the 'concept' of transcendence as an abstract thought or idea. We have used the word 'concept' more in keeping with its significance as 'notion' and as 'understanding of'. The study is a reflection on experience and to this end we have made a synchronic study of the works of Dupré. The methodology followed is basically phenomenological and the aim of this book is to make a synthesis of Dupré's understanding of transcendence and the path towards attaining this transcendence. This study examines the Judeo-Christian concept of religion that Dupré speaks of. While it is clear that Dupré deals with the concept of transcendence in different ways, we restrict this study of the concept of transcendence to its religious aspect as connected to a supernatural divine Being. The concept of transcendence is a complex term and this study focuses on a phenomenological examination of the experience and act of religion. Besides, the approach being phenomenological, we examine primarily the experience of religion while not excluding the metaphysical and epistemological aspects.

1.9 A Preview of the Chapters

This study is divided into seven chapters. The first chapter is largely descriptive in nature and while acquainting us with religion and the topic of transcendence also presents a biographical sketch of the author Louis Dupré and his most important works. We also take a look at the development of his thought, explore the main

---

[7] These themes in the writings of Louis Dupré have been identified by George Schner, "Louis Dupré's Philosophy of Religion: An Indispensable Discourse on Fragments of Meaning" in Casarella and Schner, *Christian Spirituality*, 226.

[8] George Schner, "Louis Dupré's Philosophy of Religion," 227.

themes he studies and present a general idea of the argument he follows. The second chapter examines the concept of transcendence in general which functions as a sort of basis for our study of transcendence in the works of Dupré.

The third chapter takes a look at Dupré's understanding of the self as subject and examines how the transformation of culture has led to a loss of transcendence. This loss has led to a metaphysical search beyond the self, for transcendence. An attempt was made to overcome this alienation through an initial synthesis of nature and grace which was consequently challenged. The fourth chapter examines how through the religious attitude we become aware of and gain knowledge of this religious object especially through faith.

Chapter five is a deeper look at Dupré's explanation of various aspects of religion and the truth of religion, especially from the phenomenological aspect of experience. To this end, we examine a number of philosophers who influenced Dupré's thought, from whom he borrowed, or on whom he comments, such as Husserl, Blondel and Duméry. The sixth chapter is basically an attempt to show a possible path toward transcendence, a synthesis that can be arrived at through the threefold path of purgation, illumination and union with God which then leads to a vision of the beyond and to transcendence. Chapter seven engages in a critical appraisal of the concept of transcendence in Dupré and our justification of transcendence.

We accept that the transcendent must by nature be beyond our reach. Nevertheless, we believe that as human beings it is our nature to strive to understand it and describe it in ways and methods that are in keeping with our limitations and possibilities. Not to attempt to attain transcendence would be to surrender to an inferior existence. Hence, this study can best be described as a journey of exploration through examining religion, religious attitudes and the concept of transcendence. It is therefore a search which indicates openness to the beyond, a search for transcendence. As Dupré says:

> "Ours is a time of change in which painstakingly a new culture is being formed. It already appears that the men of the coming age more than their predecessors are interested in sounding its transcendent depths. If philosophers have nothing to contribute to this exploration, philosophy will not fulfill its task."[9]

Man is a unique part of the universe and has a special role to play as a human being. Due to his questioning nature man enjoys a privileged position among all other living things. Because of his social nature he cannot live isolated from other human beings and so in most cases he lives in community. This social nature is just one of the many aspects that there is to the human being. From among all the other aspects we focus our attention on man as a questioning animal in search of

---

[9] Louis Dupré, "Philosophy and the Religious Perspective of Life," *Proceedings of the American Catholic Philosophical Association* 45 (1971), 8.

answers regarding the meaning of his existence, and we shall study how in religion and the religious attitude he gives expression to this constant aspiration within himself to move beyond towards an unforeseeable future which is the drive for transcendence.

Chapter 2

The Concept of Transcendence

2.1 Transcendence as a Search

Man's existence which is characterized by his search for meaning is a continuous journey. His entire life is a learning experience which is not limited to any one role, but it is an interior seeking that in the process of searching opens up newer areas and possibilities for improving the quality of his existence. On the one hand man is confronted by his own physical limitations and the limitedness of his existence which blocks him and does not allow him full control of his individual existence. But on the other hand he also realizes that he has a great potentiality and limitless possibilities and so this urges him to always look for the 'beyond' and the 'not yet'. He is aware that despite all the limitations placed on his existence he can always do more than what he has already done and he can be more than what he already is. It is this drive to go beyond his possibilities that is one of the striking characteristics of the human person. It is the indeterminate future, man's own capabilities and the transcendent potentiality of existence that gives a unique dynamism to human existence. This dynamism coupled with his nature to ask questions and seek answers is what opens him to the transcendent, a movement and dynamism that we refer to as transcendence. It is the dynamism of transcendence that gives a direction and purpose to man's existence and as long as life is purposeful and as long as man feels incomplete the quest continues. And this dynamism directs our efforts towards a goal which is forever beyond ourselves.[1]

---

[1] Cf. Robert M. Torrance, *The Spiritual Quest: Transcendence in Myth, Religion and Science* (Berkeley: University of California Press, 1994), 50-57.

2.1.1 A Constant Quest

This quest in most instances is the drive that exists in each and every person whereby we continuously strive to surpass our given condition. While it is true that we are conditioned by various forces, it is also true that these conditions are not independent of each other and so these forces work together in a dialectic that keeps all of them connected and together they contribute toward the possibility of man being able to go beyond himself. Hence, no single aspect is able to claim fullness and independence for itself as being responsible for this movement beyond, but it is all these aspects working together in this dialectic that results in a going out into the unknown. This venturing out into the unknown is an uncertain movement that could result in a feeling of insecurity but it is in this going out into the unknown and in this search that we fulfil our humanity. While our concern is about another realm of reality it is not that we leave behind the realm of our personal existence for another realm that is separate, but rather it is an enlarging and transformation of our human potentialities.[2]

2.1.2 A Feeling of Uneasiness

Part of man's existence consists in his having to confront the feeling of uneasiness that he experiences in his daily life. This uneasiness is because of a need for fullness and to answer this need for completeness he continues searching for that beyond. He is able to realize that there is a higher aspect of his existence which is 'more' than what it appears to be and which is operative in the universe outside of him. As he becomes conscious of this 'more' he becomes conscious that his person is continuous with a wider self and so in a way man is forced to confront transcendence. He comes face to face with his limitedness and his finitude, and it is this recognition of his contingency that opens man towards transcendence. Whether he will be able to succeed and arrive at it is not possible to say, but one thing that can be said is that it is in this drive and this quest for transcendence that we are able to move towards the fulfilment of our potential. The actualization of our potential then depends on our willingness and ability to gradually transcend that which is given and thus to explore and investigate this 'other dimension'. It is this continuous search that gives rise to further quests and it is this response to his situation that indicates transcendence. The mind when confronted by an impasse becomes aware of its ignorance which in turn gives rise to a new search. It is this impulse which is inherent to human life and existence which enables transcendence.[3]

---

[2] Cf. Torrance, *The Spiritual Quest*, 265-283.

[3] Cf. Torrance, The Spiritual Quest, 284-293.

2.1.3 The Secularization of Life

As we go through life we are overwhelmed by the level of secularization in the world today. Technological advancement has made us increasingly aware of the destructive tendencies and the challenges that these modern possibilities have posed to the quality of human life. Confronted by these challenges society seeks coherence in religious norms because a neutral society is not possible. Conflicting ideas seek supremacy and society is in search of a binding element that will serve to keep it united. Down the ages religion has served as this binding force and despite its different facets it has held a fairly central place in various societies and cultures over time. The place and role of God in the life of man has always been a point of discussion in every society. This becomes even more evident when we reflect on the human person especially from the point of view of its physical and spiritual nature. The human being is neither pure spirit nor is it pure body. It is a spirit in a body and this body is placed in the world. So

> We experience ourselves as living beings, rooted in the whole context of the life of the world of nature, the world of plants and animals. As bodies, we are part of the world of nature. But even in our corporeity we differ from the world of beings that lack consciousness… we are in a sense estranged from nature. At the same time, even through our corporeity we transcend the world of nature, and we experience this transcendence through the continual perfection of our potentialities, through our ability to adapt to ever changing conditions, through our power to transform our natural environment and create technology and culture. We are human beings thanks to our spiritual life, the life of intellectual knowledge and love.[4]

We have to accept that as human beings we are material but at the same time we are also spiritual beings and so there is a constant tension within us between this finitude of matter and the infinitude of spirit. We are constantly aware of our limitations as human beings and at the same moment we are driven by the desire to transcend this situation knowing well that we are capable of it. Naturally this is no easy task and "consists in constantly transcending the finite so that, enhanced by the infinite, we might return again to ourselves and enrich and develop our potentialities. We manifest this by constantly going out from ourselves toward something beyond, something greater, more perfect, and then returning again to ourselves."[5] We have to realize and accept our place in the universe not just as a mere part of the world or just a function in the world, but rather as a person, conscious of our being, and aware also of the all encompassing Being that transcends our being and the being of the universe. It is this awareness that distinguishes us from all other beings in the universe. We question the meaning of our own being when

---

[4] Zofia J. Zdybicka, *Person and Religion: An Introduction to the Philosophy of Religion*, trans. Theresa Sandok (New York: Peter Lang, 1991), 113.

[5] Zdybicka, *Person and Religion*, 113.

we search for the meaning of our lives. This search for a direction in our existence, the search for the foundation and source of our existence is also a search for the end of our existence and is what points us towards transcendence.[6]

We shall therefore examine what the term transcendence signifies and its meaning and connotation in various fields.

2.2 The Term Transcendence

We begin our study from the very root of the word transcendence. It is derived from the Latin verb, *transcendere* which means to climb over, to surpass or to go beyond. It is "a term describing the relation existing between two things when one is superior and extrinsic to the other, e.g. God and the world, animal and plant, and knower and thing known."[7] This term implies a separation between the two realities involved and so as a result there is a passing from one to the other which could happen in reality or through knowledge. This dynamism of the word transcendence is best understood by a splitting up of the Latin verb *transcendere* into two parts, *trans* which would mean across and *scendere* which means to climb. So, the movement which is involved in transcendence is described by the verb 'to climb across'. In speaking of transcendence we have to speak about being transcendent which can be explained as the quality of surpassing or excelling others of its kind, or going beyond the ordinary limits.[8] To be transcendent would also mean to exist apart from the material universe and so not be subject to its limitations. Scholastic philosophy would see it as being higher than and not included in any of Aristotle's categories while Kantian philosophy describes it as not being realizable in experience.[9] Hence, we can say that transcendence is the "property of rising out of or above other things… the property of being, in some way, of a higher order."[10] As we shall see a little later in this section, transcendence is best understood when seen in contrast with immanence and presence because it deals with the innermost core of religious belief. It stresses on the aspects of otherness, separation and as being set apart or marked off. But it also highlights holiness as being greater than mere morality. While we have attempted to give different definitions and explanations, transcendence which eludes a universally accepted definition, is most fittingly described from the point of view of experience.

---

[6] Cf. Zdybicka, *Person and Religion*, 113-114.

[7] *New Catholic Encyclopedia,* 2003 ed., s.v. "Transcendence," by B. A. Gendreau.

[8] Cf. *Oxford English Dictionary*, Vol. XVIII, 1989, s.v. "Transcendence."

[9] Cf. *New Oxford Dictionary of English* (1998), s.v. "Transcendence."

[10] *The Cambridge Dictionary of Philosophy* (1998), s.v. "Transcendence."

2.3 Transcendence as Experience

One of the basic experiences of the human being is his search for ultimate meaning in reality. There is a difference between the present reality which usually but not always occupies his interest, and the reality beyond which always seems to be out of his grasp. Man is constantly in search of a better understanding of this elusive reality. This goal or the answer to this search need not be arrived at by going beyond the present reality, but it could also be attained through a better understanding of or even a transformation of this reality. To go beyond, we have to look back at the present reality and that is what the concept of transcendence is, it is a going beyond by looking back.[11] Usually, the concept of transcendence deals with experience. It is concerned with the mental state and attitude that is related to one's being in the world. Consequently, it also deals with one's relatedness to persons, things, history and tradition. This is necessary because we are dealing with the interaction between the self and the world, an interaction which takes place in an ongoing process of communication. On another level the concept of transcendence also deals with God. It is true that today God is no longer used as the explanation for many inexplicable worldly experiences and events as was the case earlier. This is unavoidable because no longer is the experience of the sacred realm as universal as it once was. Transcendence once led us beyond this world but today it is sought within the world of historical and temporal experience. The problem in this situation is that experience is reduced to sense experience and other types of experience are overlooked. Eugene Long says that there are dimensions of human experiences which suggest a wider range of being than merely finite being and these point us toward the transcendent dimensions of human experience especially experiences of ultimacy which point beyond the limits of the ordinary. The challenge in such experiences is that there can be no universal proof and so our aim shall be to describe and interpret these dimensions of experience and show that they testify to this wider range of being and thus place them within the being of human existence.[12]

2.3.1 The Experience of Relatedness and Finitude

We are beings-in-the-world and hence we are related to other persons and things. Another aspect of our being in the world is that we are 'becoming'. We are unfinished essences in the process of becoming, and our being and becoming are closely related because becoming is just one of the various possible ways of being. It is our becoming that enables us to constantly go beyond our boundaries and so move into newer possibilities of being. This is also what transcendence is about, we remember the past to move to the future. We make this movement not merely

[11] Hermann Krings, ed. *Concetti Fondamentali di filosofia*, (Italian edition) ed. Giorgio Penzo, trans. Gerardo Cunico et al. Volume III (Brescia: Editrice Queriniana, 1982), 2206.

[12] Cf. Eugene Long, "Quest for Transcendence," *Review of Metaphysics* 52/1 (1998), 7.

as individuals but more importantly as individuals who are part of humankind. Experiences like suffering and death challenge our being and at the same time such experiences expose our finitude and limitedness. We are forced to confront our limitedness and the possibility of our not-being and of our nothingness. It is this awareness of our limitedness that makes us aware of the being that lies beyond our own limited being. This is especially seen in our experiences of the mysteriousness of the universe and the contingency of everything. This uncertainty leads us to seek for an explanation of the totality of things, and this involves a movement from contingency to necessity which is seen in nearly every moment of our existence.[13]

Paradoxically it is the experience that we have of our nothingness in conjunction with the mysteriousness of the universe that allows for our experience of freedom. Even though we are embodied and participate in material reality, we are still able to transcend other beings. We can rise beyond our boundaries and consequently we are capable of creatively shaping our own existence. We can transcend our own potential being and so we are able to give a direction to our being in the world. We are still dependent on others because we relate to them but we are also called to a higher standard of living and to a sense of responsibility. As a result of our having to follow social conventions and living in society we need to be committed to a belief in life and to meaning in life. This drive for meaning in life is what motivates us to go beyond and strive to break through limitations that bind us. If we remain only at the human aspect of going beyond it does not make sense. Our 'going beyond' needs to have a sense of direction. In going beyond we seek our humanity in its fullness, which is beyond but is not completely independent of the being of human existence. In exploring the being of our existence we confront our contingency and the limitedness of ourselves and the world, and consequently the possibility of our nothingness which as Heidegger would say leads us "to experience in Nothing the vastness of that which gives every being the warrant to be. That is Being-itself."[14] We need to have a true sense of this otherness to be able to reach for the transcendent dimension in human experience. It is basically man's freedom that suggests openness and a certain unfinishedness in the being of human existence. As long as we are free we can look beyond, and so transcendence is this process that continuously enables us to be.[15]

2.3.2 Religious Experience

Philosophy by and large reflects on the dimension that is accessible to the senses and which reason elaborates by applying scientific principles. In religious discourse on

[13] Cf. Long, "Quest for Transcendence," 7-8.

[14] Martin Heidegger, *Existence and Being* (Chicago: Henry Regnery, 1949), 353, as quoted in Long, "Quest for Transcendence," 14.

[15] Cf. Long, "Quest for Transcendence," 9-15.

the other hand we can speak of a transcendent metaphysical reality which cannot be considered as an object of ordinary knowledge. In this sense transcendence does not deal with a thing or a person nor is it a category of place referred to as the beyond. We cannot speak of it as we might speak of a property of a tangible thing. We usually refer to the experience of transcendence. Experience in general is an ontological rapport between consciousness and being, between intentionality and appearance. Appearance is the foundation of being and so it is also the foundation of this rapport with being. This foundation is the sense of transcendence and so on a fundamental level, experience is a rapport with transcendence.[16]

Experience has to be interpreted and so it has an interpreter. In religious experience transcendence is always interpreted under the divine form and under the figure of the divine. The divine belongs to religious experience not as the perceived object, but as the sense in which man feels and suffers. God is the religious name for the transcendence of the event. The philosophy of religion is a philosophical reflection on religious experience. In itself philosophy is an interpretative activity and so when we speak of the philosophy of religion it is an interpretation of an interpretation, namely of myths, ritual gestures and an understanding of the world which is arrived at as the result of the search for an answer to life and death. Religion is an interpretation of the appearance of Being, so religion should not be turned into philosophy. Religion began with humanity. It began with man who thinks but who is not a mere thing. Man has a rapport with being insofar as it appears. This appearance leads to questions and hence interpretations because man is co-involved with appearance. There is no complete and exhaustive answer to the questions of life and so it is in answering and interpreting appearance that he becomes fully man. So, man is exposed to transcendence at every step and every moment of his existence.[17]

When we speak of religious experience it is described as such because the object of the experience is religious. Something is experienced in a religious manner because of the religious status of the person who has the experience of transcendence. Ordinarily when speaking of transcendence we would use space categories and so God was defined as something 'above'. Transcendence is described as something 'above', but this explanation is not enough. Sometimes, transcendence is also described as 'beyond the senses', but again this is not sufficient because it could be beyond our senses and yet immanent. It could also be described as the extra dimension or the new dimension, but we still cannot define reality by what we know through our senses. Even describing transcendence as beyond space and time still makes it a concept related to the meaning of immanence. God is experienced in this world. It is difficult for an immanent being to experience

[16] Cf. Aldo Magris, *Fenomenologia Della Trascendenza* (Milano: Guerini Studio, 1992), 135-137.

[17] Cf. Magris, *Fenomenologia Della Trascendenza*, 137-147.

something that is beyond time and space. Transcendence then belongs to our world of thought and reflections, and is on the level of theories. We can meet or experience God in this world but just because we meet him in this world need not mean that he belongs to this world, he could belong to a world beyond time and space. Hence, transcendence belongs to a stage later than experience. While we agree that religious experience need not justify or point to something beyond time and space, yet we cannot deny that religious experience can form convictions within us because it gives religion an air of reality. Transcendence is usually brought on as a result of numinous feelings and so even though the experience has taken place in the world of space and time, the concept of transcendence has to be looked at as belonging to another level.[18]

2.3.3 Religious Experience and Transcendence

From religious experience we cannot necessarily infer transcendence. But then if we hold that religion belongs to the other dimension, and that transcendence is beyond space and time, then it amounts to saying that the religious object as well as transcendence are in the same dimension. But God cannot be described merely as 'beyond space and time', because today 'beyond space and time' has a much larger significance than earlier in history. 'Beyond space and time' is not just a mere blotting out of the consciousness of space and time but it implies that transcendence is absolutely above space and time. According to Lyttkens when religion is accepted as the fifth dimension, "It denotes that religion belongs to a sphere of its own, not beyond, but rather beside the other four. It is something that accompanies the other four and which can be seen as the core of the whole universe."[19] This fifth dimension is the unifying dimension. It is innermost and not beyond the cosmos and the universe. Hence, when we speak of the 'beyond' it is not so much in a spatio-temporal sense but in the conceptual sense that it is used. We realize then that there are many senses in which transcendence can be understood and so we shall now consider the various ways in which transcendence can be spoken about.[20]

2.4 Different Approaches to Transcendence

There are different ways in which transcendence could be understood and so we need to mention different approaches to transcendence.

---

[18] Cf. Hampus Lyttkens, "Religious Experience and Transcendence," *Religious Studies* 15 (June 1979), 211-218.

[19] Lyttkens, "Religious Experience and Transcendence," 219.

[20] Cf. Lyttkens, "Religious Experience and Transcendence," 219-220.

2.4.1 Cosmological Transcendence

From a cosmological point of view transcendence indicates a hierarchy of place, time, being or activity. It deals with a relative comparison. Transcendence is determined by the way one thing is related to another and can lead from the existence of one to the existence of the other. In this sense, the 'going beyond' indicates hierarchical steps from the lower to the higher. This type of transcendence is also based on the relationship between cause and effect. It is more of a factual transcendence in the relationship of a multiplicity of beings with a higher being beyond them. The opposite of cosmological transcendence is cosmological immanence, that is to say that God is within the universe even though he is a qualitatively higher type of being.[21]

2.4.2 Ontological Transcendence

Ontological transcendence indicates the value or the quality which makes one being superior to another. It also aims at explaining why this is so. It is basically concerned about the degrees of perfection. In this light transcendence refers to that which is above normal or which is above average. It depends on what the transcendent thing is in itself and on its ontological value. In this light God is referred to as the transcendent, the being who is the greatest in perfection, that is to say, any limitation in perfection is denied of him.[22]

2.4.3 Epistemological Transcendence

Epistemological transcendence deals with that which is beyond thought as its object, that is to say something which is known and knowable by man but which signifies a going beyond the mind. This movement beyond is aimed either towards some being known as an object existing in reality, or to some reality that is beyond sense data, or to some being above the world, such as God.[23]

2.4.4 Phenomenological Transcendence

Phenomenological transcendence signifies that it has something beyond consciousness as its object. It stresses the value of intentionality in the knowing subject and it also assures objectivity of the activity of knowing and the objective reality of the thing known. It analyses human subjectivity in order to discover the contents of man's awareness and their extra mental foundations. And it aims in a way to overcome the difficulties of the critique of reason which leads to epistemological immanence.[24]

---

[21] Cf. Gendreau, "Transcendence," 141-142.

[22] Cf. Gendreau, "Transcendence," 142.

[23] Cf. Gendreau, "Transcendence," 142.

[24] Cf. Gendreau, "Transcendence," 142.

2.4.5 Mathematical Transcendence

Mathematical transcendence designates functions and numbers that are transfinite or indefinite according to particular operational norms. So, a transcendental number would be a number that is not the root of an algebraic equation with rational coefficients.[25]

2.4.6 Religious Transcendence

As Christians we also talk of the possibility of religious transcendence in man. Due to his relationship with God man is able to fulfil many possibilities. In man's being there is an orientation towards such a relationship and he needs this relationship in order to be complete. Man needs God. This aspect of man by which he is directed towards something beyond is what we refer to as transcendence because it is a movement that goes beyond the order of scientific knowledge and secular values. He wants to go beyond himself to that order of being and perfection which he realizes is greater than himself and the world in which he lives. This is referred to as religious transcendence because man is directed towards a relationship with God and not just mere knowledge of God and morals. It is a personal relationship to which he is oriented, a relationship with God which takes place within a community.[26]

While there are different ways of looking at transcendence yet the concept of transcendence is challenged and sometimes denied because of the questions about the possibility of metaphysics. Usually that aspect of metaphysics which is denied is a metaphysics that leads to an inferential knowledge of the existence of God. Metaphysics is a philosophical study of reality as it is in itself and not just reality as it appears or as mediated by language. Yet, it looks for a basis in man and the world so that it can legitimately assert the meaning and existence of God. Hence while it would be acceptable for some people, others would deny the possibility of objective talk on the subject of transcendence. Another reason for the denial of human transcendence is that man's orientation to an absolute and unlimited value is questioned.[27] It is interesting to note that in the whole effort to grasp the meaning of transcendence, whether it is from the epistemological or metaphysical point of view, or even from the point of view of the deity, the 'beyond' is very clearly understood either as the deity beyond the world or the transcendental beyond sensibility. What seems to be lost in this understanding is the whole aspect of the 'movement' to the beyond. It seems as if we have restricted

---

[25] Cf. Gendreau, "Transcendence," 142.

[26] Cf. John Farrelly, "Religious Reflection and Man's Transcendence," *The Thomist* 37 (January 1973), 1-2.

[27] Cf. Farrelly, "Religious Reflection and Man's Transcendence," 3-5.

our understanding to extra-worldliness and as a consequence we have ignored "the directional idea of a movement beyond the world."[28]

So when we speak of transcendence we refer to the sacred and when we speak of the sacred from the many thinkers we refer to Rudolf Otto for whom the concept of the spiritual reality and the experience of the spirit and experience of God are essential. His interest is in the rapport between the non-rational factor in the idea of the divine and reason which brings man to religious experience. Together with this we also look at the aspects of the numinous, of feeling and of God as the totally other.

2.5 The Sacred and the Holy

Some phenomenologists speak of the sacred as the object of religion. But sometimes the sacred is intended in such a way as to exclude the divine. On other occasions the sacred intended as the Divine is the principal defining content of religion and also of the object of religion. This gives rise to a certain ambiguity. Most often the sacred today is identified with the Sacred intended as Divine, but it is not always clear whether we are referring to the content of religion or to the object of the religious experience. Sacred could be used for Divine, or merely as something connected to religion. The problem arises because in many religions and especially in the ancient cultures religion is distinguished from but is not separated from other activities. So it cannot be considered a separate sector. They involve the entire human sphere be it religious or civil. Culture and religion tend to be identical in ancient society.[29]

It is interesting to note the distinction that is made between the terms 'sacred' and 'holy.' In English 'the sacred' and 'the holy' have nearly the same connotation and are often used in place of each other. The use of the German word '*das Heilige*' as a noun, as was used for instance by Rudolf Otto, gives the term 'the holy' its actual connotation. The term 'holy' is generally used to refer to an attribute of the divine, or even to an attribute of God. The Latin word for holy is '*sanctum*' and this term in general applies to a divine power, or to the behaviour of an individual or a saint who is considered to be holy.

On the other hand the term 'sacred' is of more recent usage. It is more often used in connection with objects of veneration, and is not used so much in connection with the divine or with persons connected to divinity. Also in Latin the term is '*sacrum*' and not '*sanctum*' as used for holy. The *sacrum* has more to do with human veneration than with divine power. Magnani has pointed out that this confusion between the holy and the sacred came about because while

---

[28] Robert A. F. Thurman, "Transcendence and the Sacred in the Mahayana Middle Way," in *Transcendence and the Sacred*, ed. Alan M. Olson and Leroy S. Rouner (Notre Dame, Indiana: University of Notre Dame Press, 1981), 104.

[29] Giovanni Magnani, *Storia Comparata delle Religioni: Principi Fenomenologici* (Assisi: Cittadella Editrice, 1999), 523-526.

the term 'sacred' excludes the divine or God, in the new terminology it began to be used with reference to God. This was the case with Mircea Eliade who used the term *le sacré* to mean divine. The German *das Helige*, Latin *sanctum* and the English holy refer to God or the divine. We can neither say that God is sacred nor that the sacred is God.

2.6 Ultimate Reality

When speaking of religious ideas we necessarily have to talk about the ultimate reality. It deals with the topic of God, or gods, that some religions have only one God while other religions have many gods. Speaking in terms of God is a sign of a bias toward monotheism and so we acknowledge that while we speak of the ultimate reality in the singular we could as well be speaking in the plural of ultimate realities. This ultimate reality could be the creator or the world on which all else depends or even the goal of human existence. It could be looked at from a metaphysical, epistemological or even as in the majority of cases from an ontological point of view. Keeping in mind all these possibilities, when speaking of the ultimate reality from the point of view of religion we are generally concerned about an ontological ultimate reality because it is this that is the object of ultimate religious concern. Besides, it is also the object of the human orientation especially from the aspect of human life and its religious dimension. It is necessary to point out at this stage that even if there is no ontological ultimate or nothing ontological to refer to ultimately, what is important is the orientation and the drive of the religious path, the quest for God and the drive for perfection and liberation.[30]

When we refer to ultimate reality we are speaking from the background of religious life and this term has to deal with a religious truth. While it is true that the ultimate is what is most important for human life in general, we have to accept that it is religion that has enabled us to comprehend and define in a better manner those aspects of life that are most related to the ultimate. This ultimate reality is of necessity very vague and difficult to define due to its vastness and also because of the different religious traditions that look at it from different points of view and hence interpret it differently. Different religions and different religious thinkers also look at reality in different ways. When we combine this with the vastness of reality and the fact that it can be studied by different traditions leading to different interpretations, we cannot but accept that this is going to lead to many different understandings of the ultimate reality. Yet, every religion which is in search of purity, holiness, perfection and truth has to accept this ultimate reality, because otherwise the ultimate reality becomes completely anthropomorphic and meaningless since it is no longer ultimate. This ultimate reality could be the first cause, the last goal, the final truth, that which is most real, or that which is most

[30] Cf. *Ultimate Realities*, ed. Robert Cummings Neville (New York: State University of New York Press, 2001), 1-2.

wanted. The important thing is that it is that which is most important for a religious way of life and this is dependent on what this religious way of life accepts as the nature of reality.[31]

2.6.1 The Ultimate Reality in Different Religions

Each religion has its own way of looking at and understanding the ultimate reality. In the Chinese religion the ultimate reality is seen as harmony and transcendence, and their actualization in human life. Ultimacy in this context refers to a transcendent ideal for harmony, and when speaking about reality the reference is to empirical reality. So, the question for ultimacy in Chinese religion is to transcend reality in this sense. The ultimate reality is arrived at when there is ideal harmony and transcendence, and this is made real through actualization in human experience. "The ultimate in Chinese religion is a process of realization and experience, part of the world yet not accessible with worldly means, and thus the opposite of the Western concept of God, which is substantial and static, entirely beyond the world, and accessible only by transcending the world completely."[32] Judaism presents God as the ultimate reality. All the meanings of ultimacy apply to God who is "the uncaused creator of everything else, the goal of existence, the ground of intelligibility or wisdom about the world, superlative excellence, and goodness."[33] It is interesting to note that for Judaism the ultimacy of God is always conceptualized in contrast with the limitations of human life, and so from this human perspective God as ultimate gives unity and coherence to life. God is ultimate also because he is absolutely unique and despite anthropomorphisms used for God, God in not really like humans and actually is beyond human comprehension.[34]

Islam considers ultimate reality as something stable, fixed and objectively 'out there' quite much in keeping with Judaism. Ultimate reality was the deity itself, with divine attributes including eternity and transcendence. God is not confused with the created world. He is the creator and as divine will has an effect on personal and political realities since he is present in the world. In the cosmic order every entity has an assigned place and is fully integrated into the system, but it has no rational, moral or ontological ultimacy. Its reality, structure and significance is derived wholly from God. The ultimate reality is described in the Quran by ninety nine names, but these names do not have any real reference because God is beyond all names. Yet, he is expressed throughout all of creation

---

[31] Cf. Robert Cummings Neville and Wesley J. Wildman, "Comparative Conclusions about Ultimate Realities," in Neville, *Ultimate Realities,* 151-153.

[32] Neville & Wildman, "Comparative Conclusions about Ultimate Realities," 158.

[33] Neville & Wildman, "Comparative Conclusions about Ultimate Realities," 158.

[34] Cf. Neville & Wildman, "Comparative Conclusions about Ultimate Realities," 159-160.

and his unity embraces the world.[35] We shall not go into the details of Hinduism, but broadly it holds that "Ultimate Reality is that which cannot be surpassed; that from which all realities, persons and things come, that on which they depend, and that into which they return upon dissolution."[36]

In general we can say that the ultimate reality is often conceived in both ontological and anthropological terms, and refers to human experience. Symbols are also used for this ultimate reality to express the striving for that which is of ultimate importance to human beings. Some of these symbols are drawn from the anthropological conceptions of ultimate reality while others are drawn from ontological conceptions of ultimate reality. There are a variety of representations of the ontological ultimate. They could be earthly personifications and could also be principles and philosophical representations which are so transcendent that they are beyond much of positive knowledge. This is evident especially in Judaism, Islam and Christianity which use a highly personalized language for God. He is spoken of as the creator of the universe and is presented as a personal being in relation to other personal beings in a field of interaction. Greek philosophical thinking was used to explain what it meant for God to create, judge, govern and fulfil the world in an intermingling of the philosophical and personalistic aspects of the ultimate reality. By and large we realize that the personal aspect appeals to popular religion and the more philosophical aspect is what appeals sophisticated thinkers and writers. Popular religion tends to be devotional while the philosophical aspect of religion does not always lead to devotion. What is significant is that whether it be personal, or whether it be philosophical, whether it be ontological or anthropological, it leads us to a better understanding of the ultimate reality.[37]

2.7 The Problem of Transcendence

When we speak of transcendence we are not dealing only with the concept of transcendence but our concern is also about whether there is an absolute transcendent being. We try to attain a better understanding of what this being is and why it is higher and better than other beings while at the same time knowable yet enigmatic. If it is transcendent, then can it be known? How can it be known? How does that which is transcendent enter into the world and world view of the immanent? These are some of the issues that are part of the problematic of transcendence. We have chosen to remain with the problem of transcendence from the point of view of trying to understand this beyond, but more importantly how we are able to be aware of, give expression to and move toward this beyond.

[35] Cf. Neville & Wildman, "Comparative Conclusions about Ultimate Realities," 160-161.

[36] Neville & Wildman, "Comparative Conclusions about Ultimate Realities," 162.

[37] Cf. Neville & Wildman, "Comparative Conclusions about Ultimate Realities," 165-168.

2.7.1 The Difficulties that are Encountered

Down the ages different thinkers have spoken of the Absolute as transcendent in many and varied ways. Plato considered the transcendent as the nature that is more perfect than, and which stands apart from this world. Augustine on his part would consider it as the justification of the value of human knowledge in its truth, necessity and certainty. The great thinker Thomas Aquinas saw the transcendent as the cause of this world in its beginning and also as responsible for its continuance with respect to its essence and existence. Bonaventure understood it as an explicit infinite reality which is implicit in any knowledge and expression with respect to the finite universe. And we also mention Phenomenology which deals with the transcendent as the object that is implied in human consciousness and which demands the presence of the other as the cause and the horizon of meaningfulness.[38] Many others have written volumes on this subject but we limit ourselves to these few considerations which are relevant to the scope of this study.

There are different ways of reasoning that could lead toward the absolute as an existent whose reality cannot be denied. It depends on the framework in which the thought about the transcendent is developed. This is the case particularly when we consider the extra-mental existence of the transcendent and the possibility of our mind to know anything that lies beyond consciousness. Most of the explanations that were offered dealt with the possibility of the mind to transcend itself. They also dealt with the possibility of the mind to know things other than itself and to deal with the substance, soul and God. This gave rise to questions about objects which are beyond thought and whether they exist at all. Some would accept that knowledge can grasp things existing in the world. A decisive point in this thinking was Descartes who with the concept of *cogito ergo sum* introduced a chasm between the mind as spirit and matter as extension. As a result of this partition the objectivity of knowledge had to be guaranteed by a higher power which does not depend on the very activity of knowing. Kant limited knowledge to the phenomena of verifiable sense perception.[39]

Another problem we face when speaking of transcendence, especially of divine transcendence, is that such an experience of transcendence is ineffable, God is beyond description. Verbal expressions of our religious experiences very often have little or no meaning for those who do not share these experiences because God is different from everything else. Nothing is equal to God. Even though, God is beyond description philosophers of religion still attempt to discover special ways of using language so as to coherently describe God. Besides, even if words are inadequate we can always use art and symbols to help us in this task. We realize that we can stretch language without actually rupturing it. By pushing it to its limits, language can be a tool to describe the transcendent.

---

[38] Cf. Gendreau, "Transcendence," 142.

[39] Cf. Gendreau, "Transcendence," 142.

Transcendence in a way forces us to use analogy to affirm intentions and to express attitudes. We must realize that analogy does not make a statement of fact but is an aid and so must be treated with respect. God in himself is beyond knowledge. Not that we cannot have any knowledge at all about God but we need to accept and realize that our knowledge of him is always a limited knowledge. This is so, not because God cannot be known. He can be known, but it is our capacity for knowledge of God that is limited because we do not have the necessary tools to know him. So while we know that he exists and that he is transcendent, we also know that he is beyond description and beyond knowledge. So, the problem is how to conceive this transcendence with our inadequate experience and our confused conceptualization. What would be helpful to us in our effort is greater experience because greater experience does lead to fuller awareness. Hence, when we deal with the concept of transcendence our problem will be to examine how we can go beyond our limited knowledge toward a fuller knowledge of God, and how by removing these limitations we can give expression to this movement beyond ourselves to that which lies beyond us.[40]

2.7.2 Many Possible Understandings of Transcendence

One of the problems about the concept of transcendence is that there are many possible answers and many and different ways of looking at transcendence. And so while studying the topic we have to be clear that different people look at it from these different angles and so if we attempt to give answers, the answers in themselves may be correct, but then they could be the answers to the wrong question and hence become irrelevant. As we have said earlier trying to understand transcendence is a quest and a search. So while we try to understand transcendence the effort itself to go beyond and attain that which is greater than us is the movement towards transcendence.

Considering the different aspects of transcendence, the general way of looking at transcendence is as an experience that takes us beyond the ordinary. It could be just a temporary sensation that can be arrived at through music, silence, a religious ritual or even through the use of chemical substances. It is a basic yearning that is present in each one of us as part of our being human. It is our capacity for transcendence that is a cause of our dissatisfaction with our way of being and consequently our desire to be and achieve more than what we are just now. It is a longing for a reality that seems to be beyond us. Most of us live our existence on the rational level, but since we are not merely rational beings, the feeling and affective part that is in each one of us strives to attain something more. We are blessed with a dynamism that takes us further, to the beyond. The mysterious beckons us always. Transcendence is not merely a cognitive concept

[40] Cf. W. Donald Hudson, "The Concept of Divine Transcendence," *Religious Studies* 15/2 (June 1979), 198-209.

and so we have to follow it also with our heart. With our mind we try to grasp as much of this concept as possible but then at a certain moment our quest forces us to let go of all constraints and participate in the experience that is transcendence.

Another aspect of this concept of transcendence as we shall see in the next section is that transcendence is connected with the concepts of immanence and presence. This aspect of transcendence is largely connected with the Christian understanding of transcendence as divine transcendence. Hence, transcendence from this point of view is seen as a characteristic of God. God is understood as the 'wholly other' and as beyond this world. He is beyond and independent of this world, yet his being is closely related to us and hence to the reality in which we live. And so the concept of transcendence is closely related to immanence.

2.8 Transcendence and Immanence

At the heart of most persons is the feeling that there is a presence that is much greater than man and the world put together. Most persons strive to grasp and understand this presence in their own way gradually working toward a meaning in life. Naturally, since the synthesis that is arrived at is the fruit of different beliefs, ways of thinking and world views, it gives rise to conflict and any number of differences of opinion. And yet if transcendence has to be meaningful to us, in a certain sense it has to be immanent or else it would be of no significance to us at all. Hence, it is imperative that transcendence also be a presence that is immanent. The problem arises because we believe that everything that exists has to be accessible to reason. And yet transcendence is a direct challenge to this principle that everything lies within the grasp of reason. Today, increasingly man realizes that not everything lies within the grasp of reason and that he has not yet arrived at many answers. Transcendence at times seems to be only an absence while what man is searching for is a meaningful presence.[41]

Christianity's answer to this question was the mystery of the Incarnation. But still this is a doctrine that is accepted only by Christians and entirely on faith. Yet, other religions too have not succeeded in giving a satisfactorily universal response to the question of the presence of transcendence. And this is not surprising because this presence is not just an idea to be thought of like some metaphysical entity, nor can it be reduced to something that is merely material. Transcendence has to be present in such a way that while it is beyond our grasp, yet we are within its grasp.[42]

Transcendence is not so much concerned about the spiritual as seen in opposition to the phenomenal, but it is more about the entire spiritual experience as seen from the point of view of the partial spiritual experience. Due to our human limitations the whole is not accessible to us. Still we are able to access

---

[41] Cf. Boeve and Ries, *The Presence of Transcendence*, vii-ix.

[42] Cf. Boeve and Ries, *The Presence of Transcendence*, ix.

at least a part of the whole through experience, through the conscience and through the symbolic language of those who have had the experience and which they have used to share their experience with others. In this way the transcendent is mediated through the immanent, especially through symbolism and anthropomorphism. At the same time, we have to accept that without this beyond our existence is meaningless because if there is no beyond then we should be able to have all the answers. But we realize that we do not have all the answers. Hence we look to the beyond for the answers which we do not as yet have, and as we gradually grow in our knowledge and experience of transcendence we are able to understand ourselves better and thus our existence becomes more meaningful. The correlativity between immanence and transcendence is unavoidable and inescapable. Transcendence needs an immanent expression.[43]

This is the problem that we have to confront. We need to explain the relation that exists between immanence and transcendence. Immanence is generally understood as an identity. This identity is understood in different ways. It could be understood in the pantheistic sense or it could also be understood in the Christian sense that "God is the constant and efficient Cause from which all at every moment derives its living."[44] From this point of view then things remain in existence because God is thinking of them. Where there is the thought of God there he acts, and where he acts there he is immanent. Transcendence and immanence are two aspects of the same thing. God's transcendence is immanent and his immanence is transcendent. Since there is no interval between his thoughts and his acts God is necessarily present. An artist can be absent to his painting and the painting can still continue to exist in his absence even though it represents the thoughts the artist once had. But, God cannot be absent from creation because they represent the thoughts he is thinking just now. We cannot say how the thought of God will be manifested in nature. This depends on God. We also have to accept that not all thoughts in nature are directly his. This is not to say that they are of another being but there are thoughts that lack his presence. Our duty is to be aware of his presence, the lack of which makes evil possible.[45]

Christianity presents this union of transcendence and immanence in its understanding and use of the medium of prayer. As Holmes describes it, "the whole life of prayer may be described as a continuous passing of the external presence of God into the internal shrine of the human spirit; we hold converse with Him Who is without that He may penetrate more deeply and possess more completely the spirit that is within. Prayer is the co-operation of the human

---

[43] Cf. Gabriel Daly, *Transcendence and Immanence: A study in Catholic Modernism and Integralism* (Oxford: Clarendon Press, 1980), 143-146.

[44] W. H G. Holmes, *The Presence of God: A Study in Divine Immanence and Transcendence* (London: The Macmillan Co., 1923), 6.

[45] Cf. Holmes, *The Presence of God*, 6-12.

action with the Divine."[46] Where God's thought is, there he is present, immanent and transcendent. The presence is an exterior presence but only so that he may enter within. His presence is dependent to an extent on our acceptance because it is our acceptance that allows the presence to make an entrance. So we can say the Eternal dwells within us and we dwell in the eternal. Prayer is the life of union with God. This entrance of the presence within us is not a 'once and for all' event, but is a process that takes place gradually until we are completely filled with his presence and we are united with him. God is not beyond the universe. We see and recognize his presence in nature, a presence that sustains it in being from moment to moment. This is the outer presence. From this outward presence the believer turns inward, and God is no longer seen as 'outside' in nature and the universe, but as dwelling within. As we grow in prayer we grow into a relationship with transcendence and gradually the veil that hides his presence is removed and we are able to perceive his presence in the world, within ourselves and yet beyond.[47]

2.9 Transcendence and Being

The term transcendence for a long time was associated and characterized as a being, even if it was understood to be the supreme being. Understood in this sense it was in accordance with philosophy. But then there was a conflict when philosophy attempted to grasp this transcendence. The problem was that philosophy was limited and could not escape the determination of beings as presence. While philosophy did go beyond beings, it was only in the direction of the 'what' of beings and so it had no way of dealing with that which absents itself completely. So, transcendence is understood as those realities which were excluded from the order of presence and hence which overflow the limits of philosophy. This problem arose because philosophy was considered as the metaphysics of the presence, but it could not deal with what is other than presence. Hence, "it became possible to deplore philosophy's inability to envision a radical alterity, an alterity that nonetheless persists in calling upon us; and thus it also became possible to appeal to the necessity of renewing thought, in such a way as to enable it to embrace that which it had previously grasped only by disfiguring it."[48] So from this point of view philosophy has no access to transcendence, whether it is understood as being, as God or as the Other.[49] It is "unable to grasp transcendence, insofar as this is understood according to the category of an excess with respect to presence."[50]

[46] Holmes, *The Presence of God*, 90.

[47] Cf. Holmes, *The Presence of God*, 90-94.

[48] Marlène Zarader, "Phenomenality and Transcendence," in *Transcendence in Philosophy and Religion*, ed. James E. Faulconer (Bloomington: Indiana University Press, 2003), 107.

[49] Cf. Zarader, "Phenomenality and Transcendence," 106-109.

[50] Zarader, "Phenomenality and Transcendence," 109.

2.9.1 Pan-entheism

Another way of speaking about transcendence is from the point of view of God who pervades the world and souls. He is in the world and at the same time is beyond. According to Magnani it is best perceived in the doctrine of pan-entheism, which signifies that 'all is in God'. Even though, God is beyond the world he is still considered real and eternal and as a personal God has a certain personality and transcendence. The Divine is considered to be of two elements namely the eternal and the temporal, or in other words, the Divine in itself and the Divine as manifested in creation which is seen in some way as his body. Hence there is something relative and at the same time something absolute. This does appear to be contradictory but in pan-entheism this distinction between God and creature is never clear. The universe is part of the being of God. Pan-entheism is different from pantheism which also claims that 'all is God' but which identifies God as the totality of the real. The world and the souls are considered co-eternal with God and so in some way are necessary to him. So, God is not the positive infinite of monotheism who is simple and does not have participation in the sense that he has no parts in himself. In pan-entheism God is not properly the Absolute and there is missing the idea of total creation of the total being and the metaphysical participation. So for pan-entheism God is immanent and transcendent, relative and Absolute.[51]

From the point of view of Christian monotheism God is absolutely transcendent in the mysteriousness of being and in his sanctity. But at the same time God is close to creation, which contains him and is sustained by him and will be saved by him. The inaccessible God is also the God who is present to man and talks to him through creation or through the mediation of his prophets and also his son. He is within the soul of the just person. In fact in the experience of the mystics, God is close to creation, and makes himself present within the soul to him who searches. The way to look for God is within the inner recesses of the self, because it is by going deeper into the self and transcending the self that he is found. But even the mystical knowledge of God is not perfect.[52] And this is unavoidable because the divine transcends all things human and created.

2.9.2 The Insufficiency of the Scientific Means to go Beyond

While we are aware that there is a possibility of the transcendent revealing itself or perhaps even working within our world of space and time, transcendence is a consequence of numinous feelings and of the striking impact of a numinous presence. When we speak of transcendence we speak of it as being beyond space and

---

[51] Cf. Giovanni Magnani, *Religione e Religioni: Dalla Monolatria al Monoteismo Profetico* (Roma: Editrice Pontificia Università Gregoriana, 2001), 86-87.

[52] Cf. Giovanni Magnani, *Religione e Religioni: Il Monoteismo* (Roma: Editrice Pontificia Università Gregoriana, 2001), 357.

time in the sense that it belongs to a higher level. When religion is looked at as the fifth dimension then transcendence which lies beyond the four dimensional world, in practice is identified with religion. Hence in religious experience the religious object would be transcendence. Yet practically the problem of demonstrating that religious experience has an objective reference is not yet resolved. Besides we are also faced with other problems that concern the 'beyond'. For instance, it is difficult to attribute some content to this transcendence and so we cannot speak of it in personal terms as we would of a personal God. Also 'beyond space and time' was formulated at a time when the world and the universe were considered to be much smaller. Today we know much more about the extent of the universe and so the 'beyond' has a much larger significance today than years ago.[53]

Still from the religious point of view to speak of transcendence as 'beyond space and time' seems to be the best possible description. It expresses the faith of the believer in an unlimited power and in the majesty of God. While the phrase does have a negative connotation it also sheds some light on the power and supremacy of God. A dynamic predicate instead of this static one would be more in place but this seems to be the best possible description from a practical point of view. One of the difficulties that such a description gives rise to is that of explaining how that which is 'beyond space and time' is able to act in this world. Besides, being of a higher level of knowing it cannot be of the level of concrete experience but has to function as an interpretation on a higher level.[54]

2.10 Dupré and Transcendence

In speaking about transcendence Dupré says:

> It refers to that particular quality by which the source and terminus of the religious relation surpasses absolutely the mind's and all other reality. It introduces separation into the most intimate union, negation into the most affirmative assertion. It provides the dynamic tension without which the religious act would grow slack and eventually collapse in its own immanence. Transcendence marks religious practice before it becomes a principle of reflection. Both in an individual and in a culture it requires time and religious attentiveness to attain its full potential. At the same time it provides the initial impulse to a movement that, from the very beginning dissatisfied with 'things as they are,' continues to increase the distance between the given reality and man's ultimate aspirations. The principle of transcendence directs his spiritual life.[55]

[53] Cf. Lyttkens, "Religious Experience and Transcendence," 218-219.

[54] Cf. Lyttkens, "Religious Experience and Transcendence," 219-220.

[55] Louis Dupré, "Transcendence and Immanence as Theological Categories," *Proceedings of the Catholic Theological Society of America* 31 (1976), 1.

According to Dupré it is this dynamism that helps man to move towards and also attain his greatest achievements. Yet if transcendence is not firmly rooted in the immanent then it can be self defeating because it becomes a negation of the immanent. The problem in the world today is the ignorance and gradual decline in the awareness of transcendence. Dupré holds that the distinction between the sacred and the profane is inadequate to explain the nature of religion. He holds that we have a concept of transcendence "in which the sacred and the profane are mutually exclusive and share the same plane of reality."[56]

The awareness of transcendence was strongly affected by the strong movement toward objectivism seen in a strong way from the sixteenth century onwards. It was the one-sidedness of this approach which according to Dupré affected the mind's capacity to conceive a genuine transcendence. It reduced our view of nature and the world became a presence-at-hand and gradually closed itself to contemplation. Everything, even the Absolute, was reduced to Spinoza's substance, the objective category par excellence. This objectivist view of transcendence had a drastic effect on the religious character of our entire culture because it gradually led to the awareness that causal dependence was incompatible with genuine freedom, and this would lead to atheism.[57]

Dupré holds that the divine transcendence is a paradox because it can be consistently held only as long as God is conceived as being fully immanent. Mystics and holy men have always held that as God becomes more and more immanent in us he becomes more transcendent to us. As we get closer to him he goes further away. Yet when man is most autonomous he is most dependent because the only dependence that is compatible with full autonomy consists in God's immanent presence, and this presence becomes more intensive as man partakes more directly in God's own autonomy.[58]

2.10.1 Transcendence and the Religious Act

According to Dupré the notion of transcendence can be established independently of the religious act. Its content though is a religious matter. Even so philosophy has to be able to reflect on the sacred or else the sacred has no meaning. We also have to realize that not all philosophies are such that they can deal with the religious phenomenon. Nor can religion claim to have full rational support. Some deal with the transcendent dimension in such a way as to see God as the keystone of the system while others are openly agnostic.[59]

[56] Dupré, "Transcendence and Immanence as Theological Categories," 2.

[57] Cf. Dupré, "Transcendence and Immanence as Theological Categories," 2-8.

[58] Cf. Dupré, "Transcendence and Immanence as Theological Categories," 9.

[59] Cf. Dupré, *The Other Dimension*, 138-139.

Dupré makes a distinction between "the thought of a necessary being and the necessary thought of a necessary being."[60] The first deals with a very fluid concept of reality which can include or exclude the notion of a transcendent necessary being while the second deals with a universe of which God is a necessary component. We are not so much concerned about proving the existence of God, but we are more concerned about being open to the transcendent. Our open ended philosophy seeks to deal with the ultimate ground of the mind and the universe as in an actually existing religious experience. We seek to deal with the God-hypothesis as it is presented by religious man. We determine the specific nature of the religious act in and through its various expressions, especially through a rational study of symbols. While philosophy does respond to the need to reflect systematically on one's faith we have to be careful not to substitute the living experience with rational speculation. We should not pretend to understand that which we describe as lying beyond all understanding. Yet, religion must constantly seek to be clearer lest it get lost in lower forms.[61]

2.10.2 Rationale for Metaphysics and Philosophy of Religion

Dupré refers to the philosophical reflection on the religious act as the philosophy of religion. He also says that philosophy of religion is distinct from general metaphysics which does not use God talk in the strict religious sense. Philosophy of religion on the other hand embraces the full content of the religious experience. The desire to formulate a unified philosophical system to reflect upon religious experience may attempt merging it with general metaphysics. According to Dupré Hegel is one of those who attempted this. "For Hegel the 'system' of philosophy that begins with *Logic* and ends with the *Philosophy of Spirit* has no other content than religion."[62] He quotes Hegel who said, "Philosophy has its own content, its need and interest common with religion; its object is the eternal truth, that is, nothing but God and his explication. Philosophy explicates itself only when it explicates religion and while it explicates itself, it explicates religion."[63] Philosophy of religion has the same general objective as philosophy as such. It does not remain at pure thought but studies religious representation as externally manifested. Philosophy of religion does not consider the finite forms of the Spirit in nature but concentrates directly on the Idea in its infinite form as absolute Spirit.[64] This closeness between philosophy of religion and metaphysics leads to

---

[60] Dupré, *The Other Dimension*, 139.

[61] Cf. Dupré, *The Other Dimension*, 139-142.

[62] Dupré, *The Other Dimension*, 143.

[63] G.W.F. Hegel, *Vorlesungen über die Philosophie der Religion*, ed. Georg Lasson (Hamburg, 1966) I, 29, as quoted in Dupré, *The Other Dimension*, 143.

[64] Cf. Hegel, *Vorlesungen über die Philosophie der Religion*, 31-33, as quoted in Dupré, *The Other Dimension*, 143.

a 'religionization' of metaphysics and could lead to the autonomy of philosophy being challenged. If philosophy insists on autonomous reflection on the religious experience without sacrificing its independence, then it ends up reconstituting basic religious concepts to the extent that religious concepts are no longer recognizable as such. But it can also serve as an independent critical interpretation of a received experience and this is what philosophy of religion is.[65]

In this light when speaking of Hegel, Dupré says that Hegel accepts the unique authority of Christian revelation but he also holds that faith comes into its own only when it has philosophically thought out the representational content of this revelation. So philosophy is not considered merely as a reflection on faith, but it is faith itself reaching its own truth. Philosophy cannot be a substitute for religion but religion must also become philosophy. This does not mean that we must stress the cognitive aspect to the detriment of the faith aspect but just that both are important and each has an identity of its own. Our aim is not to change religion into an intellectual insight but only to use philosophy to shed light on religion and our religious experience. This task of maintaining the relationship between the two is difficult. We have to attempt to correctly interpret the nature of the religious experience while not negating the autonomy of philosophy.[66]

2.11 Conclusion

All in all we can say that while it is difficult to arrive at a universally accepted definition of transcendence we realize that it is a notion that we cannot do without and so we need to speak about it and try to understand it better. This is so because the nature of man does not allow him to be limited to the worldly dimension of his existence. His nature drives him on with a constant desire to escape from this ordinary level of existence to the beyond, thus helping him to add more meaning to his existence here in the world. Increasingly man is beginning to accept that the answer to his quest cannot be found only through scientific means. While beginning from experience he has to reach out to that which lies beyond his grasp. It is for this reason that he looks towards religion, and that is the direction in which we have chosen to look and the path that we have followed in this study. What seems to be universally accepted is that transcendence deals with a metaphysical realm that is beyond or above the rational. Our daily and ordinary experiences which are in this world often seem to point beyond. Whether such an ontological realm exists or not is not our immediate field of study, but we constantly attempt to make sense of the experiences which point to this beyond. We are interested in transcendence since it continuously offers newer possibilities and enables the mind and the soul to strive for higher goals thus allowing man to give vent to the dynamism that lies within him which is in keeping with the

---

[65] Cf. Dupré, *The Other Dimension*, 143-145.

[66] Cf. Dupré, *The Other Dimension*, 145-147.

dynamism of the entire universe. Transcendence is characteristic of man and the universe he inhabits and it is through religion that he is able to reach toward this reality and give expression to his experience of transcendence.

The considerations in this chapter have enabled us to examine transcendence from the phenomenological aspect of religion and experience, because these will serve as the guideposts in our understanding of the concept of transcendence in the writings of Louis Dupré. We have seen how transcendence is a response to the feeling of uneasiness that man experiences as a result of the secularization of life. Transcendence which in general signifies 'to climb across' puts the human being's experience of relatedness and finitude in perspective, particularly from the point of view of religion and the religious experience. It is the religious experience of the sacred and the holy which points towards and leads us to the ultimate reality. Transcendence is a complex concept and it becomes necessary to understand how the transcendent as immanence and presence is part of our existence, a complexity that allows us to be in relation with God. Christianity holds that we share part of our being with the beyond, a paradox that we try to understand through the concepts of participation, causal efficiency and freedom. These are best expressed in the act of religion.

In the next chapter we discuss the religious subject who sometimes has to confront alienation, but who also has an inner dynamism that directs him toward the religious object, a dynamism which is expressed in the religious attitude.

Chapter 3

The Religious Subject

When we consider our existence, we are struck by the fact that we are not just living beings, we are persons made up of body and soul, spirit and flesh, with rational and physical faculties. In most cases philosophers are concerned with man's situation with respect to his surroundings which would include the world, the universe at large, society and his family. Basically it is the religious thinkers who are concerned about the inner life of man and of things beyond this material world. As a result of this approach the concept of man was developed along very mundane lines.

As man deepened his knowledge and awareness of himself he realized that there was more to himself than meets the eye. As a result the consciousness of his environment gradually led to a deepening of the consciousness of his self, and he became "aware of the passive side of selfhood: its dependence and insufficiency."[1] Paradoxically this awareness of his so-called 'weakness' actually worked to his advantage because it was the process of going deeper into himself and trying to understand his inner life that led to a growth of the self.

When man is alone by himself and has nothing to do, he cannot but think. Reflection and consciousness are as much a part of his nature, as his physical abilities and capacities. And when man begins to think and reflect, invariably he begins to confront himself and his existence. Questions about who he is and what is his role and place in the world force him to try and learn more about himself so that he can be clear about where he stands with regard to himself, with others and with the whole of creation. Only when he is clear about who he is, namely—his identity, the present existential situation of his life and his destiny, namely—where he is headed, is man able to have a certain equilibrium about himself, his

[1] Louis Dupré, *Transcendent Selfhood: The Loss and Rediscovery of the Inner Life* (New York: The Seabury Press, 1976), viii.

existence and the meaning of his existence. It is in this search for his identity that we can say philosophy begins.[2]

3.1 The Self as Open to Transcendence

In this discovery of himself there are two aspects that are indispensable and form the core of man's journey towards finding the meaning of his life. These two aspects of the inquiry are experience, and the reflection on that experience. While it is true that without experience there would not be anything to reflect on, at the same time we cannot deny that without reflection, experience by itself would actually lose much of its significance. It is therefore interesting to note two conclusions that Dupré makes concerning the self. The first as we have just mentioned is that "Man's view of himself develops in the dialectic of spontaneous experience with reflection upon his experience."[3] The second conclusion is that a philosophy of man cannot be accomplished and constituted by one man at one moment of time, for the simple reason that it must continually develop with experience.[4] In reflecting on himself man gradually becomes aware of himself as subject. Dupré presents the process of self discovery as taking place in four philosophical stages. The development we notice is from one stage of consciousness to the next.

3.1.1 The Philosophical Stages of Self Discovery

3.1.1.1 The Discovery of the Subject

Among the many emotions that man experiences, perhaps the first experience he has is one of wonder and awe. Before he can even begin to turn back on himself, man is aware of and astonished with himself and his place in the universe together with other objects. It is from this initial feeling of awe and wonder that man goes on to philosophize in pursuit of his search for wisdom. While this feeling of awe and wonder gave man a lot of self-respect, it also enabled man to realize and accept that his fate was closely linked with that of the cosmos. Hence, harmony with the world was necessary so that man could be in harmony with himself. Perhaps none recognized and accepted this fact as much as the Greeks, and it was very clearly evident in their concept of the *polis.* As Dupré says, "In the city man's life was integrated with the world order and it acquired its proper dignity from the national religion, culture, and morality."[5]

From looking outside and around, it did not take very long before man spontaneously turned inward and began to look within himself. Together with self-reflection was born the first true ethics with the soul within as the guiding

[2] Cf. Louis Dupré, "The Philosophical Stages of Self-Discovery," *Thought* 39 (1964), 411.

[3] Dupré, "The Philosophical Stages of Self-Discovery," 412.

[4] Cf. Dupré, "The Philosophical Stages of Self-Discovery," 412.

[5] Dupré, "The Philosophical Stages of Self-Discovery," 416.

principle.[6] This "newly discovered subjectivity is not *per se* opposed to the objective world order—it merely opens another dimension in this order."[7] There exists a basic harmony between man's inner life and the rest of the universe. Thus, man discovers himself as a subjective universe of his own.

3.1.1.2 The Content of the Subject

As man begins to go deeper into himself, he becomes aware of himself as a subject and that he is different from the rest of the universe, and thus he discovers his individuality. In a way this happens because the bond between the individual and the group is broken. With this, man begins to feel lonely and consequently even his relationship with the universe is gradually severed and he reaches complete anonymity. Stoicism as a philosophical reflection on this new experience taught man that it was within himself that he could find harmony with the universe. It was in the depths of one's personality that one found the key to harmony with the rest of the universe.[8] Yet, as Dupré points out, "The Stoic subjectivity remains abstract and empty: it is a withdrawal in a self which has no further determinations than to be a self."[9]

What was needed was some positive content to this subjectivity. Christianity provided this content with its emphasis on personhood, and on the aspect that the person has an eternal and well defined destiny. In the Kantian notion of the person as an absolute end, Dupré sees a laicised reflection of the Christian understanding. So there is no need for a withdrawal from the world, but rather the world itself is part of the drive within man to search for meaning and purpose of the self. Medieval man is well aware of the importance of the position he holds in the universe, and he is especially mindful of his special calling to understand the meaning of the universe.[10] Regarding himself, he considers his own existence as part of the universe, and hence he seeks to understand his own significance outside himself, namely in God and in the world. "As a person man is for himself; yet the principle of his activity is mainly the other-than-himself. Subjectivity is there, but only in a latent, implicit state."[11] The awareness of this search for meaning leads to a new awareness of the dignity of the person.

3.1.1.3 The Isolation of the Subject

Man became increasingly conscious of his control over the world. More importantly he accepted the principle that the laws of the mind had to run parallel

[6] Cf. Dupré, "The Philosophical Stages of Self-Discovery," 416.

[7] Dupré, "The Philosophical Stages of Self-Discovery," 416.

[8] Cf. Dupré, "The Philosophical Stages of Self-Discovery," 417.

[9] Dupré, "The Philosophical Stages of Self-Discovery," 417.

[10] Cf. Dupré, "The Philosophical Stages of Self-Discovery," 417.

[11] Dupré, "The Philosophical Stages of Self-Discovery," 418.

with the laws of nature. As a result of this, the mind had the basic elements for the understanding of the universe in itself. Therefore, the resources for the purpose of understanding both the world as well as the self lay in the mind. So man believed that the truth of himself and his world was within himself. It was Descartes who introduced the insight that the mind was an independent form of being and it was this insight that evolved into a metaphysics of consciousness. Man did not see himself as a part of nature, but through consciousness he is essentially opposed to nature. He knows nature through consciousness, so nature is described in terms of consciousness. Descartes described the world as *res extensa*. His understanding of the world as a determination of the mind was a reversal of the earlier understanding that held that the self was determined by nature. Descartes' consciousness was not constitutive of reality because he held that the human mind was separated from the reality of things. Yet consciousness itself does not create truth. It only exposes an objectivity by submitting itself to a transcendent realm of being which is revealed in the mind but whose ultimate reality remains beyond the grasp of the mind.[12]

Kant on the other hand does not allow consciousness to be submissive to a transcendent reality and would claim that consciousness is to be explained exclusively by itself. The conditions for intelligibility are to be found not in external reality but in consciousness itself. Truth and falsity are in the mind. Morality and truth are determined by the intention of the agent. While such a sequence of thought established the autonomy and independence of man, it ended up in man being separated from the universe. Due to this isolation from reality, man was not capable of knowing the real thing. Thinking and willing are subjective.[13] This line of argument points out the failure of subjectivity itself because, "when the subject takes over the role of the object and denies that the latter can have any intelligible content which is not integrally constituted by the subject, it forfeits all claims for a content of its own."[14] Kant's subject of freedom is empty and devoid of content.

When subjectivity is thus made into a universal principle the human aspect loses its objectivity. In order to understand the true nature of subjectivity then, it is imperative to maintain a separation between the subject and the object each with a content that is its own, and only this will help us understand the true nature of subjectivity. Subjectivity cannot be arrived at by opposing a non-substantial subjectivity and a substantial reality as an independent form of being. Consciousness and objective reality are related. The problem is how to relate them without reducing one to the other.[15]

[12] Cf. Dupré, "The Philosophical Stages of Self-Discovery," 419.

[13] Cf. Dupré, "The Philosophical Stages of Self-Discovery," 420.

[14] Dupré, "The Philosophical Stages of Self-Discovery," 421.

[15] Cf. Dupré, "The Philosophical Stages of Self-Discovery," 421-422.

3.1.1.4 The Subject and the Object

Subjectivity and the objective world, and their relation is the very problem that Hegel tackled in his dialectic of freedom. "He shows how on the one hand subjectivity as freedom expresses itself in the real and, through labor, civilization, law, science and art, creates an objective, spiritual world."[16] So he saw freedom and reality as complementary aspects of one totality which he called, the Spirit. The subject and the object are made up of each other in a dialectical opposition. Hegel sees man as an historical being. There is a development at the heart of the self, which is "no longer seen as a static being, but a self-creating process… The notions of self-development and dialectical opposition of subjective freedom and objectivity are synthesized in Hegel's view of man as an historical being."[17] It is in becoming aware of his historicity that man transcends his historical situation and becomes trans-historical. Marx's philosophy challenged the reduction of man to the objective world. Man originates from nature and his consciousness is determined by nature, but man is not nature. When man relates to nature in a thing-like way it leads to his estrangement. He refuses to identify man as merely a development of pure consciousness.[18]

Kierkegaard in his philosophy challenged the notion that freedom takes on absolute proportions in man. While he agrees with Hegel that man constitutes himself in freedom, this freedom is not an autonomous self-realization, but consists in his freely choosing a self that is given and also dependent on a transcendent power. Such a choice naturally seems to be self contradictory because this immanent striving in the long run is bound to get stranded in a transcendent limitation. The solution he says is to be found in the attitude of Abraham, who in faith resolved this tension between the immanent and the transcendent. "To surrender oneself and one's immanent values to the transcendent, and, at the same time, to remain steadfast in one's conviction that one must and will regain the entire sphere of immanent freedom within the transcendent, that is the paradoxical achievement of faith."[19] It is in this search for his authentic self that man realizes his true self. In Kierkegaard's explanation of freedom, Hegel's dialectic and subjectivity are sustained but this dialectic of freedom breaks through the constraints of its immanence because it is related to an ulterior term which remains forever transcendent.[20]

It was in Existential Phenomenology that the view of man as a relational being reaches its completion. According to existential phenomenology, the essence of the human subject is to *ek-sist*, to posit itself in the world. Man's freedom is a

---

[16] Dupré, "The Philosophical Stages of Self-Discovery," 422.

[17] Dupré, "The Philosophical Stages of Self-Discovery," 423.

[18] Cf. Dupré, "The Philosophical Stages of Self-Discovery," 424.

[19] Dupré, "The Philosophical Stages of Self-Discovery," 425.

[20] Cf. Dupré, "The Philosophical Stages of Self-Discovery," 426.

freedom through the body and so it is bound to a situation in the world. And yet, while man is 'in' the world, at the same time he is not 'of' the world. "Through consciousness he constantly negates this world and asserts his otherness... He exists only in a constant dialogue with this world... he never becomes a part of this world—he remains forever a subject intending an object."[21] From this we can say that man does not merely belong to the world of things, but he is the meaning-giving principle of this world. His essence is not something finished but it develops gradually. Uniquely his freedom is not autonomous and self sufficient, but is always connected to the world and also to the transcendent. It is a freedom within a given situation, and yet it is a freedom that leaves him in control and allows him to go beyond himself.[22] It is a dialectical movement of freedom which in the process of creating objective reality creates itself.[23]

3.1.2 The Nature of the Self

From the point of view of understanding the concept of transcendence it is imperative to understand the self, because transcendence arises from the capacity of man to go beyond himself. Dupré makes a differentiation between the 'self' and the 'individual'. As individual, man is part of this world. It is in his individuality that man has a body, possesses life, and is very much this-worldly. As self, man surpasses this world. This aspect of man is seen in his capacity and ability for reflection and recollection which takes him beyond the limits placed on him by his bodiliness. This means that when he dies to his individuality and when the individuality is overcome, then the self is born.[24]

3.1.2.1 Self and the Person

The concept of person includes both selfhood and individuality. Objectively speaking, in the words of Boethius, the person is just an individual substance of rational nature. But there is more to the human being than this. The person also has a subjective mode of being besides being a substance, and it is from this point of view that we can speak of selfhood.[25] Human life is the first condition for personhood but then, Dupré says, "Personhood is a dynamic category in which distinctions between undeveloped and developed stages are crucial."[26] Every individual human life has at least a minimal personhood. But personhood is not equivalent to being human because personhood is a dynamic concept.

---

[21] Dupré, "The Philosophical Stages of Self-Discovery," 427.

[22] Cf. Dupré, "The Philosophical Stages of Self-Discovery," 427-428.

[23] Dupré, "The Philosophical Stages of Self-Discovery," 414.

[24] Cf. Louis Dupré, *Transcendent Selfhood: The Loss and Rediscovery of the Inner Life* (New York: Seabury Press, A Crossroad Book, 1976), 31.

[25] Cf. Dupré, *Transcendent Selfhood*, 32.

[26] Dupré, *Transcendent Selfhood*, 32.

Every individual human life has a potential for achievement, which can become an actual achievement, and it is this "degree of actualization" that enters into the essence of personhood. Personhood is a larger and all encompassing concept. But selfhood while being similar is more about the individual identity of the person. In a sense it is the subjective core of personhood. To reach selfhood man has to develop his sense of self-awareness, and so it needs a power of recollection and reflection. The objective expression of the individual is the person, and the subjective principle beneath the person is selfhood.[27]

3.1.2.2 Self and the Body

Joseph Maréchal in his book *Studies in the Psychology of the Mystics*, has made an interesting analysis of mystical states. He explains how the mystic can obtain a vivid awareness of bodily presence unsupported by sense perception.[28] This opens up an interesting perspective of the self because when we follow this line of thought it would point towards a relative independence of the feeling with regard to the presence of actual sensation. Along similar lines would be the many instances of the memory functioning without the support of the body which would give rise to the entire problem of the relation between the mind and the body. According to Dupré, the states of consciousness cannot do away with the body altogether, because even the mystic remains bodily oriented. The mystic's "body alone provides the stable vantage point which directs his experiences even when they transcend its ordinary capacity. Without any connection with a body the human mind would become totally disoriented."[29] The body is more than a mere instrument of the mind because it helps one to define one's relation to oneself and to the world. Usually experience indicates an operative union of mind and body. This union of mind and body indicates that personal identity is connected to a particular mind-body relation. According to Dupré most people "regard the body as an object in the world through which the mind acquires information that may be acquired in other ways. But the body is not a part of the world: it is my viewpoint with respect to the world."[30]

3.1.2.3 Self and Consciousness

The self also cannot be equated to self consciousness because there could be many instances when for long stretches of time the self loses all consciousness. But because it loses consciousness it does not mean to say that it has lost its selfhood. Some philosophers and depth psychologists accept the existence of a "dark side" of

---

[27] Cf. Dupré, *Transcendent Selfhood*, 33.

[28] Cf. Joseph Maréchal, *Studies in the Psychology of the Mystics*, trans. Algar Thorold (New York: Magi Books, 1964), 55-145, as quoted in Dupré, *Transcendent Selfhood*, 83-84.

[29] Dupré, *Transcendent Selfhood*, 84.

[30] Dupré, *Transcendent Selfhood*, 85.

consciousness, that is a layer of selfhood which is sometimes unconscious. Beyond the self that was object-oriented, William Ernest Hocking posited "a reflective self beyond the excursive, object-oriented one. This subphenomenal foundation explains how the self can remain constant after interruptions of consciousness and lapses of memory."[31] Basically it is this reflective self that gives humans a personal identity, because while the body has an important role to play in the personal identity of the self, it cannot be its ultimate foundation.[32] More and more we see that the unconscious self interferes with the conscious self. Often when this happens the self is led beyond the boundaries of the ordinary world and in this it reveals the working of an inner power. This deeper self is not very much dependent on the body, which naturally leads to the question about whether the self could altogether do away with its dependence on the world. While he accepts that there is no conclusive philosophical answer, Dupré says that the, "mind seems to be so essentially and definitively determined by the body that it must forever maintain an essential relation to the body, if it is to preserve its identity."[33] At the same time, to say that a mind can do without complete embodiment seems to be only a hypothesis, while a relatively embodied self with its own unconscious core seems to be more plausible.[34] As Dupré says, "The self is essentially more than mere self, that transcendence belongs to its nature as much as the act through which it is immanent to itself, and that a total failure on the mind's part to realize this transcendence reduces the self to less than itself."[35]

From this discussion we can say that, "To survive individually the mind must maintain a permanent relation to an individual body. The body itself need not be permanent, but the mind must permanently retain the essential bodily orientation."[36] Bodiliness of some sort is an essential condition. While accepting that the mind in ordinary circumstances cannot function in total independence from the body there are a few functions that are not directly dependent on the actual presence of the body apart from its general physiological conditions. Hence, we can say that because of the relative independence of the mind with respect to the body it is possible that there be certain states of consciousness that do not require the actual presence of the body, though naturally there has to be some connection with an actual body. Sometimes, the mind can function without the contribution of the senses.[37]

---

[31] Dupré, *Transcendent Selfhood*, 89.

[32] Cf. Dupré, *Transcendent Selfhood*, 89.

[33] Dupré, *Transcendent Selfhood*, 90.

[34] Cf. Dupré, *Transcendent Selfhood*, 89-90.

[35] Louis Dupré, "The Mystical Experience of the Self and its Philosophical Significance," *Proceedings of the American Catholic Philosophical Association* 48 (1974), 162.

[36] Dupré, *Transcendent Selfhood*, 90-91.

[37] Cf. Dupré, *Transcendent Selfhood*, 90-91.

3.1.3 Self as Subject

3.1.3.1 From the Self to the Subject

The self had a role to play in the total order of being. This role took on an added meaning with a change in the understanding of the term *subject.* Subject was usually translated as *hypokeimenon* which meant that which lies under something. From the most elementary level of being it gradually came to be understood as the ultimate source of meaning which earlier had been attributed to God or to a divine nature.[38]

The deepening of the understanding of the subject can be attributed to Duns Scotus who assigned a distinct mental reality to the known and called it the *esse objectivum* in the mind.[39] The 'objective' being was ideal, in contrast with the 'subjective' being which was extra-mental and real. This distinction between the real and the mental would be broadened in nominalist philosophy. The subject still referred to the *suppositum* of being and its qualities. But there was the human mind which while belonging to the substantial subject, in its activity was ideal in nature. So the mental subject came to be regarded as the source of the ideal qualities which earlier had been considered as inherent in all other *supposita.* These ideal qualities were bound to the mental subject as objects, that is to say as being for-the-subject and so the entire order of reality was reconstructed in terms of the ideal. And in this process the self lost its own substantial content in the exercising of its cognitive and volitive functions. Earlier humanism had prepared for this transition by speaking of the second human nature created by humans through culture which raised them above the rest of nature. But the person was still a power *within* Being, as a substance. Renaissance philosophers developed this concept into the person as constituting meaning and value, a power that was earlier attributed either to nature or to the creator. Tomasso Campanella said that the person surpasses nature and ceases to be part of nature by thought and in artistic achievement, while for Giordano Bruno the person not only shaped himself but also gave meaning and form to the universe. It was the person who subjected nature to human purposes.[40] Gradually there was a shift of emphasis, and more importance was given to the shaping of nature according to the needs of human beings.

This turn towards the subject gradually became inevitable and the self had no option but to function as a subject, the meaning giver. The traditional world view was being challenged and there was a prevalent existential crisis that gave rise to a heightened anxiety. The normal reaction would have been to take refuge

---

[38] Cf. Louis Dupré, *Passage to Modernity: An Essay in the Hermeneutics of Nature and Culture* (New Haven: Yale University Press, 1993), 112.

[39] Cf. Duns Scotus, I Sent. dist. 36, q. un., no. 45-47. *Opera omnia* (Civitas Vaticana, 1950), vol. 6, 288-289, as quoted in Dupré, *Passage to Modernity*, 112.

[40] Cf. Dupré, *Passage to Modernity*, 113.

in religion. But religion, specifically the Christian dominated culture of the west, was going through its own turmoil and unfortunately had no solution to offer in the face of the prevailing crisis and in fact it was religion that lay at the heart of the turmoil. In this confusion there was a return to the ancient sceptics and to the conviction that one could lead a morally respectable life even without possessing certainty. Gian Francesco Pico della Mirandola made an attack on worldly learning and concluded that since philosophy does not give certainty, the mind ought to turn to divine prophecy. Montaigne's scepticism arose from a fundamental doubt about the capacity of the mind to have certainty in any area. In his *Apology* he wrote of the need to find one thing of which we could be absolutely certain or else we could not be certain of anything. It is the self that is the source of all uncertainty.[41]

3.1.3.2 The Contribution of Descartes

Descartes' approach to this prevailing epistemological crisis was interesting because of his approach through 'doubt'. He attempted "to restore the foundations of human knowledge by converting moral uncertainty into philosophical doubt and doubt itself into a method for attaining certainty."[42] Descartes notes that many of our preconceived opinions which initially are accepted, later on are proved to be wrong. This leads to a doubt about all truths, even those that seem to be most reliable. Ironically it is from this extreme doubt that arises the indubitable truth of the existence of the thinking subject as he explains in his *cogito ergo sum.* God is an important part of the Cartesian system, and once the existence of the deity has been established Descartes goes on to reinforce his belief in the world around him. Descartes also uses the deity to develop a method for the search of truth through our 'clear and distinct ideas' that are innate, which he would say are implanted in our mind by God.[43]

Descartes' argument which proves the existence of God by clear and distinct ideas, and which then uses the existence of God to render clear and distinct ideas as trustworthy is circular and seems to avoid the possibility of an evil genius which may interfere with thinking. Descartes overcomes this problem of a totally unpredictable God, though without much philosophical justification, by saying that while God is omnipotent his omnipotence is limited by a moral attribute. And so while God has the power to deceive he cannot will to deceive us. Dupré feels that the way Descartes conceives of the self shows an openness of the self towards transcendence.[44] In fact, Descartes concludes the third Meditation in which he lays the foundation of the self's cognitive ability with these words,

---

[41] Cf. Dupré, *Passage to Modernity*, 114-115.

[42] Dupré, *Passage to Modernity*, 115.

[43] Cf. *Cambridge Dictionary of Philosophy* (1995) s.v. "Descartes, Rene," 195.

[44] Cf. Dupré, *Passage to Modernity*, 116.

"[Before I pass on to other truths] I should like to pause here and spend some time in the contemplation of God; to reflect on his attributes and to gaze with wonder and adoration on the beauty of this immense light, so far as the eye of my darkened intellect can bear it."[45]

With his introspection Descartes says that the basis of all ideas is the mind, and not God. In this sense the self becomes the foundation even of the idea of God. Descartes identifies the self with mental substance. He describes this mental substance as the opposite of bodily substance. He describes it as, "'*une chose qui pense, et non-étendue..., et qui ne participe à rien de ce qui appartient au corps*' (a thinking thing, and not extended..., not participating in anything pertaining to the body)."[46] Yet in this description he fails to provide an aspect that would be a positively distinguishing mark from bodily substance. He only shows that consciousness exists as an irreducible mode of being, and so can be applied to different substances. The foundational self seems to be an emptiness. But it is the mind that defines the real in the ideal categories and controls it through *praxis*. What is significant is that Descartes sets the notion of selfhood in a direction that would result in it being a functional notion, in the sense that it would be the source of meaning and value. The self-making through self expression can be traced back to early humanism. For the humanists the expressive power of the self was mediated through the integration of the self with nature and also through its intrinsic dependence on a transcendent reality. For the rationalists on the other hand, the existence of the world and God was founded on the thinking subject because it was the thinking subject that defined and established them. The self therefore had only a foundational role.[47]

3.1.4 The Subject, Morality and Religion

3.1.4.1 Descartes

Descartes developed a metaphysical theory on the basis that the mind is a different kind of being. Instead of defining the self in terms of nature he defined the material world in rational categories. But he did not consider consciousness as a component of reality. It was Kant who took this final step. "Kant declared the mind to be self-sufficient both in its knowledge of itself and the world. Thus, the subject changed from a principle *parallel* to the objective world into a principle *constitutive of* objectivity."[48] This principle had a major effect on ethics and

---

[45] Rene Descartes, *Oeuvres*, ed. Adam-Tannery (Paris: Vrin, 1964) 224, as quoted in Dupré, *Passage to Modernity*, 117.

[46] Descartes, *Meditations* IV, AT IX, 42, as quoted in Dupré, *Passage to Modernity*, 118.

[47] Cf. Dupré, *Passage to Modernity*, 117-119.

[48] Dupré, *Transcendent Selfhood*, 34.

morality because now the morality of an act was not determined by the object of the act but rather by the intention of the acting subject.[49]

This aspect of ethical consciousness is significant in our study of the self because it was through ethical consciousness that philosophy came face to face with the transcendent dimension of the self. The discovery of transcendence does not signal the end of our moral striving. On the contrary it is religion that provides the strongest motivation for the ethical endeavour. It is the religious ideal that drives man forward in his search for the attainment of moral ideals in his life. As Dupré writes, "It is not only in the awareness of moral failure, then, but also in the need for a transcendent foundation of the moral law, that the ethical attitude may turn into a religious one."[50]

3.1.4.2 Kant

Kant in an inadequate definition described religion as the ability to perceive the moral imperative as a divine command. What he was trying to do was to give divine sanction to a moral system. But later in *Opus Posthumum* he says that, "The religious interpretation is not added to the perception of duties as duties, but is given immediately and necessarily with them."[51] That is to say that the categorical imperative implies the existence of God because, "The categorical imperative of the command of duty is grounded in the idea of an *imperantis,* who is all-powerful and holds universal sway. This is the Idea of God."[52]

3.1.4.3 John Henry Newman

Cardinal John Henry Newman based the transcendent character of this moral obligation on the conscience. For him the conscience was more than a mere sense of morality that man possessed. It was more of an authoritative dictate.[53] In this sense "there is One to whom we are responsible, before whom we are ashamed, whose claims upon us we fear."[54] Naturally this insight is only acceptable to those who have a sense of the religious, so it cannot be taken as a *proof* for the existence of God, but rather it has to be accepted as an indication of the religious mind's actual perception of transcendence in the moral order. Newman therefore seems to be saying that the divine sanction adds weight to the moral obligation because it emphasizes its transcendent origin.[55]

---

[49] Cf. Dupré, *Transcendent Selfhood*, 34.

[50] Dupré, *Transcendent Selfhood*, 38.

[51] Dupré, *Transcendent Selfhood*, 38.

[52] Immanuel Kant, *Kants Opus Posthumum*, ed. Erich Adickes (Berlin, 1920), 108, as quoted in Dupré, *Transcendent Selfhood*, 38.

[53] Cf. John Henry Newman, *An Essay in aid of a Grammar of Assent*, ed. I. T. Ker (Oxford: Clarendon Press, 1985), 74.

[54] Newman, *An Essay in aid of a Grammar of Assent*, 76.

[55] Cf. Dupré, *Transcendent Selfhood*, 39.

3.1.5 Conclusion

From all this we can say that there is a distinction between transcendence from the point of view of religion and moral self-transcendence. Religious transcendence has a deep impact on moral self-transcendence. Man is never content with the prescribed and the given but is always seeking to go beyond that which is required and necessary. He seeks ever new responses to a transcendent calling. Why man looks for and accepts the more difficult option is not easy to explain, but his pursuit of transcendence is undeniable. This voluntary nature of his pursuit is the very call to transcendence. If man is able to transcend his normal human nature in observing these 'rules' of divine perfection, he is no longer 'bound' by these rules. It is this propensity to go beyond and let himself be taken to limits beyond his self that induces him to do things that from an immanent ethical viewpoint would seem to be superfluous.[56]

The person is a complex entity and in fact has been described as an ensouled micro-cosmos. The human person is a synthesis of the spirit and the world. His incarnated spiritual nature is articulated through symbolism, especially through symbolism in words. It was phenomenology that has shown how the body "is the primary symbol that constitutes all others. The human body projects its spiritual inwardness upon the outside world. Through the body I take a position in a world already coordinated and symbolically endowed by earlier human projections."[57] Sometimes, in special moments and through unique symbols the person succeeds in giving expression to the depth and interiority of his personhood. It is in these singular moments that the body truly reveals itself as a manifestation of spirit. In these moments the mind is able to perceive the permanent in the transient and the universal in the particular. It is when the mind is able to make this connection and is able to see in the singular instance a reference to the whole of reality that it has attained in some part the *essence* of the real. Each symbol is singularly perceived and creates its own meaning, but when all are taken together and seen in relation to each other and the whole, then the whole totality becomes meaningful. And this is what in the West is called 'culture.'[58]

3.2 Transcendence that is Challenged in Culture

Every person has received being as something already given. So our life long task is to make sense of our existence and to make it meaningful so that our existence in the world may be of some significance to ourselves and also to the others around us. We are human beings and so we live in community, we are not isolated. As members therefore of a group, culture is an important aspect of our existence. Let us therefore make a deeper study of what Louis Dupré has to say about culture.

---

[56] Cf. Dupré, *Transcendent Selfhood*, 40.

[57] Louis Dupré, *Metaphysics and Culture* (Milwaukee: Marquette University Press, 1994), 7-8.

[58] Cf. Dupré, *Metaphysics and Culture*, 9.

Dupré speaks about culture as the embodiment of mind. This is so because it is the formation and use of symbols that gives a particular direction and identity to the life of a society. It is through culture that a group has a special way of looking at and interpreting experiences which enables it to make its existence significant. This meaning that is sought is first expressed in the act of naming things and putting order in creation. Human beings are unique because of their ability to control nature through *techne*, or a craft which Aristotle would say helps towards achieving a good that lies beyond the activity itself. Earlier the Greek *paideia* and the Latin *cultura animi* emphasized the aspect of cultivating an existing nature, but the modern concept separates culture and nature by aiming at a conquest of nature. The ancients did not seem to make or consider any such separation. Earlier culture was seen as a fostering of and developing an already existing nature. Modern man wants to create a second nature. Culture earlier meant cultivating, while today it is seen in the context of domination of nature.[59]

More than supplying society with norms and values, the purpose of culture is to provide society with a help to cope with the material conditions of existence. More than the mere satisfaction of physical needs it enables the human being to fulfil and give expression to the spiritual and rational powers that are part of his being and which cannot be satisfied by mere bodily gratification. Culture therefore deals with our existence and also our drive and ability to be fully human. In this sense being human is the same as being cultured.[60]

Ancient grandeur and heroism serves as one of the means to idealize life. Hence law, ritual, art and manners in society help a community to remain as an organic unity. Early philosophers were not very clear in their acceptance of this unity as having an existence. Kant said that as a moral being the person is distinguished from the realm of nature. While being linked to the world as a natural being, in his freedom man has a moral vocation beyond this world, and it is culture that bridges this gap between nature and man's moral vocation. The problem arose because there was a clash of interests as happened with culture which was supposed to unite the objective to the subjective in a higher union and harmony. But this is very rare especially in the modern times. This difficulty in a way was unavoidable due to a gradual transformation that took place in culture which would lead to the loss of transcendence and alienation.[61]

3.2.1 The First Transformation of Culture: The Subject as the Source of Rationality

According to Dupré, it was "in the early Italian Renaissance that the idea of fostering and developing an existing potential started giving way to man's need

[59] Cf. Dupré, *Metaphysics and Culture*, 12-13.

[60] Cf. Dupré, *Metaphysics and Culture*, 14-15.

[61] Cf. Dupré, *Metaphysics and Culture*, 16-19.

to assert himself independently from nature's arrangement."[62] This was seen in the process of socialization. To be fully "human" man had to go beyond his given humanity. This is reflected by Pico della Mirandola who in *Oratio* describes man as a 'Prothean' being. Having no nature that is proper to himself, man is able to take on all natures. Dante in *De vulgari eloquentia* claims that the source of national cultures which lay in the origin of vernacular languages was due to a technical enterprise that was taken up in defiance of a divinely established order. So at the base of the new concept of culture is the decision to surpass ones allotted nature even if it involves an act of rebellion. This is reflected also in the use of the term *humanitas* which was an invitation to go beyond the limits of ordinary mankind. In attaining this *humanitas* man so to say, became the new creator of his nature and in this joins the divine Maker.[63]

Traditional Christian cosmology considered that the world was created by the measure, number and rule of divine Wisdom. The hierarchical order in the world reflected that Wisdom and it was basically this cosmic order that also determines man's place in this whole complex while also prescribing the norms of his behaviour. Later the idea of an intrinsically rational world order disintegrated. The rationality of the world was derived from its divine character. "For the Greeks and medieval Christians, Arabs and Jews, a rational logos, variously interpreted, *inhered* in the *given* nature of reality. It definitely did not emerge from a human mind imposing its own categories upon a world devoid of a rational necessity of its own."[64] But this security in the immanent rationality was challenged, and astronomists like Copernicus, Galilei and Kepler concluded that the rationality of the universe lay in mathematical structures which are an operation of the mind but are hidden behind the primary qualities in the physical world. And so nature is subjected to a breaking down into simpler elements that are quantifiable, and this analysis was the scope of most of modern scientific theory. This analysis is followed by a synthesis, which does not simply put together the previously analysed reality, but in fact results in a new reduced reality—the world of physics. This reality which no longer 'reveals' but only answers the questions we raise and responds to our demands, is a much truncated reality. So, nature becomes a calculable and predictable force, a sort of shortened reality whose intrinsic meaningfulness which earlier was articulated in the final causality and inner teleology of nature is transposed to the *res cogitans*.[65]

---

[62] Louis Dupré, "The Modern Idea of Culture: Its Opposition to its Classical and Christian Origins," in *Ebraismo, Ellenismo, Cristianesimo II*. Ed. Marco Olivetti. *Archivio di Filosofia* 53 (1985) 470.

[63] Cf. Dupré, "The Modern Idea of Culture," 470-471.

[64] Dupré, "The Modern Idea of Culture," 472.

[65] Cf. Dupré, "The Modern Idea of Culture," 472-473.

As the subject became the sole source of rationality, thought took on a new aspect. Thought was no longer contemplation but it now became a method of categorical structuring. The subject began to impose its rationality on a vague world. The application of the method of the physical sciences led to a transformation of the concept of reason. "While the Greek *theoria* had required the soul to be purified before being allowed to the divine act of contemplation, the subject now immediately adopted an attitude of domination culminating in the conception that *real* is only the objective, that is, what has been constituted by an autonomous subject."[66] Reason thus took on a practical orientation. Objectivity and practical control ended the rule of contemplation. Fabrication became the order of the day and this resulted in an unlimited instrumentalization of the world.[67]

For a long time science developed but there was little or no development of technology. Even so, methods, attitudes and other related factors were being developed as a result of which there was a steady ordering of nature which would give rise to the technological revolution that now controls our lives. Modern technology unlike ancient and medieval technology, is not content with just being a part of the work of nature, but aims at full control over nature. This naturally leads to a confrontation. The Greeks did not strive to control nature and its processes, but were careful to restrict all instrumental activity within the fixed boundaries set by nature. When the craftsman 'created', it was primarily to adjust oneself to nature. Modern technology on the other hand aims at the control of nature without regard to its immanent processes. As a result man is caught up in the technological enterprise and because of this attitude everything is a *function* and nothing refers to the *beyond*. Earlier technology was man's handmaid, but now he is slave to technology. Technology has become the face of reality today and with it has vanished the importance and significance of transcendence.[68]

Purpose and act coincide in the smooth functioning of the system but while this assures the smooth functioning of the system, man becomes just an essential part of the 'economic' and 'social processes' of the system. Technology has now begun to be equated with reality and so the possibility of transcending it becomes all the more remote. As Hans Jonas so correctly wrote, "If we equate the realm of necessity with Plato's 'cave', then scientific theory leads not out of the cave; nor is its practical application a return to the cave: it never left it in the first place. It is entirely of the cave and therefore not 'theory' at all in the Platonic sense."[69] As Hannah Arendt noted, it is precisely in the moment when man

---

[66] Dupré, "The Modern Idea of Culture," 474.

[67] Cf. Dupré, "The Modern Idea of Culture," 474-475.

[68] Cf. Dupré, "The Modern Idea of Culture," 475-476.

[69] Hans Jonas, *The Phenomenon of Life* (University of Chicago Press, 1982), 11, as quoted in Dupré, "The Modern Idea of Culture," 476.

becomes most worldly that the world itself has lost all its intrinsic meaning, and is reduced to a mere mental abstraction. "What started by being a pure object ends up being devoid of any substance, a mere projection of the subject. Everywhere man encounters only himself and his own fabrications in this closed, autistic universe."[70] He does not encounter his own essence.

3.2.2 The Second Transformation: The Meaning and Role of the Self

The second transformation of modern culture is connected with the meaning and the role of the self. Starting with the *Timaeus* and many books influenced by its content, man is presented as a micro cosmos of the entire world order. This particular view of man as micro cosmos was well received by Christians because in this way man was seen as a reflection of the cosmos, because man is an image of God who is mirrored by the cosmos. Man who is seen as the crowning of God's creative activity has a special duty to return this creation to its creator. The universe is endowed with a meaning by its creator, and it is man's duty to discover and express this meaning. It is through the fulfilment of this duty that man finds meaning in his existence.[71]

With the advent of the modern age, the analogy between God and the creature was no longer possible and the world was considered as an arbitrary effect of an omnipotent and inscrutable God. Francis Bacon rejected the world as an image of God and man as an image of the world. He held that the works of God do reflect his omnipotence and his wisdom, but they were not a reflection of the image of God. They reflected his characteristics but did not reflect God. The heathens too did not accept that man was a reflection of the cosmos. They saw man as a comprehensive but brief image of the world. Reality is deprived of having an immanent God-given meaning and this meaning has to be supplied by the subject.[72] Dupré quotes the words of Max Horkheimer:

> The more all nature is looked upon … as mere objects in relation to human subjects, the more is the once supposedly autonomous subject emptied of any content, until it finally becomes a mere name with nothing to denominate. The total transformation of each and every realm of being into a field of means leads to the liquidation of the subject who is supposed to use them. This gives modern industrialist society its nihilistic aspect. Subjectivization, which exalts the subject, also dooms him.[73]

---

[70] Dupré, "The Modern Idea of Culture," 476.

[71] Cf. Dupré, "The Modern Idea of Culture," 477.

[72] Cf. Francis Bacon, *The Advancement of Learning in Works*, ed. J. Spedding and R. L. Ellis, III, 349, as quoted in Dupré, "The Modern Idea of Culture," 477.

[73] Max Horkheimer, *The Eclipse of Reason*, as quoted in Dupré, "The Modern Idea of Culture," 477.

Romanticism was a reaction to the increasingly rationalist, objectivist culture. It tried to free the self from this very limiting task that had been imposed upon it, namely that of constituting an objective universe. But the modern consciousness realized that the subject had been so completely absorbed in its task of bestowing meaning upon all things that no content was left in itself. This was especially clear in the psychological sciences which while intending to understand the subject, only ended up in reducing it to an *object* of observation and analysis. The Greek and medieval Christian world view in spite of their basic cosmological orientation had taken man as the measure of the real. But it was rather interesting to note that in a strange paradox, this modern attitude which was subject-oriented resulted in a de-anthropomorphizing and an ultimately dehumanising attitude.[74]

This gave rise to a whole new style of literature dedicated to the 'death of the subject'. In this period there is a certain anti-humanism that exhibits an antagonism towards man. Ortega y Gasset in his essay *The Dehumanization of Art* (1925), showed how this aversion of the human person was expressed in modern art. This expression brings to the fore the sense of defeat that is encountered in the attempt to return man to the central place he held in the universe of meaning, a position he had held since the Renaissance. When Nietzsche spoke of the *religion of man* as a phenomenon of decadence, and even earlier when Marx spoke of the absolute primacy of *praxis*, it was just an anticipation of this awareness of defeat. What we notice here is actually the final stage in the development of western thought. It started with the belief in the intrinsic rationality of the world order with the subject who supplied the rationality to the world order which was of the subject's making. Marx carried the principle of creativity one step further and included the subject in the productive act itself. The subject no longer came before the creative activity but rather was an outcome of the activity. "Through his productive activity man creates both *himself* and his world. Thus Marx radicalized the modern rule that meaning and value are not *given* with the nature of reality, but *constituted* by the living deed."[75]

3.2.3 The Third Transformation: The Disappearance of Transcendence

This brings us to perhaps the most significant predicament of the modern age, namely the disappearance of transcendence. For most societies in the past, the integrating factor was religion. All values were subordinated to a transcendent principle because there was a general feeling of dependence. But once man realized as he did in modern culture that the powers of control over the universe and over human beings lay within himself, he no longer felt the need of relating

---

[74] Cf. Dupré, "The Modern Idea of Culture," 478.

[75] Dupré, "The Modern Idea of Culture," 479.

all aspects of his existence to a transcendent principle.[76] As Dupré says in *The Other Dimension*:

> Science, art, philosophy, and morality have emancipated themselves from their religious origins to the extent that apparently they can exist as well without religion as with it. The scientist is no longer puzzled by the parallelism between the laws of nature and the laws of the mind, since he knows that all laws are laws only for the mind... what artists dimly felt in the past, they now bluntly assert, namely, that the work of art is not an imitation of nature, subject to an extrinsic code, but that it creates its own norms and reality. In his moral behaviour also man has assumed full responsibility over himself: he has no more use of a divinely imposed, unchangeable code of conduct. Even religion can be accommodated in this man-centered universe as a symbolic expression of the human mind, structured according to immanent schemes.[77]

This assertion of the self and the simultaneous negation of the beyond and the transcendent is what in general terms could be called secularization. But often secularization is understood as a transformation of traditional religion into another sort of religion, or religion under a new appearance. Instead with Hans Blumenberg, Dupré describes "the new phenomenon as an original *self-assertion* which often continues to use religious language to express a wholly new cultural attitude."[78]

This change was brought about not because of any one particular condition, it was caused by a series of conditions which made it possible without actually causing it. What happened was that in the Old Testament there was a very strong awareness of the exclusive lordship of Yahweh. They held that God alone was holy. But consequently this lays the ground for a de-sacralization of the real, since if God alone is holy then nothing else can be holy. Christianity did attempt to re-sacralize the world through the dogma of the Incarnation, but this divine humanism also made it possible to have a "secular" humanism. This secular humanism came to the fore especially in the thirteenth century when in Christianity the "humanity" of Christ was given prominence in a Christian humanism. The Renaissance culture also concentrated on the human which could become autonomous with ease. In religious thought too the human was given more and more autonomy and by the thirteenth century theologians began to make a distinction between human nature with an intrinsic law of its own, and the order of grace which they described as being 'added' on. By the sixteenth century this distinction became a separation. The concept of man as *natura pura* ensured that grace would always be something extrinsic. And when the Reformation declared that human nature itself is corrupt it completely detached the divine order from the natural realm.

---

[76] Cf. Dupré, "The Modern Idea of Culture," 479.

[77] Dupré, *The Other Dimension*, 21.

[78] Dupré, "The Modern Idea of Culture," 480.

The Enlightenment in its turn relegated religion to the sphere of "feeling" and turned it into a principle of ultimate appeal, and this in a world which in all other respects was self-sufficient.[79]

For centuries this 'secular' attitude had co-existed with a strongly religious world view. The religious crisis of the modern culture began towards the end of the seventeenth century when objectivism began to dominate the intellectual world and challenged the possibility of genuine belief in God. Its dominance is seen in Spinoza who expressed the divine reality as the substance, the objective category *par excellence*. By the end of the eighteenth century the real was reduced to being objective and this effectively excluded the possibility of transcendence. The relation between the Creator and creation was taken to be one of efficient causality and so it bound up the idea of God to that of a mechanistic universe. Since the time of Aristotle, God was spoken of as the first cause, but this causality was always indwelling. Towards the middle ages we notice a transformation in this notion of causality taking place. Conceived as a *virtus inhaerens*—a power that was immanent in the creature—according to this understanding there was no need for the continued impact of the First Cause. As a result divine causality becomes an external force. And this would lead to the eventual conclusion that apart from the initial impact, God was just an inert support of the being of the world and to a large extent his presence was superfluous.[80]

By the eighteenth century, the idea of God was no longer a dominant theme in western culture. Many anti-theistic trends which began in this period such as scientific positivism, social determinism and axiological humanism continue even today but these do not dictate the religious condition in the world today. Secularism today no longer defines itself in negative terms with respect to faith. Not only is it not anti-religious like it was earlier but it seeks an all comprehensive openness even incorporating values earlier thought to be religious into a synthesis that is more accommodating. The religious experience which once was the integrating factor, is now just one of the many experiences in a fragmented world view. Culture can only move forward. But 'forward' need not always be in the same direction. A step in a different direction would be the acceptance of the predicament of our culture and an acceptance of the fact of the loss of transcendence.[81] As Dupré says in Transcendent Selfhood:

> Our predicament is due not to a lack of faith but to a lack of inwardness. To profess a belief in God and to observe certain rules of ritual and moral conduct is not sufficient to regain it. Faith itself is permeated by objectivism. What is needed is a conversion to an attitude in which existing is more than taking, acting more than making, meaning more than function—an

---

[79] Cf. Dupré, "The Modern Idea of Culture," 480-481.

[80] Cf. Dupré, "The Modern Idea of Culture," 481.

[81] Cf. Dupré, "The Modern Idea of Culture," 482-483.

> attitude in which there is enough leisure for wonder and enough detachment for transcendence. Culture requires freedom, but freedom requires spiritual space to act, play, and dream in. Such a space is not provided by leisure alone: leisure itself becomes suffocating without spiritual content. The space for freedom is created by transcendence. What is needed most of all is an attitude in which transcendence *can be recognized again.*[82]

3.2.4 The Loss of Transcendence

Metaphysics reflects the conditions of the culture in which this reflection takes place. It never takes place in a vacuum and often serves as the unifying factor in culture. But then in order to have a metaphysical synthesis it is necessary that the culture in which this synthesis happens must itself be coherent. The sharing of an overall vision of the real and the acceptance of a common framework of reference enables communication hence individuals are able to understand one another. In the past there was an integration of the cosmic, anthropic and transcendent components of culture in a common world view. But in the modern age with the fragmentation of culture metaphysical reflection becomes difficult. The component principles have become isolated from one another and so justification of a cultural unity that has ceased to exist is no longer possible.[83]

In the Greek culture, *kosmos* was the integrating factor and it included physical nature, men and gods. The Christian world view on the other hand separated the divine from the human and cosmic components, yet all were intrinsically united in the Creator. In the theology of the middle ages the Creator God was withdrawn from nature, the only bond being one of efficient causality. Meaning was supplied by human reason. So culture was now divided into nature, the meaning giving mind and the inscrutable God, with the transcendent component gradually withdrawing from culture. The existence of God was not denied, but tradition lost its former authority since meaning and value was supplied solely by the human subject. As a result there was an abundance of symbolic creativity in various fields, but as they were deprived of an inclusive unity they held mere fragments of meaning and did not serve as guideposts for better living. It was in this sense a very fragmented creativity, especially because the human subject was reduced to a mere function.[84] The most striking fact of the situation "is not the actual loss of faith in God, but the development of a mentality closed to genuine transcendence ... fundamentally the objectivist attitude and its subjectivist counterpart had affected our vision of transcendence."[85] There is a general loss of transcendence which is seen in the direction that our entire culture has taken.

---

[82] Dupré, *Transcendent Selfhood*, 17.

[83] Cf. Dupré, *Metaphysics and Culture*, 42-43.

[84] Cf. Dupré, *Metaphysics and Culture*, 43-48.

[85] Dupré, *Transcendent Selfhood*, 14.

This is very well demonstrated in Karl Marx and Friedrich Nietzsche, both of whom are important critics of some aspect of our culture and civilization.

3.2.4.1 Karl Marx

Karl Marx understood that our way of knowing is rooted in a socially and economically determined attitude toward reality. Man has surrendered himself to thinghood and so he is more concerned about *having* than *being*. Marx held that all spiritual achievements can be interpreted in terms of production relations and he believes that control over one's objective world is the essence of humanization. His ideal is that of man who *makes* himself in the process of *making* his world. Marx is concerned here with the relation between the human subject and the world. Man has to provide for himself and so he uses his mind. The use of tools leads to excess production than is necessary and this gives rise to newer needs. The earliest basic activities are not determined by the activity itself, but by choices that are made which form and reveal attitudes. As culture progresses there are more choices to be made, but while the earlier choices were open choices, now the choices are determined by culture and there are fewer alternatives. True reflection and imagination is needed to perceive the alienation. According to Dupré, this one sided orientation towards objectivity runs through our culture. This lack of critical reflection reduces the crisis of our culture to merely technical difficulties which can be overcome by scientific research and development. But to really grasp the seriousness of our situation we need to understand the fundamental significance of history and existence as essentially temporal. Our search must be metaphysical rather than merely historical.[86]

3.2.4.2 Nietzsche

We consider Friedrich Nietzsche as another significant critic of our culture because he linked the crisis of our culture directly to its secularization. He held that the Socratic ideal of science had led to a culture that was based on science and this illusion that science would lead us to the depths of being was what was largely responsible for the crisis. Yet he does not focus directly on the link between the development of the scientific spirit and the loss of transcendence. He wrote of the death of God and blamed the waywardness of our culture on Christianity. In *Thus Spake Zarathustra* he describes the predicament of our age in a parable[87] that speaks of the three metamorphoses of the mind:

> First the camel goes burdened under a heavy weight, the weight of transcendence which wearies existence but at the same time ennobles it with respect. Then, in the desert, the camel is transformed into a lion: the slave

[86] Cf. *Transcendent Selfhood*, 8-10.

[87] Cf. *The Portable Nietzsche*, ed. Walter Kaufman (New York: Viking, 1954) 137-13, as quoted in Dupré, *Transcendent Selfhood*, 13.

> throws off his burden and becomes free. But the freedom of refusal remains empty and merely trivializes life by undermining all moral and metaphysical values. Yet in the end the lion turns into a child, symbol of a new beginning in innocence. Only the childlike overman can redeem mankind by allowing the will to power finally to follow its unrestricted course.[88]

So, it appears for Nietzsche that only the uncontrolled freedom of the will can save modern culture from its destruction. According to Dupré it was precisely this attitude and desire to subordinate, control and dominate nature and culture that led to the crisis. Yet according to Dupré Nietzsche's diagnosis describes culture as a system of values. The loss of faith in God leads to a mentality that is closed to genuine transcendence. So by destroying its foundation the system itself could be destroyed. Nietzsche established a "clear connection between the devaluation of values and the loss of transcendence. This alone makes him perhaps the most significant critic of our culture."[89]

3.2.5 Loss of Inwardness

At some point our culture took a turn that led to our present predicament. "Culture originates from a succession of decisions by which we create, refine, and constantly revise a system of values."[90] Culture does not simply develop naturally but takes a particular direction according to decisions that are made which constantly refine the system of values. There is a general tendency to continue earlier trends. The longer a particular trend has existed the more difficult it is to bring about a change. So, any choice that is made marks the beginning of conscious innovation. The objectivity in the early Christian and medieval ages was balanced by an inward trend. But in the modern age the ideal of objective science has made a remarkable mark and left its effect on the whole of culture. This trend was so widespread that even the realm of intrinsically subjective experiences was reduced to a physical causality. The inner experiences of man began to be interpreted according to schemes derived from science and mechanics. As a result of this objective trend the universe was deprived of values since they had no transcendent support. Values do exist but they are now merely preferences that are historically conditioned. This affects the various areas of culture. Art becomes private expression, systems of thought are isolated and the person ends up living in a universe that is fragmented and which supports only ephemeral ideas and transient values.[91]

This was one of the main obstacles in the modern age. When the component principles of culture broke up there was no longer a transcendent support and the

---

[88] Dupré, *Transcendent Selfhood*, 13.

[89] Dupré, *Transcendent Selfhood*, 14.

[90] Dupré, *Transcendent Selfhood*, 15.

[91] Cf. Dupré, *Transcendent Selfhood*, 15.

real no longer appeared as a unified totality. The moderns were not looking for a unity that would last for all eternity, but they were looking for a unity that would be open and which would also allow for indefinite change. This unity

> ... would have to consist in an apriori of fundamental *givenness* that unites the three dimensions of time while fully respecting their differences and preserving the undecidedness of the *not yet*. This ideal apriori embedded in culture and required for the possibility of metaphysics, is not a homogeneous transcendental, a single entity fully given at once. The apriori of givenness consists not in a present reality but in a unifying principle of reality partly already disclosed, yet in part still hidden in an indefinite future. The totality we moderns need is a unifying horizon of meaning.[92]

Dupré holds that this horizon of totality is compatible with the ontological novelty that is gradually emerging. Modern ideology in general defends the totality of the fact and usually rejects any total vision. Socialism and communism have shown that anticipating the future as a fact that can be engineered in the present, ends up in dehumanizing the person. The closed totality of the late middle ages eschatology, like communism is a denial of a transcendent openness of the future. Positivism exalted science, while Marx and his theory of the necessity of a future socialist world projected the future as being controlled by and originating in the present. The problem though is not the acceptance of a projected totality, but rather our inability to conceive of a *totum*. The horizon of totality of the earlier ages continued even after the centre of meaning shifted from nature or God to the human subject. So instead of forming a new synthesis which could serve as a unifying principle, the principle of subjectivity splintered cultural reality into a multiplicity of mental constructions which were hardly related to each other.[93] It was this fragmentation that gave rise to alienation, a topic we shall consider in the next section.

3.3 Alienation a Block to Transcendence

One of the goals of human existence is that man needs to become aware of and accept his situatedness, and especially the wretchedness of his condition. Man needs faith to awaken this feeling of insufficiency within himself. William Hocking says that religion heals the alienation between man and his world. But then it has been religion itself that has brought about this distance.[94] Yet we have to remember that while the concept and experience of alienation are a part of the religious attitude, alienation need not be only religious. Basically, "Man is

---

[92] Dupré, *Metaphysics and Culture*, 49-50.

[93] Cf. Dupré, *Metaphysics and Culture*, 51-54.

[94] Cf. William E. Hocking, *The Meaning of God in Human Experience*, 238, as quoted in Dupré, *The Other Dimension*, 419.

a stranger to himself because *he is estranged from the sacred*."[95] So in spite of the strong movement towards secularization, this concept of alienation highlights the importance that the religious interpretation of his existence holds for man. But then interpreting alienation only in terms of religious alienation does not reveal the comprehensive meaning of the term.[96]

3.3.1 Different Aspects of Alienation

Initially it was basically in the philosophies of Hegel and Marx that the concept of alienation began to be widely used and rose to prominence. Today we can differentiate between different connotations of alienation. Alienation can be social, economic, psychological, existential-philosophical or religious. Very briefly we shall describe the various understandings because the religious understanding of alienation while different from the other connotations, depends on the secular meanings to give a complete picture of its complex significance. Hegel in a passage in the *Phenomenology of Mind* describes a state in which the mind is unable to recognize its cultural creations as its own creations.[97] Besides, there is also the desire of the mind to flee into another world, into the world of the beyond which is believed in because of faith. So the term alienation while being a cultural-religious definition cannot avoid using a social and political description. This term owes its widespread use in a special way to Feuerbach and Marx. They borrowed the term from Hegel and gave it an entirely new meaning. For Feuerbach the true alienation is man's projection of human qualities on to a God.[98]

3.3.1.1 Socio-economic Alienation

Marx in his concept of social alienation stressed that the roots of man's alienation was a particular form of objectivation the roots of which lay in man's social-economic condition which had separated man from the product of his work. Alienation also ended up in separating man from the productive activity itself. This is especially true of industrial labour which dehumanizes man. There are three aspects to Marx's concept of alienation. Man is estranged from his producing activity, from the product of this activity and from his fellow man. The effect of this alienated labour is 'private property' which in turn serves to perpetuate the alienation in man. Later in his writings Marx wrote about 'fetishism', a general attitude in which commodities became ends rather than means. Herbert Marcuse speaks of *progressive* alienation as characteristic of contemporary capitalist society. Modern day society allows man to satisfy only some of his desires. These desires

[95] Dupré, *The Other Dimension*, 419.

[96] Cf. Dupré, *The Other Dimension*, 419-420.

[97] Cf. Hegel, *Phänomenologie des Geistes*, ed. Johannes Hoffmeister (Hamburg, 1952), 347; *The Phenomenology of Mind*, trans. J. B. Baillie, 509, as quoted in Dupré, *The Other Dimension*, 420.

[98] Cf. Dupré, *The Other Dimension*, 420.

which he is allowed to satisfy are those that kill the urge within him to transcend the object-oriented system of today. The urge to go beyond is curtailed and left frustrated which results in alienation.[99]

3.3.1.2 Cultural Alienation

Man's alienation at the same time cannot be attributed only to the socio-economic system. Alienation has gradually come to be considered also as a state of the mind. Erich Fromm in his book *The Sane Society* defines alienation as a "mode of experience in which the person experiences himself as an alien."[100] In various ways he feels or is made to feel the he is not part of a group. He feels that he does not 'belong'. This is not to say that alienation is an individual phenomenon or feeling, because there is a connection between such a state of mind and a particular state of society which could itself be attributed as being the cause of this state of mind. The question that arises is, "Why would man adopt structures which keep him from developing his full human potential?" The problem perhaps lies in the egoistic needs of man. The selfishness in man and the fear of being deprived of necessities in the future gives rise to a 'hoarding mentality'. As Erich Fromm asserts, it is this hoarding mentality that gradually gives rise to a possessive society, and in turn such a society reinforces the hoarding mentality. Hence man's vision is obscured and his personal growth is blocked. His vision is restricted to his family, his group and to the people he feels are his own. His world becomes very limited and is restricted to the few people who share his background. The way out of this alienation would be to modify the social structures and to change our ideals.[101]

Yet even before this drive towards hoarding and possession, there is the whole movement towards 'civilizing' society which could also be considered as one of the roots of alienation. Freud described how cultural progress can impose a burden upon man because as society 'progresses' and becomes increasingly cultured it imposes restrictions on his aggressive and sexual instincts as a result of which man forfeits his happiness and ends up being alienated because his needs and drives are controlled due to his being a part of a particular group.[102]

3.3.1.3 Existential Alienation

Cultural development alone does not give a complete explanation of alienation. Albert Camus and some existential philosophers would consider alienation as an

---

[99] Cf. Dupré, *The Other Dimension*, 422.

[100] Erich Fromm, *The Sane Society* (New York: Fawcett Publications, 1968), 11, as quoted in Dupré, *The Other Dimension*, 422.

[101] Cf. Dupré, *The Other Dimension*, 423.

[102] Cf. Sigmund Freud, *Civilization and its Discontents*, trans. James Strachey (New York: W. W. Norton, 1962), 81, as quoted in Dupré, *The Other Dimension*, 423.

integral and unavoidable part of human existence. Heidegger speaks of man who is estranged from himself and describes it as a fall into 'inauthenticity' which is a reduced and thing-like state of being. Man's existence is reduced to "the groundlessness and nullity of inauthentic everydayness."[103] While his main task is that of becoming himself, inevitably man gets distracted because of which he loses his way and ends up being alienated. But if he does not realize and accept his alienation man ends up being comfortable in this world and is at peace with himself, that is to say, in his inauthenticity. According to Heidegger, a return to authenticity is possible only through a feeling of anguish. This is so because anguish causes man to question his existence in the world. It is in this situation when man no longer feels at home in this world that this anguish makes him aware of the nothingness that surrounds his existence. It is against this nothingness that he is able to come to terms with Being and it is this feeling of anguish that returns existence to its aboriginal state and thus overcomes alienation.[104]

3.3.1.4 Religious Alienation

Alienation in itself is not a religious act because, to confront one's estranged condition is not a religious act in itself. In the Judeo-Christian tradition alienation is connected to sin. Sin is seen as a deliberate breach with the divine and so alienation from a religious point of view stresses the moral aspect and is connected with death and suffering.[105] Luther highlighted the need for man to be aware of the wretchedness of his condition, an awareness that was basically religious.[106] Kierkegaard too stressed this negative aspect as inherent to religion because according to him it is only through this consciousness of sin that one can have a religious attitude, a consciousness that is usually arrived at due to an experience of alienation. In his book *Sickness Unto Death* Kierkegaard presents sin as despair. Despair is a mixture of existential inauthenticity, religious perversion and a commitment to moral evil. It is that free act of man in which he rejects his given self and in that same moment chooses an impossible self. It is in this refusal to accept his given condition that despair becomes religious. This refusal to be authentic is the same as the existential concept of alienation and Kierkegaard equates this refusal to be authentic with the religious category of 'sin'. It is the moral and religious perversion which is the root of all alienation. Sin, despair, death and suffering are all elements that contribute towards a religious consciousness of

---

[103] Heidegger, *Being and Time*, trans. Edward Robinson and John Macquarrie (New York: Harper and Row, 1962), 222-223, as quoted in Dupré, *The Other Dimension*, 424.

[104] Cf. Dupré, *The Other Dimension*, 425-426.

[105] Cf. Dupré, *The Other Dimension*, 427.

[106] Cf. Martin Luther, *Selections from his Writings*, ed. John Dillenberger, trans. Karlfried Foelhlich (Garden City - New York: Doubleday, 1961), 502, as quoted in Dupré, *The Other Dimension*, 430.

alienation. Because of this he would say that sin is intrinsically a religious category and is best understood within the religious experience.[107]

3.3.1.4.1 Sin as Alienation

To understand sin in all its complexity we have to understand it from the perspective of a personal relationship. Initially there has to be a dialogue with the sacred, and so sin is a violation of this personal bond through some ritual or ethical transgression. Naturally the physical deed is not as important as the internal disposition and so sin leads to a diminished selfhood. While the starting point is God it ends up in a shift towards the self that feels guilty, and so the self becomes the centre of decision. The awareness of sin is a key point in the development of religious consciousness. Yet the individual is not the end and so alienation necessarily entails a trans-individual aspect, a communal power and solidarity with the entire human family that gives it its ultimate significance. It is from the point of view of solidarity in sin, and in light of the relationship between the self, the community and the transcendent that the concept of alienation as sin is best understood.[108]

It is from the understanding of sin as an action of one person with effects for himself and others that gradually the concept of solidarity in sin developed. Sin remains a personal act of rebellion, but it also extends beyond the individual act in space and time. The myth of Adam as the initiator of sin introduces the concept of a 'corporate personality' where the individual represents the entire community. Later on the idea of sin, especially Original Sin, would be understood as concupiscence, the desire for the sexual act. Kant emphasized the moral aspects of the myth, stressing that man has to bear responsibility not merely for his acts, but also for his evil disposition.[109] So we begin to see that there are two important aspects of sin, namely, sin as a free act and sin also as an innate disposition. Though man is normally inclined towards evil, he has to bear responsibility for the inclination as well as for the act. And yet at the same time we cannot deny the fact that there is also a certain solidarity in sin, in the sense that the actions of one person have an effect on other members of society because man does not live in isolation but lives in communion with others. It is in this context of solidarity with others that sin results in the alienation of man from others due to his acts.[110]

---

[107] Cf. Dupré, *The Other Dimension*, 430-432. For Kierkegaard's views see, Kierkegaard, *Sickness Unto Death*, trans. Walter Lowrie (Princeton: Princeton University Press, 1967), 153 and *The Concept of Dread*, trans. Walter Lowrie (Princeton: Princeton University Press, 1967), 14.

[108] Cf. Dupré, *The Other Dimension*, 433-435.

[109] Cf. Immanuel Kant, *Religion Within the Limits of Reason Alone*, trans. Theodore M. Greene and Hoyt H. Hudson (New York: Harper and Brothers, 1960), 36-37, as quoted in Dupré, *The Other Dimension*, 439.

[110] Cf. Dupré, *The Other Dimension*, 436-440.

3.3.1.5 Self-Alienation

When we think of the self there is always the possibility that the self is vulnerable to alienation because the human being in the world today is often not in touch with the deeper self. Human beings today tend to be satisfied with a superficial existence. One of the threats to selfhood is that there are opposing forces that one encounters in the course of existence. If one yields to any one of them more than the others it tilts the balance to one side thus disturbing the balance of being, and at the same time upsetting the balance of the self. "Routine work drudgingly performed, conventional values unquestioningly accepted, objective ideas never interiorized gradually erode the very possibility of growth and development. A person may spend a lifetime in this closed but safe universe without ever approximating genuine selfhood."[111] At the same time, some individuals could also be so overwhelmed by the self's infinite potential that they find it difficult to achieve concrete selfhood. So instead of seeing a possibility towards development of the self they feel crushed by an overpowering sense of responsibility and a terror of endlessness which leads to their downfall. This brings to the fore the complexity of the self and the fragile condition of the mind. As R. D. Laing has shown, in every person there is a self that is interior to self, and a self that is exterior. Due to this duality the inner self feels threatened by the look of the outsider and often creates an 'outward persona' which it thinks is acceptable to the other or as it imagines the other expects it to be. The problem is that this 'created' outer self is often in conflict with the inner self and hence leads to schizophrenia.[112]

This alienation of the self and the isolation that it leads to is most evident in the experience of suffering. Every individual has to confront suffering at some point or the other of his or her existence. In this experience of suffering the individual feels most isolated and alone because ultimately my suffering is 'mine'. The others may support me or comfort me, but it is I who suffer and it is I who have to bear the pain. So this suffering arouses in the person the feeling of insufficiency. Paradoxically it is this awareness and acceptance of one's inadequacies that leads to genuine transcendence. As Dupré says, "… Religion is not a desperate attempt to cope with matters that cannot be handled otherwise, but a positive vision in which personal suffering is *needed* for spiritual growth."[113] It is through the awareness and acceptance of this fundamental insufficiency that the person begins to feel the need for salvation, and thus penetrates deeper into itself, moving towards the heart of the self where the person is no longer alienated but one united and complete whole.[114]

---

[111] Dupré, *Transcendent Selfhood*, 43.

[112] Cf. Dupré, *Transcendent Selfhood*, 42-44.

[113] Dupré, *Transcendent Selfhood*, 49.

[114] Cf. Dupré, *Transcendent Selfhood*, 48-49.

3.3.1.6 Conclusion

According to Dupré authors like Rousseau, Hegel, and Simmel held that culture by its very nature separates the human being from an original state of immediacy. No culture is able to completely avoid alienation because the unique character of each culture produces a unique form of alienation. The problem as Dupré presents it is the fragmentation of the classical synthesis of God, world and man in the modern epoch. Initially reason was considered to be a principle that was immanent in the real itself, but later it came to be considered as an exclusive attribute of the mind. It was the mind that imposed rationality on the real. Reason was no longer inherent in the very nature of things but was detached from reality. "Reason no longer enlightens the real from within: henceforth the entire burden of conveying meaning falls upon the person who must find his way in an opaque and dark world."[115] And this is the main aspect of the human person that we speak about when we speak and reflect upon alienation. It is the reference to this phenomenon of the human subject who by modern considerations has been emptied of any content he previously possessed and is now reduced to being a mere function. It is this dehumanization of the human person that we understand as alienation.[116]

From all that we have said about alienation it has to be accepted as one of the unavoidable aspects of the human condition. But then given the dynamism of the self it is unthinkable that man would sit back and accept this situation which basically goes against his being man. This is especially so when alienation is looked at from the perspective of the drive towards transcendence that is part of the constitution of man. The issue of alienation when studied in connection with the concept of transcendence is best understood by studying two related concepts of nature and grace because it is in the connection and relation between these two that Dupré presents his solution to the problem of man's situation of alienation.

3.3.2 Alienation and Transcendence in the Light of Nature and Grace

We shall now make a study of these two concepts of nature and grace making a quick run through history. To guide this historical recapitulation of the relation between grace and nature we shall depend on the argument as presented by Dupré in his book *Passage to Modernity: An Essay in the Hermeneutics of Nature and Culture.*

[115] Dupré, *Metaphysics and Culture*, 48.

[116] Dupré, *Metaphysics and Culture*, 46-48.

3.3.2.1 An Initial Synthesis

3.3.2.1.1 The Form Principle

Early Greek philosophy was a search for the ground of nature. There was an effort to understand the relation from the more fundamental to the less fundamental. This was explained by the form principle. The form constituted the intelligible essence of the object, but it also surpassed the object. In *Parmenides* Plato presents form as being both transcendent as well as immanent, and so there is a dialectic at work.[117] Aristotle instead said that the place of the ideal form was within the real. The ultimate justification of reality is beyond the appearing reality in the unmoved mover, and so it has a transcendent foundation. Aristotle refers to a divine presence in nature, as for instance, "In *De Anima* a divine agent intellect illuminates the mind by its active indwelling in the soul. It unites the soul with God in intellectual contemplation."[118]

3.3.2.1.2 The Concept of Nature

After the fourth century, Christian thinkers often used Platonic categories in theology in spite of basic differences that tended to be overlooked, as for instance in the case of the term 'nature'. For Christians nature owed its existence to a free act of God, but for Plato and for most of Greek thought, nature was divine through itself. Hence the Christian concept of 'creation' separated God from nature, while the Greek concept of 'emanation' does not accept a clear cut separation. Platonism placed the image of God as being primarily in the mind. The body too has traces of the divine but is on a much lower level. As a consequence later on it was the body that was held to be responsible for the evil inclination in man. It was Irenaeus in particular who taught that something created by God could not be evil and so even after the fall the image of God in the human person still continues existing.[119]

Like Irenaeus, neoplatonic philosophy too held that the fall had not separated the soul from God. It held that it was the presence of God in the person that deified the person and in deifying the person the cosmos also is deified. In this Greek Christian theology we see that man exchanges a nature with God due to grace. The divine nature is not natural, neither to man, nor to the cosmos, but it is given and received. Nature and grace are not completely separated because they have an innate capacity for reception. It was Augustine who advocated neoplatonic theology in the west. He agreed with the Greek Christians that God's image in man did not exist in the same way that the original exists in a copy, but its existence was as a presence. The difference was that for the Greek fathers the

[117] Cf. Dupré, *Passage to Modernity*, 167.

[118] Dupré, *Passage to Modernity*, 168.

[119] Cf. Dupré, *Passage to Modernity*, 168-169.

nature of the image was according to the archetype, but for Augustine it worked the other way around, the idea of the archetype was constructed on the basis of its human image.[120]

3.3.2.1.3 Grace

Later in time a separation would take place between the order of nature and the order of redemption. Perhaps this separation could be traced back to the so called medicinal view of grace. Augustine stressed that due to the fall, nature was wounded and incapacitated and hence needed to be cured. The remedy to effect the cure was grace. But gradually this cured nature was understood as being an entity nearly independent of the original nature. This was quite different from the Greek Christians who held that grace led to the deification of the human nature. We are not saying that Augustine is responsible, but perhaps as Dupré says, "… his anti-Pelagian writings unquestionably planted the seeds of two conflicting doctrines, neither one of which he would have accepted and both of which in their own way caused a break between nature and grace."[121] One doctrine of late medieval theology holds that grace superimposes a different reality on nature, that is to say, grace is added to nature, while the other doctrine of the Reformation sees nature as being independent and self-sufficient. According to the second doctrine nature is so corrupt that grace is unable to transform nature, so it just covers its sinfulness. Here grace is seen as something extrinsically imputed to nature.[122]

3.3.2.1.4 Nature and Grace

Initially the dispute about the relation between nature and grace was epistemological. Aristotle considered nature independent of its destiny in grace. Albert and Aquinas joined nature and grace together. The problem lay in the conflicting concepts of nature held by Aristotle and Christian theology. For Latin theology the term nature signified human nature. Hence, Duns Scotus would speak of the 'natural' desire towards a 'supernatural' vision. On the other hand from an Aristotelian perspective, nature is endowed with its own immanent teleology, a natural theology that could end up in a theological dualism because the end was proportionate to the means and hence 'natural'. Hence, Aquinas felt that the Aristotelian concept of nature was inadequate to express the complete Christian meaning of *natura elevata*. When Aquinas speaks of 'nature' he refers to human nature as it concretely exists, integrated within the context of grace but formally is independent of what we know of the context through revelation.

---

[120] Cf. Dupré, *Passage to Modernity*, 169.

[121] Dupré, *Passage to Modernity*, 170.

[122] Cf. Dupré, *Passage to Modernity*, 170.

Hence nature has a transcendent openness to grace and has a *desiderium naturale* towards a fulfilment in grace.[123]

3.3.2.1.5 Natural and Supernatural

Sixteenth century theological dualism gave rise to the terms 'natural' and 'supernatural'. For Aquinas supernatural referred not to a new order of being added to nature, but rather referred to the means used to attain the final end, a means that was more than the power of nature alone. God is called the *agens supernaturalis* and nature is the effect of a supernatural agent. Another factor that led to the separating of nature from the divine was the way in which the causal relation between God and creation was understood. The difference was regarding the immanence of the cause in the effect. Plato's fundamental doctrine was that of participation. Aristotle too held the immanence of the cause in its effect. Natural substances all contain the source of motion and change within themselves.[124]

Catholic theologians held that God created the world *ex nihilo*. Aquinas himself was somewhere between the participation of Plato and the efficient causality of Aristotle. Speaking of the creature's dependence on God Thomas Aquinas says, "Being is innermost in each thing and most fundamentally present within all things, since it is formal in respect of everything found in a thing... Hence it must be that God is in all things, and innermostly."[125] We see here that participation is balanced by an efficient causality. In his brand of Christian Aristotelianism Aquinas had achieved quite a balanced synthesis. Yet this was a complex synthesis because his distinction of *nature* and *supernatural* had separated one reality into its two formally distinct aspects. Later others would treat them as two different orders of being thus threatening the synthesis.[126]

3.3.2.2 The Disintegration of the Medieval Synthesis

3.3.2.2.1 The Separation of Nature and Grace

Grace and nature were gradually separated into two quasi-independent orders of reality. Dupré is of the opinion that they could have been maintained in perfect harmony, especially because Aristotle's concept of nature was flexible in the sense that it had a potential for growth since he considered nature to be a matrix of development. The threat to this synthesis and the subsequent separation of an order of pure nature from that of pure grace was mainly the work of the nominalists who led the resistance against Aristotelianism. The concept of an unrestricted divine power as held by the nominalists left little place for predicting

[123] Cf. Dupré, *Passage to Modernity*, 170-171.

[124] Cf. Dupré, *Passage to Modernity*, 171-172.

[125] Thomas Aquinas, *Summa Theologiae* I, Q.8, a.1., as quoted in Dupré, *Passage to Modernity*, 173.

[126] Cf. Dupré, *Passage to Modernity*, 173-174.

the order of nature. Grace was given randomly by a divine decree and did not depend on the moral condition of the receiver. As Bouwsma says, "... man could no longer count on the mediation either of reason or of other men in closer contact with the divine than himself. His salvation depended on an immediate and personal relation with God."[127] In this atmosphere, mystical and devotional movements responded to the religious need and especially union with God through experience helped to bridge the gap between a transcendent Creator and his creation.[128] Scotus posited that "in order to receive the infinite, human nature itself be endowed with an infinite receptivity and hence naturally disposed toward a union with a "supernatural" reality."[129]

3.3.2.2.2 God's ***Potentia Absoluta*** and ***Potentia Ordinata***

Ockham tended towards an understanding of human nature as an independent entity rather than as being a relational entity as was held earlier. Hence, his position in a way was a preparation for the concept of nature as a self-sufficient reality. The traditional concept of God's power made a difference between God's sovereign power over all creation, the *potentia absoluta*, and the manner in which he exercised this power, the *potentia ordinata*. After Ockham, nominalist theology initiated two changes in the understanding of God's *potentia absoluta*. It now had neither moral nor rational limits and included anything as long as it did not imply a logical contradiction. The second change was that *potentia absoluta* and *potentia ordinata* were seen as two independent and successive moments in God's power. God possesses absolute power but in a second moment he entrusts part of the power to secondary causes. This was the explanation of the late nominalists for the intrinsic coherence of the order of nature.[130]

3.3.2.2.3 The Beginning of the Dualism

Early Scholasticism on the other hand held that "God did not surrender his sovereign power to secondary causes. His primary causality remained fully operative in the secondary causes."[131] *Human nature* was understood as part of a concrete human condition but which was controlled by a supernatural destiny. The human being had a natural desire for a vision of God and an openness towards a transcendent vocation. *Pure nature* as an independent reality was seen only in late nominalist theology. Gradually, this dualism between nature and a

[127] William J. Bouwsma, "Renaissance and Reformation," in *Luther and the Dawn of Modern Era*, ed. Heiko A. Oberman (Leiden: E. J. Brill, 1974), 136, as quoted in Dupré, *Passage to Modernity*, 174-175.

[128] Cf. Dupré, *Passage to Modernity*, 174-175.

[129] Dupré, *Passage to Modernity*, 176.

[130] Cf. Dupré, *Passage to Modernity*, 176-177.

[131] Dupré, *Passage to Modernity*, 177.

supernatural realm became an integral part of Catholic theology. One consequence of this separation was the development of 'natural theology' or what is also called 'philosophical theology'. This science of God is founded exclusively on rational arguments. Once nature was taken to be independent, in order to understand it fully there was a need also to understand its transcendent cause. But while most arguments were based on nature, it was difficult to start from a religiously neutral position. Even Thomas Aquinas whose proofs would later become the supporting factor for the whole of natural theology presupposed a monotheistic idea of God. There was always a movement from nature to God, but it was no simple task to begin from a religiously neutral starting point.[132]

3.3.2.2.4 The Separation

It was in the sixteenth century that the realm of nature was separated from the realm of faith. This was resorted to in order to prove the existence of a Creator of the cosmos but without taking help from revelation. The way this was attempted was to show that nature was autonomous but had a tendency towards natural transcendence. So, according to Dupré, "Natural theology began an earnest attempt to restore to a concept of nature a transcendent orientation that had been severed from it."[133] This was understandable because they wanted to separate the discussion from the theological ambient in which it would usually take place. This endeavour naturally was no easy task given its vast and difficult scope, and also because "the fundamental problem was that the new natural theology continued to argue on the basis of God's immanent presence in nature (both human and cosmic) after having defined nature as an independent, self-sufficient entity."[134] It is this sense of separation of nature and grace which took man further away from his roots. This is the aspect of alienation that we refer to when we deal with man and his relation with God and the world. It is in this sense that man feels alienated because he is separated from his roots, or as Dupré would say, the synthesis between God, man and the world has been destroyed. Given the human dynamism and intellect, the human person does not sit back and suffer this alienation. He goes in search of that which will help him to live a fuller and more meaningful existence. That is what he does and it is the search for ultimacy that makes man what he is, giving expression to the capacity for transcendence that is present within each one of us.[135]

This division gave rise to a Religious Naturalism which attributed a divine quality to nature, a quality that was independent of the supernatural realm that theology dealt with. In order to study one of the forms of this religious naturalism

---

[132] Cf. Dupré, *Passage to Modernity*, 177-178.

[133] Dupré, *Passage to Modernity*, 179.

[134] Dupré, *Passage to Modernity*, 180.

[135] Cf. Dupré, *Passage to Modernity*, 179-180.

we shall consider the religious naturalism of Nicholas of Cusa and his attempt to bridge the gap caused by nominalist thought between nature and its transcendent source. Perhaps, the genius of his thought was his "rethinking the relation between God and nature in such a manner that God is no longer the pinnacle of a cosmic hierarchy but a spiritual center that unfolds itself in the cosmos."[136]

3.3.2.2.5 The Religious Naturalism of Nicholas of Cusa

For Cusanus restoring divine immanence in nature meant defining predictable borders to the nominalist idea of God's *potentia absoluta*. This meant a different explanation of the concept of possibility. According to the nominalists God was omnipotent and so could create anything or do anything that he wanted, as long as it was not a logical contradiction. As Dupré explains there are two issues present here. One is a realm of infinite possibility which is subject to God's absolute power and another of limited actuality which is subsequently chosen by God's ordained power. Cusanus saw possibility and actuality not as two separate concepts but as complementary elements of one creative act. Both originate with each other because creation includes the totality of all that can be realized. For him, the actual world is the only possible way in which divine reason can be expressed because previous to the act of creation there was no Leibnizian choice between two possible worlds. Whatever is, is the best that could be possible.[137]

Cusanus holds that the act of creation is the explication of God's Being, thus implying an intimate union between God and the creature. The universe is in the mode of multiplicity what God is in a unified way. It is infinite since it includes all that in fact exists and also that which could exist. He understood the world as the otherness of God's Being, and God as the non-otherness of created being. God is the principle through which all things are identical with themselves. The absolute is not 'other', but as he is the ground of the world, God constitutes his own essence and also the essence of the world. Usually the relation to another would imply a separation. But God's self-identity is such that he is more the thing than the thing itself. Neoplatonic philosophy saw the One as opposed to the many, but for Cusanus this not-otherness is the highest mode of being. So the created cosmos is distinct from the divine unity, but God's immanence gives the created cosmos a unity, and this coincidence with uncreated being conveys its self identity. So that which characterizes God's Being also describes the creatures innermost reality.[138]

To further explicate this difference between the Creator and the creature, Cusanus uses the metaphor of one-point perspective used by painters which explains that "although infinite in its identity with the absolute, created being

[136] Dupré, *Passage to Modernity*, 186.

[137] Cf. Dupré, *Passage to Modernity*, 186.

[138] Cf. Dupré, *Passage to Modernity*, 187.

is a broken infinity that reflects various but always limited perspectives of the uncreated infinite."[139] Like a mirror, each fragment presents a different view of God's face, though none shows his full countenance. Due to this limitation of creatures to reflect the divine essence completely, Cusanus holds that the divine presence more than being a likeness or an image is in symbolic ciphers which are made up by the human mind. While he rejects any analogy between the sign and the signified, he holds that finite symbols are able to give expression to the presence of an invisible infinite. Cusanus completely overcomes the nominalist dualism between the human order and the divine order when he explains that in the Incarnation the hypostatic union of the divine and human nature transforms nature as a whole and together with it the whole of creation also is transformed. This decision is not influenced by the 'Fall' because for divinity there is no before or after. As divine person Christ ontologically precedes created nature and it is through his humanity that created nature is able to participate in the divine nature. So for him nature and grace are insolubly united.[140]

The problem with Cusanus is that his philosophy cannot be separated from his theology and as Karl Jaspers pointed out:

> His philosophy does not presuppose particular articles of faith, but it does imply a fundamental attitude of faith, which he explicitly calls Christian. Because Cusanus regards his mind as a copy of the divine original, philosophical faith and revealed faith are for him identical... What we call the duality of his thinking was to him no such thing. He does not recognize multiple sources of faith, but only one, the Christian.[141]

Cusanus' synthesis while correcting the nominalist theology had many internal contradictions of its own. At this moment it is not our intention to delve into these contradictions but we would like to draw attention to his insight that grace is united with nature in one single order of being. This insight would lead him to the concept of a universal religion. Besides all religions reveal only a part of the truth about the divine *Logos*, and no single faith can totally explain the conceptual depth of God's Being. All true worship is one and a religious unity of all believers can be obtained only if all people understand and accept that all religions emerge from one source only and that all the different rituals relate to this same source which is within and yet beyond the human being.[142]

---

[139] Dupré, *Passage to Modernity*, 187.

[140] Cf. Dupré, *Passage to Modernity*, 188.

[141] Karl Jaspers, *Anselm and Nicholas of Cusa*, Vol. 2. of *The Great Philosophers*, trans. Ralph Manheim (New York: Harcourt, Brace, Jovanovich, 1974) 58, as quoted in Dupré, *Passage to Modernity*, 188.

[142] Cf. Dupré, *Passage to Modernity*, 188-189.

3.4 Conclusion

This study of the self in some of its aspects as described by Dupré highlights the fact that the human being is very much 'this worldly'. And yet given the dynamism of his personality man cannot remain in his situation and passively accept all that life has to offer him. He realizes that if his existence is to be of any significance it has to be in the context of his relationship with the world and more so with others who form a part of his culture. But then with the transformation that has taken place in this culture he realizes that the transformation of culture has radically altered his self and in the process he has lost contact with his deeper self. This message comes across very strongly in his experience of alienation, an experience that highlights the fragmentation of his existence and especially the loss of the synthesis that in earlier ages gave meaning and significance to all the various aspects of the human existence.

Alienation is not a situation that man is comfortable with, and so he has to strive to break out of the chains that bind him down to a meaningless existence. To break free, man has to be able to give expression to the dynamic striving that is part of his selfhood. This drive that pushes him to look for that which can complete his existence is the drive of transcendence. It is the urge within him to search for that elusive transcendent which can help him to put all the various aspects of his existence into a unity and a synthesis that is meaningful. So his goal in life is to search for and discover the elements of his existence and then merge them into a significant unity that we refer to as a union of nature and grace. One of the crucial elements is the ultimate reality, and so in the next section we shall deal with this religious object and the drive of the religious subject towards this beyond.

Chapter 4

The Religious Object

To a religious person, just about any object or event could be sacred. It is not that all of these events or objects are sacred in themselves, but rather it is the religious attitude of the subject that makes them into sacred symbols. Because of the religious attitude we can discover the sacred in almost every domain of human existence, but at the same time this does not mean that religion is solely a subjective experience. This so-called religious attitude is always directed beyond the self, and this religious object is not created by man, but rather "it is revealed to him in a disposition to perceive a deeper reality under the appearance of objects and events."[1] The present chapter is going to be a study of the Religious Object, often referred to as God.

4.1 The Religious Attitude

What man sees is a depth of being so great that it overwhelms him because it is a reality so rich that it can only be described in terms that cover a variety of concepts. Everything that exists has a dynamic and creative characteristic because it is transcendently real. But generally it is because of the religious attitude in the human person that he is able to uncover the 'ultimate reality' which is an absolute which is the basis on which all things find their foundation and on which even the self depends for its being.[2] The religious perception of absolute reality according to Dupré is symbolical and dialectical. "Sacred reality is grasped directly *in* the appearance of relative being—not as the conclusion of a logical process. The absolute shines directly through the relative. Yet the two never coincide."[3]

---

[1] Dupré, *The Other Dimension*, 13.

[2] Cf. Dupré, *The Other Dimension*, 13-14. Also see Mircea Eliade, *The Sacred and the Profane*, trans. Willard R. Trask (New York: Harper and Row, 1961), 12.

[3] Dupré, *The Other Dimension*, 14.

What we have to realize is that nothing is sacred in itself and yet every object is potentially religious. What makes a thing sacred is the fact that the absolute appears through the finite object. In fact as Mircea Eliade writes:

> The sacred tree, the sacred stone are not adored as stone or tree; they are worshipped precisely because they are *hierophanies*, because they show something that is no longer stone or tree but the *sacred*, the *ganz andere*... By manifesting the sacred, any object becomes *something else*, yet it continues to remain *itself*, for it continues to participate in its surrounding cosmic milieu... In other words, for those who have a religious experience all nature is capable of revealing itself as cosmic sacralitiy. The cosmos in its entirety can become a hierophany.[4]

4.1.1 The Religious Attitude as Dialectical

4.1.1.1 The Sacred and the Profane

The religious attitude can be best described as dialectical. As Dupré says, "The religious attitude is *dialectical* insofar as it is a relation (and therefore an opposition) to a transcendent term."[5] This is especially so because it is always seen in connection with a transcendent term. When we speak of the sacred it has to be always in opposition to a profane or a non-sacred reality. This is necessary because when we think or speak of the sacred it is always of the sacred as separated from the ordinary realm of existence. And yet at the same time while it is different and separated from reality, it does not mean that to encounter or to experience the sacred one has to withdraw from reality. For one with a religious attitude, the sacred is all positive while the non-sacred reality lacks a certain depth of existence.[6]

The profane is a term that is usually used to contrast the striving towards an ultimate reality and indicates the shallowness of ordinary life. This dialectical understanding of the sacred and the profane is significant because it is this opposition that enables us to clarify the transcendent. It is not an easy task to define that which is profane since that which is profane for one group could be sacred for another group. "The term *transcendent*, so essential to religion, develops dialectically and takes various meanings in different contexts. It is always transcendent *in relation to* what surrounds it."[7] This is the job of the profane. It informs us of the surroundings and helps by making the background clear so that the sacred can stand out in contrast. Yet at the same time, it is interesting to notice as Dupré points out, that in most cases where the absolute is the point of reference, it usually overwhelms and absorbs that which is relative. But in the

---

[4] Eliade, *The Sacred and the Profane*, 12.

[5] Louis Dupré, "Secular Man and His Religion," *Proceedings of the American Catholic Philosophical Association* 42 (1968) 80.

[6] Cf. Dupré, *The Other Dimension*, 15-16.

[7] Dupré, *The Other Dimension*, 16.

case of the dialectical opposition between the sacred and the profane this is not the case. We see that the sacred does not overcome the profane completely, and perhaps the reason for this is the ambiguity with regard to the sacred. The sphere of religion is obscure when compared to other fields of knowledge and experience in the rest of the world which are much clearer. Ordinary reality is easier to deal with and less challenging than the sphere of the sacred. Even so, this ambivalence between the sacred and the profane is not enough to stop the profane from being overcome by the sacred.[8]

The sacred, because it is unable to overcome the profane by attraction, absorbs it by an internal negation. The profane is not seen as another form of being but as Roger Caillois describes it, it is "an active nothingness."[9] It has this special capacity for integrating and reconciling opposites into an ultimate unity. But this is possible since the sacred in embracing all opposites actually transcends all distinctions. It is precisely this quality which enables religion to be the integrating force of life in community.[10] In this connection Dupré quotes Hegel who says:

> All that has worth and dignity for man, all wherein he seeks his happiness, his glory, and his pride, finds its ultimate centre in religion, in the thought, the consciousness and the feeling of God. Thus God is the beginning of all things and the end of all things. As all things proceed from this point so all return back to it again. He is the centre which gives life and quickening to all things and which animates and preserves in existence all the various forms of being. In religion man places himself in a relation to this centre in which all other relations concentrate themselves, and in so doing he rises up to the highest level of consciousness and to the region which is free from relation to what is other than itself to something which is absolutely self-sufficient, the unconditioned, what is free and its own object and end.[11]

4.1.1.2 Power of Integration

This capacity and power of integration is an important aspect of religion because deprived of the integrative function religion can easily degenerate into a power structure and destroy the opposition. But such a destruction of the profane world only results in an impoverization of the sacred because by this destruction religion becomes ordinary and loses its reason for being. When the human person is truly

[8] Cf. Dupré, *The Other Dimension*, 16-17.

[9] Roger Caillois, *Man and the Sacred*, trans. Meyer Barash (New York: The Free Press of Glencoe, 1959) 20, as quoted in Dupré, *The Other Dimension*, 17.

[10] Cf. Dupre, *The Other Dimension*, 18.

[11] G. W. Hegel, *Vorlesungen über die Philosophie der Religion*, ed. Georg Lasson (Hamburg, 1966), Vol. I, 1-2. *Lectures in the Philosophy of Religion*, trans. E. B. Speirs and J. Burdon Sanderson (London: Kegan Paul, 1962) 2, as quoted in Dupré, *The Other Dimension*, 18.

himself he possesses this attitude for integration in his being. Through religion he is constantly moving towards this integration. Religion is a help for him in this direction especially because it is this drive that makes him fully human. But man would not be able to do this unless such a power or tendency for integration arose from within himself. This drive towards integration is part of the religious attitude and this capacity is present in every person. It is this power to go deeper into himself, to search for and achieve this integration, and in the achievement of this integration to go beyond himself which is the movement of transcendence. So when we really examine it, this religious attitude is the result of the presence of the sacred in man, and not just in man but in the whole of creation. The sacred also points out and highlights the presence of the profane, an aspect of existence that cannot be negated, because as we mentioned earlier, the sacred becomes meaningful since it is seen within a context, and this context is the profane. If there is no profane then religion becomes ordinary because there is no need for integration and hence it loses its *raison d'être*.[12]

4.1.1.3 Salvation and the Dialectical Movement

What the religious person refers to as salvation is the attainment of and the return to the original unity. Man participates in this unity through myth and ritual. Dupré says that this term salvation, "combines two essential traits of the religious attitude: dissatisfaction with empirical reality and unlimited hope of ultimate liberation."[13] It is because of these two traits that the religious attitude receives its dynamism. The process of salvation in such a scenario cannot come to a close because man never attains the absolute unity. Due to the nature of the sacred newer oppositions continually arise, and so there is a continuous process of integration that needs to take place. "Salvation, then, rather than being the final term of religion is the dialectical movement itself which proposes a transcendent reality, opposes it to ordinary existence and composes the opposites in a participation of the divine."[14]

This is one of the things that characterizes the religious attitude, that the human person is in constant quest for some sort of a relation to a transcendent reality. Not that this reality is never going to be discovered, but it is unravelled part by part in a gradual process. Given that the transcendent is infinite and we are finite this is unavoidable. At the same time, we have to accept our limitations and know that we shall never be able to completely grasp and comprehend the transcendent. Yet this is not a hindrance for a person who has a religious attitude, but rather spurs the individual on to discover more and more of this transcendent reality. While to some it may appear to be a futile project, with the

[12] Cf. Dupré, *The Other Dimension*, 19.

[13] Dupré, *The Other Dimension*, 19.

[14] Dupré, *The Other Dimension*, 19.

religious attitude this endeavour is actually the path chosen by the individual to be more human and be more himself. This is so because we realize that as we uncover more and more of this transcendent reality we are giving expression to the transcendence that is an integral part of our being human. Hence even though it will not reach an end, this activity is what characterizes the human person, an activity that expresses the religious attitude.[15]

4.1.1.4 The Rise of Secularity

We have spoken of the religious attitude in the human person, but we must keep in mind the fact that for primitive man in the archaic stage, there was no 'religious element' in his experience because his was a total experience. Since, the term 'religion' did not exist at this stage, what today we refer to as the religious dialectic did not exist in the same form at that time, and so it could not be separated or differentiated from the rest of his life experiences. Later on religion would develop from this attitude. In the second stage, different spheres of existence began to be distinguished, but religion still permeated all of existence. While there is a distinction between the sacred and the profane the concept of 'secularity' had not yet come into existence. It is only in a third stage that there is a distinction between the religious and the secular. This distinction gradually became necessary as religion gradually ceased to coincide with social life as it had been earlier. Science, art, philosophy and morality were no longer dependent on religion. With the independence of these fields the universe too became man-centred, and consequently religion which once held an exalted position came to be seen as merely a symbolic expression of the human mind and structured according to immanent schemes.[16]

4.1.1.5 The Gradual Loss of the Religious Attitude

As man gradually became more and more aware of his capabilities he was able to bring other spheres of existence under his control and with this capability he began to feel less and less under the control of a transcendent source. Where earlier he thought that the power of control of the world lay in a supreme principle, he gradually discovered that this power lay within himself. Earlier the desacralization of the world was attributed to the fact that the world had a creator who was totally transcendent, and so the finite was considered completely separate from this transcendent creator and hence was called secular. This was an effect of an overly religious attitude. With the emphasis now on man, the issue was whether secularity could in any way be considered to be compatible with a religious attitude.[17]

---

[15] Cf. Dupré, *The Other Dimension*, 20.

[16] Cf. Dupré, *The Other Dimension*, 20-21.

[17] Cf. Dupré, *The Other Dimension*, 22-23.

A characteristic of the newer form of secularization was that there was nothing that could be referred to as sacred. The holy could no longer be experienced directly, the world was totally humanized and as a result God's presence could not be easily perceived. This situation arose because modern man, "... has developed the active powers of his mind, the ability to grasp, to comprehend, to do, and to make. This has allowed him to attain an unprecedented control over his physical environment. But the unconditional commitment to the technical and the pragmatic has dulled the sensitivity of his interior life."[18] In this ambient it is difficult to find an experience that is considered religious by all people and not only by those with a religious attitude. While there were some who felt liberated because the emphasis on God in each and every sphere of life had begun to be oppressive, there were others who felt a certain 'loneliness' in a world devoid of God. They felt that while the human existence was more under the control of man, life itself has been banalized and this banalization had led to a diminished existence. So what was considered an achievement by some persons, was considered a regression by others.[19]

The question arises, "Can religion survive in a secular society?" For a long time religion had served as the integrating factor for society but with the situation in the world changing, this was no longer the case. "The sort of integration by which faith provides the final answer to every problem is definitively lost. Religion may still be the ultimate integration for religious man. But for society and its survival it is no longer necessary that the ultimate integration be religious."[20] A meaningful synthesis can be obtained even if one does not accept the transcendent principle in the religious sense. Yet for the believer it is his faith that is the all-integrating force of life. This faith is personal and private in the sense that it depends on the individual and his conviction, and not on the Church as an institution or on a society influenced by the Church. While this could be referred to as a 'private' or a personal faith, it is supported largely by a community that lives this faith, and also the fact that many of its effects are felt in public. It is the duty of the believer not to deny the autonomy of secular values but rather to place them in a transcendent perspective and thus prevent them from becoming absolute in their own right.[21]

4.1.2 Factors Giving Rise to the Religious Attitude

The question we ask ourselves is, "What are those factors that give rise to the religious attitude in man?" It is interesting to note that the secular mentality is not completely at odds with the religious attitude because much of present day belief is a remnant of past ages. We need to examine how to maintain a sense of religious

---

[18] Dupré, *The Other Dimension*, 23.

[19] Cf. Dupré, *The Other Dimension*, 24.

[20] Dupré, *The Other Dimension*, 25.

[21] Cf. Dupré, *The Other Dimension*, 26.

reality within the secular set-up of today's world. The same experiences that have made man secular also present a religious possibility to man. Experiences are ambiguous and so let us consider some experiences in order to understand what leads to or gives a person a religious attitude.[22]

4.1.2.1 The Mysteriousness of the Universe

One of the factors that leads to the religious attitude, according to Dupré, is an experience in today's world that has arisen from the great achievements of modern science. He refers to it as the sense of mysteriousness of the universe. One does not get a direct glimpse of the transcendent Creator, but rather with the new knowledge of time, space and matter that we have today, man is more and more impressed by the mysteriousness of the reality that surrounds him. That the universe is much greater than all his powers of objectivation, especially the mysterious incomprehensibility of the order in the universe, makes man reflect and search for an explanation of the mysteriousness and this opens the path towards transcendence. This awareness of the mysterious incomprehensibility of the universe according to Dupré is an essential moment of the religious attitude.[23]

4.1.2.2 The Awareness of Contingency

Another experience that Dupré speaks about is the radical awareness of contingency. Man is struck by the fact that reality is not just a fact but a puzzling fact, especially because all the happenings fail to show a justification, neither does it reveal its inner necessity. There appears to be an irrational gratuitousness and so acceptance of this contingency seems to be the only authentically human attitude. Looking for an ultimate intelligibility seems to be a futile endeavour, and he says that it is in the presence of this totally unknown that often man is able to find the transcendent. The experience of contingency when applied to his own situation is most puzzling to the human person. The awareness that he just happens to be and that he has no complete explanation about the ground of his being could lead to joyful exaltation for some persons. But in most cases there is an anguished awareness that this void is greater than him. It is in becoming aware of his freedom and possibilities that man becomes even more aware of the precariousness of his existence. "In the midst of his conquests man knows that in the end he himself will be conquered by his inherent contingency. His life and his creations carry the worm of death."[24] Dupré points out that this feeling of contingency can lead to man being confronted with the mystery of transcendence.[25]

---

[22] Cf. Dupré, *The Other Dimension*, 27.

[23] Cf. Dupré, *The Other Dimension*, 27-28.

[24] Dupré, *The Other Dimension*, 29.

[25] Cf. Dupré, *The Other Dimension*, 28-29.

4.1.2.3 The Givenness of Existence

An experience of man which contributes to his dissatisfaction with existence is that of the 'givenness' of existence. Man had no part to play in his being born and he had absolutely no choice to make about the situation of life that he would be born into nor does he have control over the day and time of his death. This has led to a feeling that existence has been imposed onto him and so he has no option but to accept the situation. His entire life therefore turns out to be a struggle to make sense of these given conditions and so in a way to be in control of, instead of being controlled by the given situation. Besides, he is also aware of the fact that just as he is, he might as well not have been. Yet this awareness of the givenness and the contingency of his existence is precisely what can help him towards transcendence because the religious dialectic that is continuously at work in his coming into and remaining in being is what can help him to break through and make the transition from contingency to religious transcendence. We must recall though that such a transition is not rationally justifiable because the justification can only be a religious one.[26]

4.1.2.4 A Sense of Community

A last experience that Dupré speaks about as giving rise to the religious attitude is the affiliation that binds man to his fellow man. A stronger sense of community and unity to other human beings has resulted in a deeper concern for the well being of the other which is expressed in the responsibility that is felt for each other. This helps man to discover the transcendent dimension because in the discovery that the person is sacred man comes to the conclusion that therefore the sacred *is*.[27]

It is the religious attitude in man that drives him towards transcendence. Various experiences give rise to the religious attitude even in secular man. This movement on the basis of certain experiences to another realm is rationally inexplicable, and for this reason some people would be able to make this transition and others would not. Apparently this seems to be merely a matter of choice but while it does involve a personal choice, this choice to a large extent is determined by the nature of the subject. As Dupré affirms, "Religious attitudes today seem to be adopted as personal and reflective answers to experiences which present themselves in a questioning rather than in an assertive way."[28] There is definitely an experience, but rather than forcing a submission, this experience invites the individual to make a decision. It is in this sense that the faith of a believer is an

[26] Cf. Dupré, *The Other Dimension*, 30-31.

[27] Cf. Dupré, *The Other Dimension*, 31.

[28] Dupré, *The Other Dimension*, 32.

active and reflective religious attitude, and not merely a passive feeling as was understood to have been in the past.[29]

This aspect of the religious attitude in the human person is important from two points of view. First of all it is important because when man has a religious attitude or at least is open to the religious attitude it enables him to do justice to his being a person. When man looks only at himself as the end and as possessing all the solutions of life, he realizes that the problems and facts of existence are much greater than himself. If he believes that he alone possesses the powers to control his existence ultimately he breaks down because he cannot find all the answers to life and so is overwhelmed by his situation. Both these aspects are connected because the religious attitude of man opens a way towards a solution and so offers him another possibility. In this way man is able to look for answers within himself, but if he does not find them he is still able to look elsewhere since he has another option. This is what gives him 'hope'. Without this possibility man is damned to a life of the 'absurd'. Besides, this aspect of the human personality is what allows for transcendence, a movement that becomes possible for the persons who have a religious attitude. It is with this religious attitude then that we continue with our attempt to understand the religious object more.

4.2 Transcendence and the Religious Object

When we speak of the religious object, very often the problem is that metaphysicians deal with a concept of the religious object as if they had invented it. And this concept they create is far removed from the religious object as it really is, and frequently this concept is independent of man's religious activity. This is seen especially when in natural theology the emphasis is on philosophy and not on God. In contrast to the idea of God as it had been secularized by philosophy, Dupré's thesis is that, "Philosophy alone never reaches the idea of God, yet that it can fully acknowledge its debt to religious faith while maintaining its own autonomy."[30] He reiterates Duméry's thoughts in saying that the philosopher only 'encounters' the idea of God. He is not responsible for it, and so it is his task to discover its significance and role in the world and not to mould and adapt this concept to fit in with his thesis. The idea of God is not the property of philosophy but rather has been borrowed from religious life.[31] Yet in a way this is unavoidable because at the root of philosophy are myth and religion. Hence, it would be hard to support an idea of God that is strictly philosophical.

[29] Cf. Dupré, *The Other Dimension*, 32.

[30] Dupré, *The Other Dimension*, 112.

[31] Cf. Henry Duméry, *Le problème de Dieu* (Paris, 1957) 15, as quoted in Dupré, *The Other Dimension*, 113.

4.2.1 The Concept of the Religious Object

4.2.1.1 Its Origins in Philosophy, Myth and Religion

The origins of philosophy are mythico-religious. Greek philosophy was a result of a rational reflection on the aetiological aspect of the myth. This reflection was usually connected with the cause and origin of all things. It also was concerned about the variety that existed in the universe which was coherent on the whole. There was a general search for the one principle that united all things. This explanation was through myths rather than through a scientific explanation. [32]

Anaximander called this principle the '*apeiron*', the indefinite. He stressed the indestructibility of this principle which was divine in the sense that it had neither beginning nor end. This was already an initial effort to define the religious aspect of reality. Heraclitus spoke of this ultimate principle as fire, a self-sufficient oneness. It develops through a harmony of oppositions, a constant movement and counter movement that maintains the original balance. Like the Ionians, the Pythagorean philosophers too were mythical-religious in their outlook and for them philosophy was an exercise in spiritual purification. While the rational nature of the number was far from religious, certain aspects of their philosophy as for example the One as the primal monad retained the original religious meaning. In his work *On Nature*—which some consider as the oldest text book in mechanistic physics—Empedocles who is regarded as the chief naturalist philosopher retains the mythical vision and seems to borrow a lot of his philosophy of nature from cosmogony. Parmenides might not have made any explicitly religious statements, but his description of the absolute as Being can be compared to the Creator-God of the Bible who is one, transcendent, perfect, eternal and identical.[33]

Socrates' life and death bore evidence to the close relationship between philosophy and the religious aspect of existence. For Socrates the new dimension of reality was essentially religious and it was his trust in immortality that empowered him to face death and dishonour, and thus fulfil his mission in life. He spoke of his discovery of the divine within the self, and this in fact would later on be the basis for all of Christian theology. Plato's doctrine of *Eros* has been referred to as a doctrine of salvation. The purpose of the *Eros* is to liberate the soul from its earth bound condition so that it can contemplate its own spiritual essence. *Eros* also enables the soul to move from physical beauty to the contemplation of the Good, the supreme form. This Good may not be equivalent to God, but he does refer to it as 'divine', but it has divine qualities. "The Good is the transcendent source of all reality and intelligibility."[34] Though Plato does uses mythical language he is aware of its limitations, and even warns against complete trust in the myth. Yet

---

[32] Cf. Dupré, *The Other Dimension*, 113-115.

[33] Cf. Dupré, *The Other Dimension*, 115-118.

[34] Dupré, *The Other Dimension*, 119.

his use of the myth as a form of expression is similar to the use of the myth by a religious man.[35]

Aristotle is perhaps the least religious and even lesser mythical of the Greek philosophers. By giving the concept of God a philosophical role, he gave a new direction to religious consciousness. He made a significant effort to completely reject mythology and anthropomorphism and combine religion and science without sacrificing either one or the other. His creativity led to conceptions such as the Divine Being and the First Cause as the unmoved mover which were of great assistance to religious speculation. But it was Plotinus who revealed the full religious implications of Plato's philosophical vision. "In Plotinus the upward flight of the Platonic Eros receives its ultimate justification from a downward process of emanation. The soul longs for the divine because it is itself of divine origin."[36] While some philosophers tried to isolate the mythical and mystical elements of Greek philosophy and concentrate only on its logical content, Plotinus showed how reason attained its summit in mystical contemplation. He does not substitute reason as the primary power of the mind but presents a higher stage of consciousness as the last step of the reasoning process. When the ultimate object of the mind is defined as transcendent, in the last stage the upward movement leaves the intellectual order and makes the transition from reasoning to contemplation.[37]

4.2.1.2 Metaphysics as Theology

Early Christians reinforced the religious meaning of Greek philosophy by fitting it into their own religious world view. According to them there were two orders of truth. One was to explain the existence of man in this world, and the other was to instruct him on the order of salvation. This position was developed by Irenaeus, confirmed by Augustine and given its classical expression by Thomas Aquinas. He adopted Aristotle's metaphysics and used it as a basis for a Christian theology of salvation. Thomas Aquinas distinguishes 'metaphysics as theology' from 'theology' taught in relation with Sacred Scripture. As Dupré explains this distinction, "The theology which is metaphysics deals with those objects of speculation which do not depend upon matter for their existence, such as God and the angels or those principles which may or may not exist in matter."[38] This sort of metaphysics could be called a divine science since it deals with God. But the 'theology' that is taught in sacred scripture is concerned about revelation and the revealed as such. It was this separation of the order of existence from the order of salvation that created the divide between religious experience and philosophical reflection. Philosophy

[35] Cf. Dupré, *The Other Dimension*, 118-120.

[36] Dupré, *The Other Dimension*, 122.

[37] Cf. Dupré, *The Other Dimension*, 121-123.

[38] Dupré, *The Other Dimension*, 124.

today is not seen as being dependent on theology, but the effort to give philosophy its autonomy has resulted in its being totally separated from the religious aspect of existence. Yet the philosopher cannot ignore the realm of experience because then his conclusions would be far from reality.[39]

4.2.1.3 Metaphysics and the Religious Idea of God

To understand the religious object using philosophy alone is insufficient. Philosophy would always be a help but independently it is unable to reach the idea of God. This according to Dupré is the basic error of philosophy especially regarding the proofs for the existence of God. Usually the idea of God was arrived at from religious sources, and so a proof cannot be formulated independent of the religious experience that goes together with the idea of God. This would hold true for Anselm of Canterbury and most of the medieval scholastics who "merely wanted to show how the existence of the finite and the contingent requires the existence of an infinite, necessary Being... They merely attempted to find *some* rational justification for their religious beliefs. Once the finite's need of the infinite is established, they did not hesitate to identify this infinite with their religious idea of God."[40] What tainted these arguments was that since from their theological reflection they knew the outcome, they just had to find a path to reach their goal. The path chosen is not always correct and hence sometimes this adversely affected the compactness of the proofs.[41]

4.2.1.4 Why Proofs are Inadequate—the Object of Religious Act

The main deficiency of these religion-based arguments is that through a process of reasoning they attempt to arrive at conclusions that are completely religious. The distinction between the phenomenal and the transcendent is not clearly defined. The problem with such arguments is that they treat the phenomenal as being fully capable of giving some positive information about that which transcends it. It thus ends up speaking of the transcendent as if it were phenomenal. When we consider a purely philosophical proof we have to be vary of two possible errors. These so-called 'proofs' for God end up in reducing God to a mere object, and they treat the finite and the infinite as equals. But God can never be only an object because by its nature the transcendent Being cannot be separated from the immanent subject.[42]

It should also be noted that even if there were better proofs and arguments for the existence of God these would still be unable to reach the 'object' of the religious act. Philosophy needs to study God from *within* the religious experience

[39] Cf. Dupré, *The Other Dimension*, 123-127.

[40] Dupré, *The Other Dimension*, 128.

[41] Cf. Dupré, *The Other Dimension*, 128.

[42] Cf. Dupré, *The Other Dimension*, 128-129.

because the object of a philosophical study of God is not the same as the God who is the object of religious experience. The object of a philosophical study of God ends up being a philosophical concept, but in a religious experience we deal with a faith experience. Philosophy deals with an absolute which solves an intellectual problem and is the product of speculative thinking, whereas the God of religion is revealed in the religious experience and brings salvation. The metaphysical idea of God is never a subject. But the God of faith is a subject. Philosophy talks about God but the philosopher rarely talks *to* him. The religious person talks *about* God but always in a context of talking *to* him.[43]

4.2.1.5 Transcendence and the Ultimate Reality

According to Dupré instead of trying to prove the existence of God we need to show that the transcendent horizon falls within man's vision of reality and that there is an urge within him to uncover and know more about this horizon. So it makes more sense to argue for the transcendence of Being and for the rational acceptability of a religious interpretation of this transcendence. Besides, one can accept this transcendence without admitting the religious idea of God, because postulating it is not the same as attaining the Divine. From a metaphysical point of view we realize that transcendence cannot be defined as clearly as would be possible from a religious point of view which has a direct confrontation with transcendence and gives it a positive content. As Dupré says, "To continue its investigation of the transcendent, philosophy must turn from metaphysics to critical reflection upon religious attitudes as they actually exist."[44] The encounter between pure metaphysics and the transcendent can happen according to two basic models, the metaphysics of being and the metaphysics of consciousness.[45]

4.2.1.5.1 Metaphysics of Being

Scholastic philosophers influenced by Maréchal's theory of the dynamism of the intellect considered the encounter with the transcendent as an apprehension of infinite being. Karl Rahner recognises the existence of transcendent reality in his concept of the 'pre-apprehension' or the *vorgriff* of being that accompanies every assertion. He describes it as "the *a priori* horizon of perception of a sensuous object presented as *a posteriori*."[46] So, Being-as-such is implicitly accepted as being the goal and horizon of all intellectual affirmation. The notion of Being itself is not completely transcendent but Being is considered as transcending all finite beings and it suggests a beyond. Hence, Rahner feels that in every particular assertion

[43] Cf. Dupré, *The Other Dimension*, 130-131.

[44] Dupré, *The Other Dimension*, 132.

[45] Cf. Dupré, *The Other Dimension*, 131-132.

[46] Karl Rahner, *Spirit in the World*, trans. William Dijch (New York: Herder and Herder, 1968) 184, as quoted in Dupré, *The Other Dimension*, 133.

the infinite Being is co-affirmed. Keeping in mind the priority of the actual over the possible, Rahner negates the possibility that this horizon be a purely negative horizon. If the horizon is pre-apprehended it must be actual rather than possible.[47]

While Dupré agrees with the pre-apprehension of Being he points out that it is not necessary that, that which exceeds every conceivable finite being must be infinite in itself. Just because the mind affirms Being infinitely does not mean that it affirms an infinite Being. In accepting the possibility of a more, it is not necessary that this notion of Being as unlimited has an actual realization. What Dupré wants to point out is that Being is the unlimited horizon of each affirmation. But this does not justify our saying that because of this pre-apprehension of an unlimited horizon an infinite Being is affirmed. The important thing to note is that when we speak of the metaphysical horizon of affirmation it necessarily raises the question of transcendence and about that which lies beyond the horizon. When the mind is able to focus on this 'beyond' aspect of the horizon of being, then it raises the question of transcendent Being. Later in this book we shall consider the way in which man speaks of this reality. These religious affirmations of the transcendent may not give new philosophical knowledge of the transcendent but they do describe new experiences of man in his relation to the transcendent. Hence, it does fulfil a meaningful purpose.[48]

4.2.1.5.2 Metaphysics of Consciousness

In the reflection on consciousness perhaps one of the most significant discoveries was that the mind has a reality of its own, a reality that is unique and hence irreducible to any other being. To know itself the mind must know something else. It is in the process of knowing what does not belong to itself that the mind is able to uncover its proper being. So from a consciousness of a multiplicity the mind by a process of elimination arrives at the form of pure self. Still this is not the end of the process because we can and must go deeper. It is precisely in this dichotomy between subject and object, between activity and passivity that the mind reveals itself as an order that has already been established which refers to an ulterior source that is also simple. This process of reduction finally arrives at a simplicity, a oneness which is dynamic and beyond order and intelligibility, and it is in this simplicity that the dichotomy of the mind is overcome.[49]

There is a restlessness about man that is expressed in the drive of the mind to go beyond itself. It is seen in the scientific, moral and aesthetic ideals of the person. It is in this self-surpassing drive of consciousness that the transcendent is encountered. It is these ideals that drive the mind ever forward and enables it to constantly try to exceed its actual achievements, and even though the ideal may

[47] Cf. Dupré, *The Other Dimension*, 133.

[48] Cf. Dupré, *The Other Dimension*, 133-134.

[49] Cf. Dupré, *The Other Dimension*, 135-136.

never be achieved, this drive never seems to be diminished. It is this drive in the person that opens up to the mystery of transcendence.[50]

What is it that lies beyond himself? Why does he want to attain it? How can he attain this beyond? These are questions that constantly confront the religious mind. What is intriguing is not so much the existence of this mysterious beyond, which could have been a mere creation of his mind, but rather that man is constantly driven to transcendence. The religious mind remains with this experience that seems to be universal to all human beings and pursues a systematic reflection on this experience. The reflective interpretation may vary, it could occur in an existential situation, in a moral decision or an aesthetic experience, but this awareness of transcendence is universal and unavoidable. Ultimately we have to accept that "Philosophy can do no more than articulate the primal awareness of transcendence. Only the religious act can transform it into an awareness of God."[51] This dimension can be seen in the human person who is searching for this beyond. It is only discovered when the person accepts that this world is not enough to satisfy all of his cravings and so looks to complete himself through the help of the 'other dimension'.

4.2.2 Some Aspects of the Religious Object

Through metaphysics we are able to arrive at the concept of transcendence, but to attain the idea of God metaphysics alone is insufficient. The idea of God can be discussed only after the sacred has been revealed in a sacred act, that is to say, only after revelation. We can recognize a transcendent dimension without having the faintest notion of God, but at the same time all the qualities that we might assign to the religious object would also be true of the idea of God.[52] Let us explore the religious object and some of its characteristics as exposed by Dupré.

4.2.2.1 The Divine Names

The first thing to be acknowledged is that this religious object cannot be attained in a single assertion. Every affirmation that is religious has to be followed by a negation to express that it negates ordinary reality. Understanding the religious object is a complex act. Even giving God a name is not a simple act, because divine names are as negative as they are positive and hence are dialectical in nature. But while the divine name might be dialectical in nature, the Being of God is not dialectical. The dialectical nature of divine names is due to the transcendence of that which is being affirmed. Any affirmation of the divine must be followed by a negation. But at the same time we must avoid concluding that because God language moves from a moment of untruth to a moment of truth, God himself

[50] Cf. Dupré, *The Other Dimension*, 137.

[51] Dupré, *The Other Dimension*, 137.

[52] Cf. Dupré, *The Other Dimension*, 323.

also makes this movement.[53] The divine names give us an insight that enables at least a partial understanding of the religious object. Names of God have to be dialectically attributed.

4.2.2.2 Power and Holiness

One of the elementary attributes of the religious object is that of power. Power remains one of the most immediate manifestations of the sacred. This is so because a powerful being has a will of its own and with this will it is able to control the lesser powerful. Hegel says that power is characterized by subjectivity, but while being the inner core of what is, it is not totally subjective.[54] Perhaps, the concepts of '*mana*[55] and 'taboo'[56] best describe this notion of power. The assertion of power is what evolves towards subjectivity insofar as it determines itself and also asserts itself negatively, with respect to the other-than-the-subject. Subjective power dominates the other. Divine power asserts itself as different. Full power requires true opposition and also total dependence. So power is only an attribute of God. It is God who exercises power, and power also manifests the Being of God. At the same time, actions such as the creative act are not just a manifestation of raw power but a power that is exercised in goodness and in wisdom.[57]

Together with this concept of power especially in connection with the religious object, there is also the concept of holiness. Holiness has been described as a value category by Max Scheler,[58] but it is unique in the sense that its value lies within itself, and does not depend on something external. It is a self-determining subjectivity.

> Religious man can appreciate the holy only after the holy has first called him to do so. We might therefore say that its value is not one of self-realization but of total self-transcendence... [R]eligious man can never face the religious "object" without being involved with it... The word God never carries a purely objective meaning: it always expresses belief in a supreme value.[59]

---

[53] Cf. Dupré, *The Other Dimension*, 324.

[54] Cf. Dupré, *The Other Dimension*, 324.

[55] Dupré, *The Other Dimension*, 325. Dupré uses an explanation of *mana* as given in R. H. Codrington, *The Melanesians* (London: Clarendon Press, 1891), 118. Here he explains "*mana*" as a power which reveals itself in physical force or any other form of excellence. This power could be impersonal or personal, since it is usually connected with the belief in spirits.

[56] Dupré, *The Other Dimension*, 325. Dupré describes 'taboo' as the negative, prohibitive aspect of sacred power.

[57] Cf. Dupré, *The Other Dimension*, 325-326.

[58] Cf. Max Scheler, *On the Eternal in Man*, trans. Bernard Noble (New York: Harper & Brothers, 1960), 169, as quoted in Dupré, *The Other Dimension*, 327.

[59] Dupré, *The Other Dimension*, 327.

4.2.2.3 God as Being

As we become increasingly aware of the power and holiness of God, Dupré says we realize that God is eminently *real.* Mircea Eliade often refers to its ontological richness as the primary characteristic of the religious object. He says that this 'sacred object' is the ultimate foundation of all reality.[60] In his description of the real he says, "the real in archaic ontology is primarily identified with a 'force,' a 'life,' a fertility, an abundance, but also with what is strange or singular—in other words with everything that exists most fully or displays an exceptional mode of existence. Sacredness is above all *real.*"[61] The notion of Being was all important to Parmenides. For Plato it was all-pervasive but not supreme, while for Aristotle there is no notion of Being as existence. Plotinus put Being under the concept of the One, but it was the Christians who took the words of the Bible in Exodus 3:14, "I am who I am" to mean that God was Being. Consequently, Christian philosophers identified God with pure Being. This conclusion was the result of theological reflection but in this way Being became the ultimate principle of explanation.[62]

This gives rise to a problem because if Being is universal then how can it be transcendent? That is to say, if God is Infinite Being, there can be nothing outside itself, and hence there is no possibility of non-Being. Besides, if God is Being how can he be the Being of all finite beings? God cannot be the Being of all finite beings as their act of existing because then mere existing finite being would add being to God. Dupré says, "God is Being, but he is not *a* being (*habens esse*); he is subsistent Being (*esse purum*), but not common Being (*esse commune*). There is, then, no common Being shared between God and the finite beings: he *is* his own act of Being while they *possess* being in an essence which differs from the act of Being."[63] Dupré also holds that the analogy of being, the theory of participation, and also the theory of causality which are mainly used by the scholastics, are inadequate to describe the Being of God. We need to find some common ground between finite being and infinite Being and here scholastics use the principle of analogy. But analogy is not sufficient because if God is not *a* being, through proportional analogy how can we relate his Being to the being of the finite being? Finite being is related to God's nature but its being is related to God's Being and God's Being is his nature, so there can be no proportionality. Also, we cannot know the Being of God's essence, we only know the finite side

---

[60] Cf. Mircea Eliade, "Methodological Remarks on the Study of Religious Symbolism" *in The History of Religions*, ed. M. Eliade and Joseph M. Kitagawa (Chicago: Chicago University Press, 1959), 88, as quoted in Dupré, *The Other Dimension*, 328.

[61] Mircea Eliade, *Patterns in Comparative Religion*, trans. Rosemary Sheed (New York: Sheed & Ward, 1958), 459, as quoted in Dupré, *The Other Dimension*, 328.

[62] Cf. Dupré, *The Other Dimension*, 328-329.

[63] Dupré, *The Other Dimension*, 331.

hence we cannot speak of true proportionality. Hence according to Dupré, "the analogy of Being does not explain how infinite Being can coexist with the finite beings... No real proportion exists between God's nature and his Being, since one is the other... The theory of analogy... cannot serve as a means for defining the Being that is God."[64] Finally he concludes that a philosophy of God must therefore move beyond a philosophy of Being because Being is only the first stage in man's dialectical attempt to name God.[65]

Keeping all this in mind perhaps a more accurate description of the religious assertion of God's 'Being' would be as a *presence*. Given the nature of God, and our limited capacity, we cannot know God as he is in himself, but we will know him and experience him as he is present to us. So what we know is not God himself, but we know a presence. What we can say then is that the notion of Being *alone* cannot do justice to the idea of God. While Being is used as a determination of the religious object we have to remember that Being also denotes the real. Everything *is* and so in Being all things are one. If God is considered to be only Being, then he would have to be equivalent and nothing more than the *One* into which the finite and the infinite unite. So we need something more than Being alone to do justice to the idea of God.[66]

4.2.2.4 Participation

The dependence of the finite upon the infinite is generally explained by the theory of participation, or of causality, or of both. For Plato participation was a sharing of a common form by finite beings. But infinite Being cannot be a common form. Boethius modified this saying that all things that exist insofar as they are, participate in Being through their being. Yet he did not talk of actual finite existence. Thomas Aquinas transformed the participation theory by reducing it to a relation of causality. He saw Being as an act of existence which for him was supreme perfection. Seen in this light, participation is understood as a perfection that is received and does not apply to being. To explain how the imperfect presence of Being in the creature depends on the perfect Being of the creator requires a causal explanation because a being which does not have Being as its essence is contingent and owes its existence to a Being that has being as its essence. The problem with causality is that then God's Being is separated from that of the creature and he becomes merely their cause. Participation is reduced to an efficient causality. We are unable to speak of an innermost presence in this case because pure Being 'causes' created being.[67]

---

[64] Dupré, *The Other Dimension*, 332.

[65] Cf. Dupré, *The Other Dimension*, 341. For his treatment of different philosophers on this topic refer to pages, 331-341.

[66] Cf. Dupré, *The Other Dimension*, 343-345.

[67] Cf. Dupré, *The Other Dimension*, 333-335.

When God is referred to as the First Cause we should see it as Tillich would, namely, as a symbol. This would involve negation and transcendence. He equates creation with participation insofar as all things that are created participate in the infinite power of Being. He calls God the *power* of Being and so present in everything without being its form, but more as a *ground* of Being. The ground of being oscillates between cause and substance and transcends both. Still he does not explain *how* cause and substance can be transcended.[68] Hence Dupré would say, "A philosophy of God must always move beyond a philosophy of Being. Being is only the first stage in man's dialectical attempt to name God."[69]

4.2.2.5 The Infinite and the Finite

To describe the existence of the religious object, Dupré speaks of the infinite in the finite. He says that "the relative cannot *coexist* with the absolute but it can exist as dependent upon the absolute."[70] There are determinations in the universe so they must have originated within the absolute. Yet they are not contradictory because these determinations do not oppose the absolute, but rather are posited by it. The relative exists through the absolute and so the existence of relative determinations indicates the existence of a self-determining absolute. If God is defined as the absolute then all relative determinations have their origin in God. Hence, if the finite and the infinite exist simultaneously they cannot be extrinsic to one another. The finite cannot explain itself because it is always in connection with other finites and so necessarily requires a reference to an infinite. At the same time, we need to remember that not every finitude refers to or implies a comparison to the infinite. Only when the term finite refers to the totality of empirical reality, then it relates to infinity. Infinity usually refers to a negation of the finite, but it is not an opposition. While it has a negative connotation, it is positive in the sense that infinite signifies a limitless limit. If it is merely opposed to finite, then infinite is limited by the finite. Finitude in fact is contained *within* infinity as the otherness of itself. In this sense the finite and infinite coexist and finitude has its function in and through infinity.[71]

4.2.2.6 God and Creatures

God is defined as infinite and if the finite is *in* the infinite then God must be part of the development of the finite. At the same time the autonomy of the finite also has to be respected. Balancing these two aspects, namely of God's being immanent in the creature and at the same time preserving his transcendence was what Whitehead attempted in his philosophy. He held that "God attains

---

[68] Cf. Dupré, *The Other Dimension*, 335-337.

[69] Dupré, *The Other Dimension*, 341.

[70] Dupré, *The Other Dimension*, 359.

[71] Cf. Dupré, *The Other Dimension*, 359-361.

actuality only in and through the world."[72] But in this sense God is not above the creative process. Every temporal actuality is a concretization of a number of potentialities. God is a non-temporal actuality that serves as the regulative principle for this process. In this view causality and creation are not unique to God. In their creativity creatures cause themselves just like God, but then God is the primary condition of the existence of all novel entities. Even so he does not precede the creatures own creativity. The uniqueness of God is his indifference to the quality and the preservation of what emerges. And while he has no aims and goals, his only purpose is the realization of each actual entity's highest possible intensity. The God of religion does not have the detached attitude of Aristotle's Prime Mover. But Whitehead seems to end up with an implied idea of a finite God.[73]

Charles Hartshorne felt that the usual concept of infinity in the religious mind was actually one of cosmic wholeness and not pure infinity. God includes the whole of creation and so the religious mind tends to regard God as a total reality. This is basically the panentheist position but in addition it also adds that only the actual is in God as actual, while the possible is present in God as potential. Usually for the religious mind, the perfect is equated to the permanent. In this case a God who grows by increasing actualization grows also in perfection. So then would we be able to say that God is imperfect? Hartshorne replies that "Supreme perfection does not require simultaneous actuality of all possible values (which is a contradiction), nor does it exclude the possibility of being surpassed by oneself but only by others."[74] God relates to creatures in two ways. His relation to creatures is first of all absolute, it does not depend on any other relations. Human relativity varies with circumstances but God's relativity is stable and has no subjective fluctuations. The second quality of God's relativity is that God remains independent with respect to each creature's particular nature. So while he necessarily relates to a universe, he also transcends it as the necessary transcends the contingent. He is the system, while at the same time transcending it. He is the cosmic wholeness and much beyond that too.[75]

4.2.2.7 Is God Contingent?

When panentheism is accepted then this naturally introduces contingency in God because then, that God exists is a *fact* and his actual existence introduces him into a web of contingent relationships. Now religion is a relationship with God. It assumes a God who reacts and responds to the initiatives of man. It would be

[72] Alfred Whitehead, *Process and Reality* (New York: Macmillan, 1929), 521, as quoted in Dupré, *The Other Dimension*, 361.

[73] Cf. Dupré, *The Other Dimension*, 361-363.

[74] Dupré, *The Other Dimension*, 364.

[75] Cf. Dupré, *The Other Dimension*, 363-365.

difficult for man to relate to a non-contingent God because such a God would not be able to get involved in the contingent play of creatures who have their own mind. No interaction would be possible and so religion would be a meaningless cult of an Absolute that does not respond to man and who is unchanged in this sense by man's initiatives. For the religious man it is important that his speaking be heard and that his supplications receive a response.[76] As Louis Dupré says:

> God must be transcendent, absolute and necessary. A God who would be only contingent would be no God at all. In his own essence God must be entirely necessary and independent of all relations which actually obtain. Yet God's essence remains an abstraction until we conceive of it as actually existent. At that moment he exposes himself to the contingent experience of a contingent world. His necessity must not be conceived in such a way as to preclude those relations. The self-sufficiency of God must be provided for *within* his outgoing relativity.[77]

In the relation of man to God there is a contingency in the relation but there is no contingency in God.

4.2.2.8 God's Omnipotence

The religious attitude always considers a communication from God to the creature. While explaining the relation there has always been a stress on conserving the transcendence of God. And hence naturally the doubt arises about how would God be able to preserve the autonomy of the creatures and yet be omnipotent. This idea of the omnipotence of God arose from the experience of power which was always present in the concept of the sacred. The personalization of the sacred leads to a conception of an agent who can do more things than any other agent, and this leads to the idea that God can do everything and that he is omnipotent. Power refers to possible things and so when it is held that God can do all things, it means that God can do all things that are possible, that is to say he can do all that does not go against the principle of contradiction. In philosophical categories God's acting would be described in terms of causality. In a certain sense there is a paradox in connection with this omnipotence. On one side there is an unlimited power to act, while another aspect of omnipotence is that which determines this power to act, a power which all things possess. God is omnipotent in the sense that he creates autonomous beings, but once they have been created he does not control them. According to this explanation if the creature is completely beyond the range of divine power, then the notion of omnipotence loses its meaning. To be meaningful, an omnipotent God must be at the origin of the autonomously acting creature *while it acts*. This involves a dependence. This dependence is fundamental yet it does not determine the direction of the activity of the creature. Sometimes, an omnipotent God might act against the self determination of the

[76] Cf. Dupré, *The Other Dimension*, 366.

[77] Dupré, *The Other Dimension*, 366-367.

creature and sometimes the creature might witness abnormal manifestations of power. Yet even in so called miracles the transcendent is never directly nor universally perceived because while he would use his power if necessary God does so while respecting the causality of nature.[78]

4.2.2.9 God as Personal

When we discuss the omnipotence of God the question that naturally arises is "Why would an omnipotent God want to intervene in the existence of creatures?" A consequent question would be, "Why would he choose to intervene only in some instances and not in others?" But this is not the main issue. The real problem is not this apparent inconsistency in God, but rather, "How can God be such that he is able to enter into *dialogue* with his creation?"[79] It is in this dialogue that God can be said to act, and this highlights the dialectical nature of the relation between God and the creatures. In order to be heard and to relate to the creature God would have to be personal. At the same time since the divine is absolute and infinite it cannot be expressed in the category of the person. The sacred in fact cannot be confined to the personal. It is the religious person who tends to personalize the sacred for the sake of worship. But the sacred cannot be restricted to the personal.[80]

When the term person is applied to God, the reference is to his self-containment and his active otherness. This is an acceptance of divine autonomy and especially of the fact that his life is not ours, and yet he is able to take initiatives, be concerned and share in our existence. It is this notion of 'personal' that is best able to express this aspect of the divine. At the same time, the use of this concept of the personal also has its own limitations. The first limitation is that of individuality because if God is the ground of all that exists, then he cannot be one particular individual opposed to the others. Paul Tillich would say in this connection that "God is called a person, but he is a person not in finite separation but in an absolute and unconditioned participation in everything."[81] So, when God is referred to as *persona*, while it signifies a self-containment, it also signifies openness towards others. As Danielou explains in his book *God and the Ways of Knowing* it is possible to enter into a communication and be in communion with him.[82]

---

[78] Cf. Dupré, *The Other Dimension*, 368-371.

[79] Dupré, *The Other Dimension*, 372.

[80] Cf. Dupré, *The Other Dimension*, 372-373.

[81] Paul Tillich, *Systematic Theology*, I (Chicago: Chicago University Press, 1951), 243-244, as quoted in Dupré, *The Other Dimension*, 374-375.

[82] Cf. Dupré, *The Other Dimension*, 374-375. Also see Jean Danielou, *God and the Ways of Knowing*, trans. Walter Roberts (New York: Meridian Books, 1965), 78-79.

Despite all that has been said, God can also be conceived without personality. A person necessarily needs other persons. But God can be conceived without others. Only in creating persons does God become personal. We establish the personal nature of God from the personal nature of man. As Dupré puts it, "God becomes a person first when man recognizes him."[83] We must also remember that when we speak of God as person it is as a symbolic notion because divine communication is not like ordinary interpersonal communication and exchange. To refer to God as person is inadequate and cannot do justice as an explanation of the ultimate reality, and yet the symbol of the person when used to describe God is necessary and irreplaceable.[84]

4.3 The Significance of the Other Dimension

4.3.1 Subjectivity and Transcendence

In his existence man is searching for a unity. He realizes that a mere putting together of many and varied independent and private worlds does not result in the unity that he is looking for. Since this search for unity is also that which gives meaning to his life, occasionally he has to stop and wonder whether he will ever be able to reach this unity. This question becomes even more important and the search more hectic in the present situation that modern man lives in. The stress on subjectivity in recent times has led to a fragmentation of culture and naturally the question arises, "Is there a connection between these two events?" One thing that seems essential and is also irreversible is the centrality of the subject in modern thought. Even so, subjectivity can be an obstacle to the desired unity if reality is reduced to mere objectivity because this gives rise to a dualism which will never be resolved. So the issue at hand is not *how* we can do away with subjectivity in modern culture, but rather whether subjectivity can be compatible with a fundamental givenness of the self, a givenness that includes even the creative subject.[85]

In the modern world unlike in the past, this givenness is not so evident nor is it as easily accepted as it was in earlier ages. In fact thinkers like Nicholas of Cusa, Erasmus, Pascal and Malebranche have given the self a central position within a reality that is fundamentally given. The fragmentation and division of the modern worldview is a consequence of the fact that the subject has been presented as the ultimate, self justifying principle. This has resulted in a limitedness that does not do justice to man nor does it allow for the dynamism in man. What is really necessary in such a situation of culture is some comprehensive principle, such that it transcends the subject, and yet does not take away from the meaning giving role of the self. For metaphysics to be possible it is necessary that a genuine

[83] Dupré, *The Other Dimension*, 376.

[84] Cf. Dupré, *The Other Dimension*, 376.

[85] Cf. Dupré, *Metaphysics and Culture*, 55-56.

transcendence be present as an essential factor which is operative within culture itself. Many critics would say that the coherence of culture has been destroyed because of belief, and so to return to the earlier coherence it would be necessary to go back to some concept of religion. But given the situation of culture in the present age it is debatable whether a restoration of transcendence at the heart of culture would be possible particularly because from the eighteenth century onwards the subject has been more and more accepted as being responsible for meaning and value.[86]

If meaning is derived *exclusively* from a transcendental subject, however conceived, then any kind of ontological givenness is ruled out. Metaphysics then has no proper object left. If however, the modern principle of subjectivity is conceived as itself dependent on a transcendent givenness that conditions its meaning giving activity, then a new comprehensive horizon could reopen the possibility for metaphysics. The turning to the subject which we see in the modern situation can no longer be a mere reflection of the classical and medieval epochs. The lack of a direct apprehension of ultimacy in a way forces us to accept that the ultimate principle is intrinsically mysterious and unnameable.[87]

4.3.2 The Mystery of Creation

Man has always been impressed by the mysteriousness of the ultimate principle. This is seen in the religious idea of creation and in its philosophical development. When we refer to God as the creator of heaven and earth, it is not a scientific theory neither is it a philosophical conclusion. Creation is first and foremost a religious symbol that has been used to give an expression to the experience of the human person as being dependent on an absolute principle. And yet while it is one of the most fundamental of religious categories it is not always seen in all religions. What it tries to explain is the existence of things that matter. Philosophy on the other hand is an attempt to explain what it is that gives existing creation the reality that it possesses. The issue here is not so much about the nature of the Absolute, but more about man's relation to the absolute and the conditions that would be needed to make this relation possible.[88]

Christian doctrine simultaneously maintained God's absolute sovereignty and the goodness of creation. For this they held that God created freely and that he created in time. The divine activity is free and also necessary but it results in a contingent reality. God is necessary and so is his creative activity, yet it leads to the necessary creation of a contingent reality. This was possible because the answer lies in the idea of absolute transcendence. God and the creature cannot be too closely connected. While the creature is a necessary product of God's activity, the

---

[86] Cf. Dupré, *Metaphysics and Culture*, 57-58.

[87] Cf. Dupré, *Metaphysics and Culture*, 58-59.

[88] Cf. Dupré, *The Other Dimension*, 377-379.

activity of God is free and unconditioned. In turn its created effect is contingent. Therefore, there is an 'otherness' that exists between the creature and the creator. Divine creativity is totally unconditioned and so a created effect can have no pre-existing necessity. Hence when we speak of creation, what we refer to is an origin in a vacuum of conditions. It is this void that surrounds the creative act that man confronts in moments of crisis and anxiety. It gives rise to the feeling of *angst* which causes man to ask questions like, why should anything exist at all, why should things be as they are and why is pain necessary. Questions like these highlight the frightening loneliness of finite being. This according to Dupré is an expression of man's deep felt need for a transcendent foundation.[89]

An acceptance of createdness is also an acceptance of dependence. Existence means dependence on the creative act and so to perceive a creature is also a perception of the creative event. In this sense "The creature is the divine act in its otherness… Yet the total dependence of all that is upon the unconditioned creative act converts the experience of nothingness into one of presence. To exist is to participate in an act of divine communication."[90] In this sense Dupré would say that pantheism is a poor expression of the divine presence because then God's presence means that all other reality is only an illusion. Instead he says that the creative act has what he would call 'another side'. The creature is the total otherness of God. But this does not mean that it is independent because there is a total dependence on God.[91] When looked at from the perspective of the creature the creator is seen as belonging to the 'other dimension' but it is the 'other dimension' that puts this created dimension into perspective, and so the 'other dimension' is necessary to make man's existence significant.

4.3.3 Revelation and Our Experience of the Other Dimension

The other dimension, if it remains completely 'other', is of no significance. The sacred has to reveal itself to man. The term revelation is usually connected with a message which can be either spoken or written. It can also be a deed or sometimes an historical event in which the transcendent is disclosed, but generally it ends up being put into words. Manifestations of the divine presence in dance, rite and sacrifice become more comprehensible when put into a verbal message. Usually this revelation demands a response of 'faith'. Religious symbols either are verbal or need verbal interpretations and Christians in fact have named God-as-manifest: the *Word*, and so the Word becomes the instrument of God's self-manifestation. Continuing the description of Karl Rahner[92] Dupré says, "In the

---

[89] Cf. Dupré, *The Other Dimension*, 387-388.

[90] Dupré, *The Other Dimension*, 389.

[91] Cf. Dupré, *The Other Dimension*, 389.

[92] Karl Rahner says, "the word of God—is not "didache" (teaching),… but proclamation in which the arrival of the thing proclaimed itself takes place. It is the mighty, creative *dabar* (word),

Word divine reality discloses itself to man: it is both the medium and the reality of God's communication."[93] But the revelation of the ultimate reality does not take place only through words. It could happen through nature, through an inner experience, through an unusual happening and in other ways too. Also revelation need not be a permanent phenomenon. What today reveals the sacred may not be able to do so tomorrow. Their theophanies need not be permanent.[94]

Dupré brings to our attention the distinction between natural revelation and positive revelation as expounded by Max Scheler. Natural revelation is that in which the divine becomes manifest in things and events, and is accessible to everyone, while Positive revelation is that in which the divine presence is revealed to a selected few through words and persons.[95] In a similar vein a manifestation of God is distinguished from a revelation of God within a positive religion because a manifestation does not reveal the ultimate reality itself, but only gives a sense or feeling of the divine.[96] Revelation need not be exclusively natural or positive. Christian revelation for instance is not exclusively verbal but takes on other forms. According to Hamann, for Christianity there is a double revelation, in nature and in Scripture. Nature must be understood through Scripture. By itself nature only gives rise to ciphers whose meaning is never clear nor evident. But it is scripture that gives the key to unravel the hidden meaning of these ciphers.[97]

Religion is a relationship that depends on the self manifestation of the divine and so has to be revealed. The mind on its part must be of a self-transcending nature in order to receive this revelation of the transcendent. So we see that there is a complex dialectic of active and passive religious attitudes. This transcending movement of the mind is what enables the person to look for and listen to a transcendent message.[98] The active element lies in the fact that the mind must compose that which it experiences as given. To enter into the consciousness it has to be made into a conscious object. So, the data has to be 'made' meaningful in the sense that the mind has to grasp, structure and articulate the data. This active disposition of the mind to a certain extent predetermines the revelation. But there are also the passive traits of the revelatory experience. In revelation we discover a reality that is given but which has to be received in passivity. Perception is

---

of God to man, the way in which the reality which is being proclaimed discloses itself, and thereby and thus becomes present to us."

Karl Rahner, "The Word and the Eucharist," *Theological Investigations*, Vol. IV, 261, as quoted in Dupré, *The Other Dimension*, 279.

[93] Dupré, *The Other Dimension*, 279.

[94] Cf. Dupré, *The Other Dimension*, 279-280.

[95] Cf. Max Scheler, *The Eternal in Man*, 161, as quoted in Dupré, *The Other Dimension*, 281.

[96] Cf. Dupre, *The Other Dimension*, 280-281.

[97] Cf. Johann Georg Hamann, Brocken, *Sämtliche Werke*, ed. Josef Nadler (Vienna, 1949-57), Vol. I, 308, as quoted in Dupré, *The Other Dimension*, 281.

[98] Cf. Karl Rahner, *Hearers of the Word*, 74, as quoted in Dupré, *The Other Dimension*, 282.

dependent on God's revelation of himself and so the subject knows God through a receptive attitude. Therefore, we can say that in revelation the religious man 'receives' revelation and at the same time he is also 'being received'. His activity and his passivity are immersed in an all enveloping reality.[99] Richard Niebuhr would say, "Revelation means the moment in our history through which we know ourselves to be known from beginning to end, in which we are apprehended by the knower."[100]

4.3.4 How the Transcendent Reveals Itself

The question is whether the transcendent can reveal itself without ceasing to be transcendent. The problem is that in order to be truly revelatory a symbol must convey the reality of the transcendent, but such a communication would destroy its transcendence. In response to this dilemma Jaspers held that such communication is done through 'ciphers' whose job is only to refer to the transcendent, but which do not comprehend nor express that which is signified. They are just signposts and are not even unique but help to point towards the beyond. Devoid of any intrinsic meaning ciphers only point beyond themselves. Thus, they help us to perceive the transcendent without compromising the transcendence of the transcendent.[101] As one of the consequences of apophatic theology Dupré says "A God who reveals *himself* must be a *revelatory God*; that is, his nature must both enable and force him to reveal."[102] We cannot speak of God as being free to reveal or not to reveal because he reveals himself only if it is his nature to reveal, that is to say only if by nature he is a revealing God. And if it is his nature to reveal, he has to reveal. He reveals because he is the manifest one and in revealing he expresses his being for another. Hegel in fact speaks of the Spirit as being Spirit only in manifesting itself, and if it does not reveal then it is not Spirit.[103] For him, philosophy completes Christian revelation, and so God can be known and the transcendent becomes manifest. Also as Hegel puts it, if God reveals he reveals something about himself. The message is always 'from' and 'about' God. In the revelation God communicates his own reality. It is not merely a message about his reality, but the primary content of the revelation is God himself because God gives *himself* in the message.[104]

---

[99] Cf. Dupré, *The Other Dimension*, 282-284.

[100] H. Richard Niebuhr, *The Meaning of Revelation* (New York: Harper and Row, 1962), 152-153, as quoted in Dupré, *The Other Dimension*, 284.

[101] Cf. Karl Jaspers, *Philosophical Faith and Revelation*, 134, as quoted in Dupré, *The Other Dimension*, 285.

[102] Dupré, *The Other Dimension*, 287.

[103] Cf. Hegel, *Vorlesungen über die Philosophie der Religion*, IV, 35, as quoted in Dupré, *The Other Dimension*, 288.

[104] Cf. Dupré, *The Other Dimension,* 288-291.

While trying to understand how the transcendent can reveal itself and yet remain transcendent we must recall that any determination is also finite, and so determinations must be negated. For this reason Hegel described God as revealing himself "not as determined, but as the *movement* which both posits and abolishes all determinations. The very act by which God differentiates and indifferentiates himself is also the act and the content of the revelation."[105] So negation is an essential aspect of the divine reality itself, and not just an aspect that shows the incapacity of the human mind before the transcendent. Besides the mind is also an active participant in this divine movement. Hence when man is able to grasp revelation he is able to understand himself *in* and *through* God. Yet while in revelation we are exposed to the inner life of God, we cannot comprehend the divine mystery completely because divine revelation is not exhaustive. In fact after all has been said and written, the mystery of God still remains, but through what has been spoken and written we are able to realize the impenetrable darkness that surrounds the divine mystery. It is for this reason that language about God must necessarily be symbolic because even though he reveals himself, ultimately he is *Deus absconditus*. Because "he reveals himself" does not mean that he is no longer concealed, but rather he is revealed as that which is hidden. And so in this sense nothing will ever reveal God as he is in himself, but through revelation we can properly grasp the relation between God and man, and in a special way this relation speaks of the one who initiated it.[106]

4.3.5 The Transcendent and the Sacred

One of the ways in which the transcendent has been described is in terms of an opposition between the sacred and the profane. While this would have been acceptable in the past, to the modern man with his restricted awareness of transcendence, a description in terms of such an opposition seems to be inadequate. Man expresses his encounter with transcendence through the symbolic complex of the sacred, but this is not the only possibility of its expression. Dupré though is unconvinced of the importance of this category in the primitive mentality. This category had an all comprehensive connotation in primitive society and so it made no sense because it had no proper name and neither was it clear what the concept signified. This is not to say that nothing was held to be sacred, but just that in varying degrees, all of life was held to be sacred and so as a natural consequence, nothing was completely profane.[107]

To describe the religious attitude solely in terms of the 'sacred' no longer seems to be adequate. It is difficult to attribute a universal significance to the term 'sacred' as used in all religions, because some religions do not even use such a

[105] Dupré, *The Other Dimension,* 291.

[106] Cf. Dupré, *The Other Dimension,* 292-293.

[107] Cf. Dupré, *Transcendent Selfhood,* 18-19.

category. These difficulties could be surmounted by increasing the connotation of the concept 'sacred', but an expansion of its meaning would make it applicable to just about anything and so such a general definition would not serve any purpose. In Christian literature 'sacred' is the main attribute of God which is revealed by God. So it is not an object of direct experience, but his holiness expresses what God is in himself and as a quality could be bestowed upon persons, places or objects. So the sacred appears to be the quality *par excellence* of transcendence. This quality, more than any other, is the distinguishing quality of the divine as such. And so while earlier we spoke of the dialectical opposition between the sacred and the profane as the primary characteristic of the sacred, it is also significant to speak of the sacred as that which encompasses all the human experiences and as that which helps it attain its ultimate integration.[108]

4.3.5.1 Loss of Importance of Sacred

In the modern world there are two interesting characteristics that we notice. The first is that today there is a strong emphasis on the transcendence of God while at the same time there is an equally strong emphasis on the secularization of the world. We cannot say definitely whether or not there is a connection between the two, but what we can say is that in the world today there is a lesser possibility of having an experience of transcendence than earlier. In this sense there is a decline of the sacred. As man discovers that the key to controlling his universe resides within himself, he ceases to feel the need of connecting each aspect of existence to a transcendent principle. As society grows more complex the integration of the different aspects of life also becomes more complex. Science, art, philosophy and morality which earlier needed religious support now manage without relating to a transcendent source. So the perception of the sacred in the world today has become gradually weaker. Nature no longer possesses the sacred meaning it once had and in fact modern man no longer feels he has a direct experience of the sacred, neither in himself, nor in this world. Even those few who do claim to experience the sacred in certain aspects of their life find that they are unable to share it with others.[109]

Despite this largely private character of the sacred, we notice a growing dissatisfaction with the fragmentation of life that this secularist movement has led to. So, man is searching for a new synthesis and while the possibility of an experience of the sacred may be waning, there is a growing interest in the sacred. Some would say that this very feeling of dissatisfaction with his life that man experiences is itself a rediscovery of the sacred. But the fact remains that raising the question does not solve the problem. It does not put life in a transcendent perspective, nor does it constitute a return to the sacred. The term

---

[108] Cf. Dupré, *Transcendent Selfhood*, 20-22.

[109] Cf. Dupré, *Transcendent Selfhood*, 22-23.

sacred invokes the idea of a direct experience of transcendence in the world, and raising the question of the sacred could hardly be described as an experience of transcendence.[110] Louis Dupré says:

> I believe the secularist revolution to have effected a more radical change, one that has not been reversed by recent trends. Because the so-called return to the sacred itself stems from a totally secular attitude... One might interpret the religious trend as a more radical (and a more sophisticated) effort to be secular by expanding the immanent world view so as to include even the *religious experience*. Thus, modern man would attempt to embellish by a sacred glow his basically secular existence.[111]

With such an attitude, even though man is no longer aware of the traditional expressions of the transcendent he does not feel the need for that other dimension and so he tries to attain an experience of that dimension without sacrificing his secular lifestyle. But then without a commitment to the transcendent he is only hoping that an expansion of the self will take him to that dimension. Without a commitment to its content much of what today is called a revival of the sacred is only a psychological exercise that passes off as being religious. But even though we notice a definite lack of the sacred quality in the life and existence of modern man, we cannot deny that he does possess a rather keen awareness of transcendence. The sacred is a category that is much more particular than transcendence, so transcendence cannot be restricted only to the sacred. Yet at the same time we have to accept that our awareness of transcendence must also undergo a change.[112]

4.3.6 The Other Dimension and the Inward Turn

Within the prevalent understanding the sacred was no longer a matter of direct experience but was moved to the transcendent realm and so trust and faith—more than a direct experience—was what was needed when dealing with the sacred. The religious worldview which earlier was an integral part of culture is now largely a matter of private preference. The synthesis of values which earlier existed in society had helped formulate and establish a religious attitude, but now attaining this synthesis was left to the individual. The origin of an acceptance of the sacred lay not in social and cultural structures, but in a personal act. This change led to a large gap being created between transcendence and the traditional understanding of the sacred.[113]

While it is a fact that the sacred is rarely experienced as objectively given or as a universally attainable reality, neither can we say that today there is absolutely no manifestation of transcendence, or that there is nothing at all that appears

[110] Cf. Dupré, *Transcendent Selfhood*, 24.

[111] Dupré, *Transcendent Selfhood*, 25.

[112] Cf. Dupré, *Transcendent Selfhood*, 25-26.

[113] Cf. Dupré, *Transcendent Selfhood*, 27-28.

sacred to us. We are perhaps at the other extreme as compared to archaic man for whom everything was sacred. Today what is sacred is generally so because of an inner conviction and free decision of the believer who holds it as sacred. Sacred in the traditional sense was a primary category of religion which on the level of experience could be directly experienced, even if this experience was passively received. In the modern sense sacred is now a secondary level of interpretation. This change came about because the centre of human piety which earlier was considered to be outside, had now moved inward where the self encounters its own transcendence. So in a world where there is not much possibility of the sacred having a voice of its own, the modern believer so to say gives it a voice by sacralizing the world from within himself. Earlier it was external things, nature, verbal revelation and ecclesiastical institutions that determined the inner experience, but now it is the inward turn of the self that determines whether and to what extent outer symbols will be accepted as sacred. This turn into the self would be vital in the movement of transcendence.[114]

4.3.6.1 Religious Faith

When we consider that transcendence is concerned with the other dimension, and that through revelation the divine communicated with this world, for this divine communication to be meaningful it is necessary that it be integrated within a particular universe of discourse. Human discourse is generally concerned about intra-mundane relations, hence the question arises: how is the transcendent capable of being expressed in the language of immanence? Hamann held that revelatory symbols were useful to this end but they were ambiguous and did not directly yield the content. According to him only faith is capable of freeing the transcendent message from the constraints of its immanent appearance.[115] Kierkegaard speaks of the paradoxical nature of revelation because of which it goes against understanding. Due to its transcendent nature there is need of faith, though faith for Kierkegaard means a going inward and hence there is a dialectic that is at play between the revealed content and the interiority of the subject.[116]

Dupré too seems to be convinced of the role of faith. According to him it is faith alone that is able to manifest the transcendent meaning of the revealed. It is faith that takes ordinary words and deeds beyond their this-worldly appearance. In this way it is faith that can transform ordinary events into religious events and simple words into revelations. Usually divine words and events appear to us but to the ordinary eye these do not appear as divine. It is faith that constitutes

[114] Cf. Dupré, *Transcendent Selfhood*, 29.

[115] Cf. Dupré, *The Other Dimension*, 294. See also Hamann, *Socratic Memorabilia*, ed. and trans. James C. O'Flaherty (Baltimore: John Hopkins Press, 1967).

[116] Cf. Ibid. Here Dupré refers to Kierkegaard, *Samlede Vaerker*, X, 272. See *Unscientific Postscript*, trans. David Swenson and Walter Lowrie (Princeton: Princeton University Press, 1944), 540.

them as revealed. Without faith the words and events are not able to reveal anything. Hence revelation and faith are inseparable. This is especially so when the transcendent is revealed as a person. A person is unique, and so the revelation of a person in order to be understood needs belief in that person. More so when a God reveals himself personally, faith seems to be the only response that such a revelation merits.[117]

Revelation does not consist of 'information' in the normal usage of the word. The truth of revelation is not so much scientific knowledge and data, but more importantly it is "the truth of a new *interpretation* of man's place in the universe. Rather than providing new information revelation opens up a new dimension in a reality known through the mind's own activity."[118] This new aspect of reality is not a completely new dimension that, so to say, has been 'added' on to reality, but rather it is an aspect of reality that has always been present, just that through the process of revelation it has been brought to full awareness. We are not in any way attempting to reduce revelation to something immanent, because by its very nature the transcendent is not capable of being 'actively conquered'. At most it can be passively received with an attitude of faith that facilitates its reception. So even though it does belong to the core of existence at most from the point of view of man we can only await its self manifestation. If man could understand or grasp it solely by his own powers it would no longer be transcendent.[119] In this light let us examine what Dupré says regarding faith.

4.3.6.2 Dupré on Faith

Religious experience is never straight forward and direct like other objective experiences. At the same time, it is not only an experience that is passively received. It is basically a call that invites a response. One cannot remain neutral in the face of the sacred. This response is what Dupré refers to as faith. In the Christian sense faith has been reduced to obedience and hope and as a result the aspect of faith as a conscious religious attitude has been neglected. Christianity stressed the importance of a reflective, free acceptance of the revealed and this acceptance was the result of a religious feeling, an environment and an authority. Faith becomes certain in the act of believing. Belief would be an understanding of things that are held to be true without a direct relation between the believer and that which is believed. Belief is different from knowledge, because what one knows is immediately present to the mind. So it is not possible to know and to believe the same thing at the same time.[120]

[117] Cf. Dupré, *The Other Dimension*, 294-295.

[118] Dupré, *The Other Dimension*, 296.

[119] Cf. Dupré, *The Other Dimension*, 296-297.

[120] Cf. Dupré, *The Other Dimension*, 38-40.

Faith is not knowledge, but it fulfils a cognitive function because the believer must understand and accept it because it is meaningful to him. The cognitive aspects of faith are belief and understanding. This cognitive element of faith is not knowledge in the usual sense of the word. There is a distinction between knowing and believing. Faith gives an assent that is different from pure cognition. Knowledge of God is to know that one does not know God. If a believer replaces faith by insight his attitude changes and he is a gnostic not a believer. Gnostic revelation is not passively received but is actively acquired. The second cognitive aspect of faith is that it will lead to understanding. Together with belief and understanding there is also the volitional element. It is this that distinguishes the assent of faith from a conclusion that is purely cognitive.[121]

The decision of the will is essential to any consent. Besides accepting a conclusion one also has to give one's assent. Assent is more than merely accepting an inevitable conclusion at the end of a process of reasoning, evidence and certitude. The assent can convert insufficient evidence into certain belief. So assent is beyond that which is strictly of the cognitive order and is the commitment of the person to a truth he sees as inevitable. Certainty results from this decision to assent and this gap between the evidence and a believing assent can be bridged only by the will. Rational man does not merely believe, but he must *decide* to believe and also decide *what* to believe. Faith always includes belief and it is this belief that separates faith from the cognitive order. Belief is of the intellectual order and faith is more of a total commitment. The commitment is determined by the intellectual act. Faith is not merely volitional and cognitive, but is also emotional because we believe in someone, and so it involves also trust and confidence, as Newman points out about our belief in God. Hence, religious faith that involves total commitment leads to a new way of existence.[122]

Now while beliefs can be tested by experience and thus converted into knowledge, faith cannot be converted into knowledge because the content of faith does not belong to the empirical world. Faith integrates empirical reality into a synthesis which cannot be experienced because the data is interpreted differently since it is subordinated to an ultimate principle. So faith does not provide new knowledge but rather creates a new attitude. Still faith does not mean that one has absolute certitude but rather it is a trusting surrender. The certitude of faith does not possess the objective certainty of knowledge because the content of faith is not mere *datum*. Faith has a certain subjectivity by which it freely accepts the content by taking a personal stance. It is this free acceptance that gives faith its certitude and a personal character. Hence, Dupré says that the acceptance of the content of faith has to be a voluntary decision because of the transcendent nature of the content of faith. Free decision is necessary where rational insight is insufficient

[121] Cf. Dupré, *The Other Dimension*, 40-44.

[122] Cf. Dupré, *The Other Dimension*, 44-47.

because the truth of faith is not truth in the ordinary sense. This truth cannot be possessed but becomes true in the commitment. Hence it cannot be expressed in universal propositions because an essential part of the truth is personal acceptance which is a decision of the subject.[123] This decision is itself a gift. As Dupré says, "Faith must be a gift before being a demand or a virtue, because, for the believer, it participates in the transcendence which it intends, and self-transcendence in the religious sense can only be given."[124] In this way faith is a participation in divine life and requires an expression in ritual worship and behaviour. This is a natural consequence of the inwardness that is initiated by the religious attitude.

4.4 Conclusion

In earlier ages it was religion that had served as the cement of society. In fact religion and culture were closely linked, and reforms and changes in one usually had an effect on the other. But today especially in the west, religion by and large is no longer the binding force of culture. Religion has gradually been moved to the fringe of society and culture. And so while the world today can boast of technical advancement, scientific achievements, and no end of material abundance, it has also resulted in a depreciation of the value of human life and an uncontrolled exploitation of the resources of the human environment. Some would refer to this as a development of culture, but we feel that "a culture cannot be truly human without another dimension. We crave for a number of things which are missing in our world. Religion, at least in the most primitive sense of the term, seems to occupy a central place in those desires."[125] Having seen in part the dialectic that is at work in the religious act we realize that it is not a simple experience but rather a complex movement by which a 'new' reality is gradually discovered. This 'other dimension' lies beyond the phenomenal dimension and in fact is in contrast with the phenomenal. Yet ultimately this other dimension is what integrates all reality into a higher synthesis. This other dimension is much the same as it was in the past, but with the change in the situation of human existence its presence is not as evident as it was earlier. In general the sacred is no longer directly experienced by the majority of persons. As a result, modern man in order to arrive at the sacred needs to use the more reflective and deliberate attitude of faith.[126]

The attempt to reduce religion and the religious phenomenon to an experience that is purely subjective is destined to meet with failure because the religious object is not a scientifically analysable object. True there is a difference between the subject and the object of religion, but at the same time it is in religion that they are united and it is in religion that this unity and transcendence is given

[123] Cf. Dupré, *The Other Dimension*, 47-58.

[124] Dupré, *The Other Dimension*, 60.

[125] Dupré, *The Other Dimension*, 6.

[126] Cf. Dupré, *The Other Dimension*, 10-11.

expression. It is in understanding this unity and its expression that we are able to make greater sense of the phenomenon we described as 'revelation', because revelation is a properly religious category. From this point of view revelation can never be described as objective information, nor can it be said to be only a subjective interpretation of an expression because it is through the symbols of revelation that the transcendent dimension is revealed, and it is in this dimension that the real reaches its unification. To have a better understanding of God and to comprehend better man's movement of transcendence we need to understand the nature of the religious expression and also the religious act.[127]

In this chapter we have examined the religious attitude which allows for a deeper understanding of our existence and being. This religious attitude arises from the dialectic between the sacred and the profane with the transcendent as a point of reference. It is this movement toward integration and unity with the transcendent that leads to salvation. The rise of secularity led to the loss of the religious attitude but other factors like the mysteriousness of the universe, awareness of contingency and others have encouraged the drive within man toward transcendence. The religious attitude thus leads man to improve the quality of his existence. In the formation of the religious attitude, the religious object had a key role to play because it was this object that led men to go in search for the beyond and the ultimate reality. The many characteristics of this beyond encourage the movement of transcendence and in and through its Being we are able to experience this presence in our world, especially in creation. God as person is attainable in the subject and in creation because it is revelation and our reception of revelation in faith that enables us to reach for and attain that other dimension. It is our sense of the sacred that also encourages an inward turn that in faith allows for an encounter with the transcendent.

Dupré says that the concept of God originates in and is developed by the religious act. And so this is the topic we shall deal with in the next chapter. This concept of God is not a philosophical discovery, nor is a philosophical argument adequate to prove the concept true or false. At the same time, it is through philosophy that this religious concept is able to receive a logical structure so that its central position in faith is able to receive some justification.[128] The following chapter will be an analysis that is presented by Dupré about the religious act. He does this by making a study of the religious experience and especially by reflecting on such thinkers like Husserl, Blondel and Duméry. We shall therefore take up this study of the religious act since it is through this act that man tries to reach out to the transcendent.

---

[127] Cf. Dupré, *The Other Dimension*, 11.

[128] Cf. Dupré, *The Other Dimension*, 11.

Chapter 5

The Religious Act: Method and Truth

5.1 A Method Based on Experience

Phenomenology reflects on the religious act but this reflection is restricted by certain conditions. When we speak of the phenomenology of religion we need to clarify three types of relations. These are, the relationship between the psycho-empirical religious experience and its transcendent object, the relationship between transcendental reduction and the givenness of a transcendental revelation, and finally the relationship between the phenomenological and religious conceptions of truth. We are concerned about how an experience of the transcendent is possible because experience is immanent in nature and hence is different from the transcendent. Yet if the transcendent does not enter into experience then the phenomenology of religion is limited to inner intentions and outer expressions such as rituals and myths, and it remains separate from the transcendent Absolute—the intended object of the religious act.[1] The basic question for Dupré is, "How could a phenomenological analysis ever result in an "essential intuition" (*Wesensschau*) of an object that lies beyond experience?"[2]

Max Scheler claims that God becomes directly accessible only by acts of faith, devotion and worship. The God of religious consciousness lives in the religious act and so by reflectively retracing the act of faith from within we can gain access to its transcendent object. Gerardus van Leeuw made a distinction between 'religion-as-experience' which was a search for the meaning of life in its totality and 'religion-as-transcendent' as given in a divine revelation. Phenomenology, according to him, deals with religion-as-experience. But this answer falls short because without reflection and without a personal motivation, merely revelation

[1] Cf. Dupré, *Religious Mystery*, 4-5.

[2] Dupré, *Religious Mystery*, 5.

and blind faith in this revelation are insufficient for phenomenology to grasp the fullness of the religious act. If the nucleus—as transcendentally given—cannot be examined phenomenologically it is not possible to arrive at that which determines the religious attitude. When the experience is separated from the revelation that informs it then the problems that are connected with the religious act are insoluble. Some philosophers influenced by Blondel, Rousselot and Maréchal held that the experience renders its transcendental object as intentionally immanent in some way. They tried "to show that all mental acts are intrinsically related to a transcendent ground of meaning and value."[3] These hold a transcendent intentionality in that they believe that all human striving moves toward an all transcending end.[4]

The religious act shows a passive attitude which is displayed by the subject of the religious act towards its object. The object then appears as providing its own meaning and is not dependent on the subject for supplying its meaning. It is this "essential transcendence of the object intended by the religious act [which] makes the outward phenomena symbolic *expressions* of what surpasses their ordinary intentionality."[5] The inner intention is closely linked to the outward expression, and these expressions are essential to the religious act. The religious act aims at a transcendent *telos*. These representations and expressions are varied and very often since they are finite forms are unable to adequately represent the transcendent reality. It is here that the 'word', especially religious language is used, because it enables a religious intention to be linked to the expression.[6] We shall begin by examining Husserl's intentions of experience.

5.1.1 Husserl and the Intentionality of Experience

Husserl's concept of intentionality according to Dupré enabled us to make a distinction between what the religious act intends and that subjective experience which some psychologists had identified as the religious act. According to Dupré, psychology deals with the empirical aspect of experience. In doing so the ideal aspect of the religious act is ignored and so the religious consciousness by which it is related to the transcendent terminus will never be attained. Any attempt to give a psychological explanation to the religious act makes it non-religious, and religion becomes an illusion. Yet at the same time while psychology may not have a sufficiently clear idea of what religion is, within its limitations it can point out the emotional components of the so called religious phenomena. Actions are never pure and so it is the psychic constitution of the person that determines his or her religious activity, especially the intentionality of the religious act and

[3] Dupré, *Religious Mystery*, 6.

[4] Cf. Dupré, *Religious Mystery*, 5-6.

[5] Dupré, *Religious Mystery*, 7.

[6] Cf. Dupré, *Religious Mystery*, 7-8.

consequently its authenticity. The problem arises because not always is the intentionality—which is controlled by the psychic determinations—what it pretends to be and so the act is not authentic since motivations are often hidden and not pure. The act remains external and does not properly reflect its inner significance. Phenomenology deals with the ideal while empirical psychology deals with the real. On this assumption it would be difficult for phenomenology by itself to adequately explain the religious act. The main challenge would be to maintain the transcendence of the religious object and at the same time to insist on the real existence of this object, and not merely its existence as an intentional being.[7]

5.1.1.1 The Immanence and Transcendence of the Religious Object

The problem with respect to the transcendence of the religious object is that if the terminus of the religious act is transcendent then it has to be at least in part an object of faith. Scheler holds that God is revealed in a symbolical manner in the structure of the world, but he is also revealed in the world itself. Through a direct non-rational intuition man knows God through these symbols. In holding the possibility of a genuine *Wesensschau* of the divine, he threatens the transcendence of the religious terminus, while also reducing the phenomenological insight to an act of faith.[8]

Van der Leeuw makes a distinction between religion-as-experience and religion-as-transcendent. Through religion-as-experience man searches for the meaning of life. But this meaning while it is revealed remains forever concealed and is never fully understood because, "it implies an advance to the farthest boundary, where only one sole fact is understood—that all comprehension is "beyond"; and thus the ultimate meaning is at the same moment the limit of meaning."[9] Hence, in an immanent experience the transcendent is revealed, but the transcendent 'as such' is not contained within the phenomenon. So, phenomenology only describes this reaching toward a transcendent which is a phenomenologically unknown being. On the other hand because the object of the religious act is transcendent it can be attained only in faith, so in 'reaching toward' the object the transcendent object is attained. The religious attitude of faith is vital because if the transcendent reality can only be an object of faith, then it is faith alone that makes the object transcendent. It is the attitude of faith that makes a reality sacred. And if so, the object of faith is beyond the scope of the phenomenologist's inquiry. While Van der Leeuw agrees that all religion is based on faith he distinguishes between theological faith which is determined by a revelation, and faith that we

---

[7] Cf. Dupré, *Dubious Heritage*, 75-76.

[8] Cf. Dupré, *Dubious Heritage*, 76-77.

[9] Gerardus Van der Leeuw, *Religion in Essence and Manifestation*, trans. J. E. Turner (Princeton: Princeton University Press, 1963), 680.

turn to when something is beyond our understanding. Only the second type of faith is open to phenomenology. Religious faith is unique because it is determined by the believer's acceptance of a 'transcendent' revelation. All faith in this sense is theological. To understand the religious act therefore the revelation in which it originates cannot be denied, and this revelation is beyond autonomous reflection.[10]

In this light how a phenomenological reflection would comprehend the religious act without a believing attitude is hard to explain. The belief therefore affects the experience as well as the object. And as this belief is part of the *noesis* it influences the understanding of the ideal *noema*. Hence if the *noema* is considered outside of faith it loses its significance. On the other hand to include the transcendent within a phenomenological reflection is to reflect within faith and hence is theology. For a religious assertion the believing attitude is necessary. The problem arises because of the relation between a detached phenomenological reflection and a live experience, a relation that is excluded in an introspective act. In most experiences the object is completely within the immanence of consciousness, but in the act of faith there is only partial immanence because the transcendent object "becomes immanent only by being experienced as *beyond attainment*. Its immanence consists in the very awareness of transcendence."[11]

5.1.1.2 Transcendence from an Objective Point of View

Through his writings Husserl added a great deal of richness to the topic of transcendence. In his books the term transcendence was generally used to refer to "any being intended by consciousness whose reality falls outside consciousness."[12] He rejected the ontological transition from the essence of consciousness to the necessary existence of the actual world which was proposed by idealism. The world does show some internal connections which are necessary for a scientific description to be possible. Yet the natural sciences by themselves cannot explain the teleology that is observed which lends coherence to the world as one unit. Hence, the 'ground' of the factual world does lie in consciousness, but the nature of consciousness by itself does not fully explain the world. The non-existence of the world is always a possibility because the fact of the world is contingent. As Husserl says, "While I am aware of the world as a self-given, uninterrupted certainty… this world still retains a continuous cognitive contingency in the sense that its bodily presence does not exclude in principle its non-being."[13] Consciousness cannot be without a world, but because consciousness is a contingent fact it

---

[10] Cf. Dupré, *Dubious Heritage*, 77-78.

[11] Dupré, *Dubious Heritage*, 79.

[12] Dupré, *Dubious Heritage*, 80.

[13] E. Husserl, *Erste Philosophie*, II, Husserliana, VIII, 50, as quoted in Dupré, *Dubious Heritage*, 81.

cannot give a sufficient foundation for reality. The foundation can be provided only by a necessary being.[14]

5.1.1.3 Transcendence from a Subjective Point of View

The question arises whether consciousness itself requires a transcendent foundation. Individual consciousness is not self-sufficient because in order to be objective it needs the cooperation of other minds. Yet a mere totality of all human minds is also inadequate. Husserl holds that the transcendental 'Absolute' which is arrived at through reductions is not the ultimate and itself has its source in what is ultimately and truly absolute.[15] Husserl does speak of the transcendence of God as an absolute, but it is different from the absolute of consciousness. He also speaks of the time-constituting ego as the absolute source of consciousness, but this again is not such that it needs no further foundation. His awareness of the insufficiency of the constituting ego led him to explore the idea of a universal teleology as directing the activity of the time-constituting ego. It is this forward moving teleological principle which is all comprehensive that lends a uniting character to the inner time flow. Husserl holds that this intentionality is based on a transconscious universal drive.[16]

Husserl calls this intentionality an 'open infinity'. He does so "because he assumes that the universal teleology—although revealed in the finite mind—is directed toward an infinite perfection."[17] It thus transcends the consciousness that is time-constituted. Deprived of an infinite and transcendent *telos* intentionality leads nowhere. It was while studying ethical considerations in Fichte that Husserl realized the universal importance of the notion of teleology and in fact considered the infinite *telos* as giving a transcendent dimension to the ethical striving of men which far surpasses the transcendental subject. As he says, "This ideal itself is only a ray of the absolute ideal, of the ideal of an all-person that infinitely transcends all contingency (*das Faktische*) as well as all becoming and all development of the contingent toward the idea; it is a pole which lies infinitely far beyond it."[18] Such a description conveys Husserl's idea of transcendence and also describes a *telos* which goes beyond each individual time-constituted being. Whether it also transcends the totality of temporal being is hard to say because while speaking of creation Husserl holds that through transcendental being the transcendent *telos* creates, not *ex nihilo* but by redeeming the world from its inner conflict between being and non-being and bringing it to full objectivity.[19] If this is the case then

[14] Cf. Dupré, *Dubious Heritage*, 81-82.

[15] Cf. Husserl, *Ideen* I, Husserliana, III, 198, as quoted in Dupré, *Dubious Heritage*, 82.

[16] Cf. Dupré, *Dubious Heritage*, 83-84.

[17] Dupré, *Dubious Heritage*, 84.

[18] Husserl, *Erste Philosophie*, III 4, 61, as quoted in Dupré, *Dubious Heritage*, 85-86.

[19] Cf. Ibid., III 9, 65-66, as quoted in Dupré, *Dubious Heritage*, 86.

the infinite *telos* is only an immanent force and cannot exactly be referred to as 'transcendent'. According to Dupré, "That Husserl had such a 'realization' in mind appears clearly enough from a manuscript of 1931 which discusses man's contribution to the process of God's 'self-realization.'"[20] Yet, Husserl also tries to maintain a purely transcendent *telos*. While it is difficult to say whether he accepted God as an absolutely transcendent and personal Being, he does refer to God as *Überwahrheit, Überwirklichkeit, Über-an-sich.*[21] God is above all truth, above all reality and indeed beyond himself.[22]

Husserl was keen to understand transcendence because there was too much contingency in the teleological process and so it was unable to account for its own being. The true absolute should be able to support itself. Hence when we speak of the problem of transcendence it is not an issue with regard to teleology but rather one of contingency. When we deal with the absolute the important question is, does the teleological process have grounding within itself or is it grounded in another? For Dupré this is a problem of causality because the contingent must have some causal relationship to the necessary. Husserl sees the problem purely from the teleological point of view and so the *telos* cannot be independent of the teleological process itself and it is a purely ideal *telos*. His understanding seems to be far removed from true transcendence.[23]

5.1.1.4 Conclusion

Dupré concludes that the transcendent character of that which Husserl referred to as absolute is unclear. The absolute is established through contingency more than teleology. Husserl did not prove the existence of a personal transcendent being because he held that its existence was a matter of faith. It is not that he was not concerned about religious problems but in a way he tried to replace the philosophical knowledge of God with *faith* which is described as "a firm belief in the ultimate meaningfulness of existence beyond the point where this meaning can be proven or even easily accepted."[24] Husserl holds that faith is belief in teleology, a view of being that grasps reality in its organic totality. But such a view is beyond all finite horizons and is no longer a rational insight but rather it is a belief. It is through faith that teleology is accepted and this relationship between faith and teleology is essential for Husserl.[25] While Husserl did make a distinction

---

[20] Dupré, *Dubious Heritage*, 87.

[21] Cf. *Husserl, Erste Philosophie*, III 4, 62, as quoted in Dupré, *Dubious Heritage*, 87.

[22] Cf. Dupré, *Dubious Heritage*, 84-86.

[23] Cf. Dupré, *Dubious Heritage*, 87-90.

[24] Dupré, *Dubious Heritage*, 90.

[25] Cf. Louis Dupré, "Husserl's Thought on God and Faith," *Philosophy and Phenomenological Research* 29 (1968), 212-213.

between the experience and the object that is manifested through the experience, he did not satisfactorily apply his theory to the alleged object of religion.[26]

Through theoretical reasoning we are unable to provide a justification for the complete meaningfulness of life. But at the same time man's ethical striving is significant because the meaningfulness of life is an accepted fact. It is religious faith according to Husserl that gives a foundation to morality. While Husserl is definitely influenced by Kant's theory of the postulates of practical reason,[27] he also disagrees with Kant when he holds that the infinite teleology is somehow *directly experienced* by the religious man when he says, "In faith we *experience* the teleology that directs us."[28]

5.1.2 Blondel and the Reflection on Experience

In speaking about religion and religious attitudes we also take into consideration the role of subjectivity because only a self that is completely aware of its subjective nature is capable of grasping its relation to the transcendent. After Kant philosophy attempted to separate the subject from the object, and the philosophy of Blondel is one of many which aims at defining the nature of the subject. Dupré presents Blondel because while others concentrated on the nature and the being of the subject, Blondel considers the subject in its *acting*. As Dupré says, for Blondel "the subject is *act*, and in acting, it discovers its own insufficiency as well as the need for a transcendent fulfilment."[29] An agnostic philosophy that *a priori* rejects the transcendent claims of religion cannot be considered a balanced treatment of religion. On the other hand the 'gnostic' way of thinking that reduces all the transcendent elements of religion to something that is completely immanent is also equally inadequate. Hence, in the treatment of religion one has to be open to the transcendent while at the same time not attempting to completely immanentize it. Naturally such a condition would be difficult to fulfil, "because religion claims to create a transcendent world *within* the immanent, and it asks the philosopher to acknowledge this transcendence while at the same time regarding it with holy fear."[30]

Maurice Blondel held that by its nature the immanent is open to the transcendent and hence revealed religion is possible. At the same time, an essential characteristic of revealed religion is transcendence, while philosophy on the other hand is limited to a study of immanent structures. Hence, it appears that

---

[26] Cf. Dupré, *Dubious Heritage*, 4.

[27] Cf. Dupré, "Husserl's Thought on God and Faith," 213.

[28] Husserl, *Erste Philosophie,* III 10, 21, as quoted in Dupré, "Husserl's Thought on God and Faith," 214.

[29] Louis Dupré, "Reflections on Blondel's Religious Philosophy," *The New Scholasticism* 40 (1966), 3.

[30] Dupré, "Reflections on Blondel's Religious Philosophy," 4.

a philosophical assertion of revealed religion is impossible. The problem is not so much the content of the supernatural order but rather that his belief requires a *transcendent* order of reality. In this regard while speaking about Christianity Blondel writes, "Not to have it as received and given to us, but as discovered and originating in ourselves is not to have it at all."[31] Philosophy can reflect on the transcendent reality of religion without giving up the immanent method but it cannot discover the transcendent order as a *reality* because then it would automatically lose its transcendence. As an *actual reality* the supernatural is beyond immanent reflection, but as a *necessary* hypothesis it is an essential part of immanent philosophy. In his *Letter on Apologetics* Blondel speaks on how philosophy can examine the structure of religion in its historical appearance without giving up its immanent authority.[32]

5.1.2.1 The Dialectic of Action

Blondel refers to the human act in its totality before the act is separated into its willing and cognitive functions. These functions have their source in the intellect and hence are united in the acting subject. Yet that which is given in the known object is rarely distinguished from that which is constituted by the knowing subject. This subjective element is important. In every phenomenon even if all the objective elements are known there is still something more to it. The mere sum of its conditions is not enough to explain the act. It is the act which produces the phenomenon. And the subject is freedom *in act*. Just as the subject cannot be separated from objective phenomena, so too freedom always appears in the context of a system of determinations, but always goes beyond the determinations. Determinism therefore is an essential part of freedom. The motive transcends the impulse which conditions it. It is the transformation of blind instinct into clear motives that enables men to create civilization and culture.[33]

Every choice of an external object estranges the subject from itself. Freedom thus progresses in a dialectical manner because it is in losing itself that it finds itself. It chooses to transcend itself, and this self-transcendence is expressed in the ascent from one determination to another. Through this constant self-expression freedom reshapes the world of facts according to its own spiritual intentions. Living action surpasses its accomplishments and as freedom increases it becomes increasingly aware of its insufficiency and of its desire to terminate in an absolute. Its impetus attains only phenomena, but it *postulates* a trans-phenomenal reality. It reveals an infinity at the heart of action and while it may never reach an actual realization it always remains an eminently real exigency. This exigency of

---

[31] Maurice Blondel, *Lettre sur les exigences de la pensée contemporaine en matière d'apologetique* (Paris, 1962), 35, as quoted in Dupré, *Dubious Heritage*, 95.

[32] Cf. Dupré, *Dubious Heritage*, 95.

[33] Cf. Dupré, *Dubious Heritage*, 95-97.

transcendence does appear as a negation but its very necessity is the foundation of all contingent action.[34]

In studying action we become aware of the discrepancy between the real and the ideal which cannot be bridged. The idea and action alternate but never coincide. Blondel concludes from the insufficiency of human action that in this insufficiency man is able to find God. Thus his argument takes us beyond the mere phenomenal order. While we have to accept that his argument does not end up 'producing' a reality because, "it makes no ontological transition from an ideal structure to a living reality… it searches the *foundations* of the phenomena of consciousness, and *interprets* what appears in the phenomena themselves. It discovers the necessity of what is merely given in the original experience, by finding the structure of its internal determinations."[35]

5.1.2.2 Our Experience of the Supernatural

The function of philosophy is to determine the content of thought and so though it does not produce being itself, philosophy is not limited to a study of merely logical possibilities. It deals rather with the discovery of the necessary *in the real.* The limits therefore in studying the supernatural are not due to the limitations of philosophy but rather due to the special character of revelation. The question arises whether the active presence of a transcendent terminus in all human action entails the necessity of a self-communication of this transcendent. It appears as if for Blondel the satisfaction of the need is a natural necessity but a deeper study will reveal that it involves only the possibility of a transcendent fulfilment. While this possibility is necessary, "The transcendent is discovered exclusively in the *existing insufficiency*—not in the necessity of fulfillment."[36] When we posit a transcendent end to human action, we can logically consider the possibility of a transcendent completion of human action. Religion claims that this possibility has already been actualized. As Blondel states, "There is an infinity present to all our voluntary acts and this infinity cannot be contained in reflection or reproduced by human effort. If we are to grasp and produce this secret principle of all action, as we want to, then it must give itself to us in a form which allows us to enter into communion with it.[37] As a hypothesis, this is a necessary hypothesis because it is based on the awareness of an insufficiency in all human action and its need for completion. Yet the realization of this hypothesis need not be equally necessary.[38]

---

[34] Cf. Dupré, *Dubious Heritage*, 97-98.

[35] Dupré, *Dubious Heritage*, 99.

[36] Dupré, *Dubious Heritage*, 100.

[37] Cf. Maurice Blondel, *L'Action* (1893). Republished by Presses Universtaires de France, 1950, 322, as quoted in Dupré, *Dubious Heritage*, 101.

[38] Cf. Dupré, *Dubious Heritage*, 99-101.

In Blondel's thought the existence of a supernatural order is completely gratuitous. It is possible to experience transcendence in the insufficiency of action, but the existence of a supernatural order cannot be experienced with the same definiteness. "What religious man *experiences*—the symbols, sacred language, psychological effects and so forth—is not properly supernatural, but is rather that through which the transcendent communicates with the immanent."[39] Insofar as the supernatural order lies beyond all actual experience it cannot be dealt with in philosophy. From the living experience of action it is possible to imply the existence of a transcendent terminus. But we cannot imply any supernatural relation to that terminus because while the experience is supernatural, it is the supernatural reflected in conscious activity—hence of the natural order and subject to natural determinations—that is experienced. As Dupré says, "There can be no reflection upon the 'supernatural experience' because there can be no experience of the supernatural *as such*. To some extent we may experience *transcendence* insofar as the immanent points beyond itself. But of the *supernatural* we can only experience the possibility."[40] According to Blondel it is this possibility that we must consider. At the same time, we have to accept that however much we might reflect upon this possibility it cannot be transformed into an actuality. To enter into the supernatural realm we need faith which by its nature is ultimately supernatural and hence from that point of view it is beyond experience. This is the paradox of faith, that faith affirms more than that which can be experienced, and that the affirmation which itself is supernatural lies beyond experience.[41]

5.1.2.3 The Contingent Character of Reflection

Philosophy considers the supernatural as a possibility but that does not mean that because it is on the hypothetical plane philosophy cannot analyze the intrinsic structure and coherence of the supernatural. Philosophy does not commit itself to the supernatural order because then it becomes theology. Man has to accept that the supernatural order is not an immanent necessity and while he might reflect on its immanent structure he cannot provide a supernatural interpretation of it. "As a philosopher he may discern a transcendent reality in the structure of the immanent, but he cannot attain the reality of living dialogue with this transcendent, for such a reality forms no part of the immanent structure of the real."[42] Philosophy respects and does not negate the transcendent dimension. It only refrains from making statements about the transcendent beyond its own scope, and restricts itself to the immanent and immanent references to the transcendent. The existence of the transcendent can be philosophically asserted but always as a possibility. From

[39] Dupré, *Dubious Heritage*, 101-102.

[40] Dupré, *Dubious Heritage*, 102.

[41] Cf. Dupré, *Dubious Heritage*, 103.

[42] Dupré, *Dubious Heritage*, 103.

a religious point of view the distinction between immanent reflection and living experience seems to replace the distinction between the transcendent and the immanent. Dupré holds that Blondel's position, "implies that what prevents philosophy from fully grasping the supernatural is not so much the limitation of the experience itself on which philosophy reflects, as the deficiency of reflection with respect to the living experience."[43] Blondel uses living action to overcome the abyss between the immanent and the transcendent since he holds that in action the supernatural becomes a reality of experience. He says, "What one cannot know nor, above all, understand distinctly, one can always do and practice: that is the use, the eminent reason of action ... Its mediation is permanent: it is a perpetual means of internal conversion."[44] Thus what Blondel denied of reflection he said could be done by the experience of action. But then if the supernatural is transcendent to thought, it also should be transcendent to practice. Action alone is insufficient for conversion it requires at least an initial act of faith in order to be meaningful. A more profitable attitude according to Dupré is that of Duméry.[45]

5.1.2.4 Conditions for Reflection on a Hypothetical Supernatural

For philosophy to be able to reflect upon the supernatural hypothesis, the reflection should be on the religious consciousness as it actually exists. The doubt arises whether philosophy can reflect upon data that is not completely given in experience and yet preserve its autonomy, because philosophy cannot depend on the authority of faith or revelation. According to Blondel there is no need to reduce religion to immanent experience. Religion is both immanent and transcendent and the data of revelation too is expressed in symbols thus becoming a part of human consciousness and so has an immanent aspect. Hence both can be considered by the philosopher. Blondel analyses the basic aspirations of human action and says revealed religion fulfils these aspirations. His analysis basically is a confrontation between religion and philosophy. He does not make a philosophical analysis of any transcendent element, nor does revealed religion become the object of philosophical reflection.[46] "The two are simply juxtaposed and the philosopher concludes that the tenets of religion correspond to the deeper aspirations of man."[47] The problem is that this approach is often influenced by religion and revelation. As Duméry says, "It is no longer the approach of the philosopher: receiving his information from the theologian, his essential aim is,

[43] Dupré, *Dubious Heritage*, 105.

[44] Blondel, *L'Action*, 408, as quoted in Dupré, *Dubious Heritage*, 106.

[45] Cf. Dupré, *Dubious Heritage*, 103-106.

[46] Cf. Dupré, "Reflections on Blondel," 19.

[47] Dupré, "Reflections on Blondel," 19.

nevertheless, to understand and to judge the religious datum as it is distributed over the various levels of consciousness of the subject who receives it."[48]

The transcendent intervention which can bring human action to completion should be an *a priori* in consciousness if it exists. That is to say, if religion is a reality for man it must become immanent and must conform to the law as of human consciousness and fulfil the conditions posed by reason. The supernatural, does not contradict the nature of action, but as shown in *L'Action*, it completes human action and so is bound to be in accordance with the immanent structure of consciousness. The task of the philosopher is to find the ideal determinations of that which is immanently given in consciousness. Philosophy of religion then passes value judgements on the basis of the ideal necessity of consciousness. But this is not done *a priori*, but it is discovered in the actual phenomenon. The philosopher does not pass judgement on the supernatural reality, but rather his value judgement is limited to religion as it appears in consciousness. He does not make judgements on the ontological status of the religious object. Philosophy affirms the necessity of the supernatural on the level of ideal condition without knowing whether these conditions correspond to a given reality. But the concrete subject can commit himself to the existence of the supernatural fact.[49]

Dupré says that Blondel concentrated on establishing the objective structures of the experience itself. He left the object largely to faith. To understand the logic, structure and intentionality of religion we need to reflect on the experience. The issue of the reality beyond the experience was taken up by Duméry who combined the method of Husserl and Blondel, especially that of transcendental reduction because religious experience deals with the *ground of experience* more than the specific 'object' of experience. Religion is not a threat to man's self-determination but rather should be seen as the source of this creativity.[50]

5.1.3 Duméry and the Reduction of Experience

Dupré holds that with the work of Henry Duméry, the tradition led by Kant of *a priori* determining the limits of religious consciousness comes to an end. Together with Blondel, Duméry's starting point was consciousness as it actually appears and as it is experienced. From there he proceeded towards examining its immanent structure, which would include its categories, schemes and specific logic. After an initially bold critique Blondel had become much milder. But Duméry was not content with merely comparing the demands of philosophy and the representations of faith. He subjected these representations of faith to a philosophical critique. As Dupré says, "Duméry, in the trail of Blondel, decides that philosophy should restrict itself to a description and rational evaluation of

[48] Dupré, "Reflections on Blondel," 20.

[49] Cf. Dupré, "Reflections on Blondel," 20-22.

[50] Cf. Dupré, *Dubious Heritage*, 4-5.

the immanent structures in which the religious impulse expresses itself."[51] It was no longer the Kantian alternative of philosophy or faith. Now even where there was faith, philosophy was fully present without deciding what religion had to be. Philosophy attempted to speak of God without even paying attention to the religious experience that had given rise to it. Duméry attempted to put the issue in right perspective.[52]

5.1.3.1 The New Way of Looking at Religious Experience

There were many philosophers in the eighteenth century who attempted to return philosophy of religion to its religious roots. Schleiermacher was one of the earliest according to Dupré. But while he accepted faith, his lack of appreciation for the intrinsic necessity of symbols became an obstacle that blocked his arrival to the end. Kierkegaard worked towards tackling the false claims of philosophy, but he did not work on what philosophy could do with religion. Blondel and Newman did manage to specify what belonged to faith and what to reason, but again they established a parallel between reason and religion which was of no use in the understanding of religion.[53]

5.1.3.1.1 Phenomenology

It was the advent of phenomenology that opened up new possibilities. Phenomenologists wanted to discover the meaning of the religious act in the act itself. They sought to reflect upon religion without ignoring the religious experience from which religion originated and at the same time without trying to define *a priori* what according to them religious experience ought to be. For this it was necessary to examine the roots of the religious experience. No experience is able to expose its own foundation completely nor can it have a phenomenological description. For religion it is an even more difficult task because to the believer religion is much more than a mere religious experience. In religious belief the believer accepts much more than is understood, seen, felt or experienced. And so philosophy must penetrate deeper and attempt to arrive at this core which is hidden behind the appearance while at the same time not become a mere constructivism.[54]

Duméry holds that philosophy can penetrate beyond the appearances and for this he begins from a phenomenological analysis of the religious experience in order to uncover its ontological foundations. Theology for Duméry is the point of reference which keeps him in contact with the exigencies of the believer while at

---

[51] Louis Dupré, "The Problem of a Philosophy of Christianity: A New Study on Henry Duméry," *The Modern Schoolman* 44 (January 1967), 161.

[52] Cf. Dupré, *Dubious Heritage*, 108.

[53] Cf. Dupré, *Dubious Heritage*, 109.

[54] Cf. Dupré, *Dubious Heritage*, 109-110.

the same time including the interpretation that religion gives of itself in theology. Faith spurs us on to reflection. The reflection on faith itself leads to newer religious experiences which in turn enables and encourages deeper theological reflection. Hence, the experience cannot be separated from the reflection because one becomes the driving force and the impetus for the other. The philosopher should not try to invert the experience but rather it is his duty to critically reflect upon the experience. He has to accept that he merely encounters the idea of God and that he has not created the idea of God. So the philosopher cannot teach the believer something new but definitely he can help the believer to have a better understanding of the religious experience. As Dupré says, "Without philosophy, the religious experience does not fully understand itself... Although, there is no God of the philosophers, the God of religion is not inaccessible to philosophy."[55] Religious experience cannot ignore philosophical reflection because religion is not pure experience while at the same time it cannot deny the primacy of experience.[56]

5.1.3.1.2 Faith and Religious Experience

Faith belongs to the cognitive order and hence is expressed in intellectual categories which come under the jurisdiction of philosophy. All experience—including religious experience—is within the jurisdiction of philosophy. But reflection on the experience can never take the place of the original experience. In the past philosophy tended to ignore the primacy of the religious experience thus violating the integrity of the religious act, and hence was restricted mostly to proofs for the existence of God. The problem is that such an attitude gives rise to a contradiction because it "implies that God's existence can be known but not his essence, while simultaneously the philosopher endeavours to show that God's essence is identical with his existence."[57] Faith makes affirmations of God on different levels of consciousness. Duméry suggests that the philosopher should concentrate on these levels of consciousness of the intellect, the will, the imagination, sensibility, and on the conditions that would be necessary to make a religious affirmation that is in keeping with that particular level. This entails a study of the religious act in and through the variety of its expressions. Such a study enables reason to have jurisdiction over the whole of religious experience as a result of which even the experience of the transcendent can be scrutinized and thus better understood.[58]

This approach can be accused of rationalism, but if it restricts itself to the limits of the immanent experience then reflection cannot intrude upon the transcendent origin of religious experience. If philosophy does not reflect on

[55] Dupré, *Dubious Heritage*, 111.

[56] Cf. Dupré, *Dubious Heritage*, 110-111.

[57] Dupré, *Dubious Heritage*, 111.

[58] Cf. Dupré, *Dubious Heritage*, 111-112.

religious affirmations it is not true to its task of clarifying the human experience in its totality. In fact for centuries philosophy remained religious in form and content and only in the middle ages was the relation between religion and philosophy changed. Revelation was dealt with only in theology and philosophy had nothing to do with revealed religion. Only after Kant, with phenomenology, did philosophy take up the connection with religion once more. "The task of philosophy is not merely to describe and analyze but also to evaluate critically on all levels of consciousness, the formation and structure of religious symbols, including the ones which the religious man considers to be strictly revealed."[59] As long as reflection is not given more importance than lived experience it is acceptable. But then the problem is how to differentiate this philosophical approach from theology. Duméry's answer is that theology and philosophy of religion reflect on the content of faith. Theology's reflection is guided by an attitude of faith, while philosophy reflects without accepting the content of faith or without any commitment to the transcendent reality that is affirmed. The reflection of the philosopher is autonomous, while that of the theologian is fully committed to the scriptures, beliefs and teachings of the religious community and the transcendent authority. Yet between philosophy and theology there is also some common ground since theology often borrows from philosophy by way of content as well as method. In reflecting on the total religious experience philosophy also reflects on theology which is part of this total experience. The philosopher of religion attempts to situate the work of the theologian within the total experience of life. Hence, philosophy and theology are linked.[60]

Duméry was influenced by Blondel especially on the relation between philosophy and living experience. Philosophy studies the logical coherence and inner system of determinations of action but it cannot replace the primary experience of the real. Yet it is because of this that the philosopher can study the transcendent reality as a self contained system of thought. He can do this because he does not discuss the reality but only the logical structure in which it is presented. When man's relation to the transcendent is considered as being possible the study of the religious phenomenon becomes a logical necessity. And according to Blondel this necessity is what is needed in order to overcome the discrepancy between the infinite impulse to action on one hand and the limited achievement of this impulse on the other hand. For the believer a transcendent completion takes place in revealed religion, a claim that has to be seriously considered by the philosopher.[61]

---

[59] Dupré, *Dubious Heritage*, 112-113.

[60] Cf. Dupré, *Dubious Heritage*, 113.

[61] Cf. Dupré, *Dubious Heritage*, 114-115.

5.1.3.2 The Theory of Transcendental Reduction

The philosophy of Duméry is not merely a critique of noetic structures but is an effort to find the foundation of the religious experience. Foundations are not revealed in the external experience and expressions, so for a total reflection we need to go deeper than the actual phenomenon. With respect to religion this becomes particularly difficult because the ultimate reality which is intended in the religious act is by nature transcendent and so must remain unknown. Duméry upheld the ultimate inability of the mind to know God yet at the same time accepted its full accessibility to the rational. He explained this by saying that beneath all forms of human activity there is a movement forward in the mind towards an ultimate principle which is beyond all determination. All activities, even cognition, desire and feeling demonstrate this movement towards absolute unity and a search for an ultimate principle as expressed in Plotinus' philosophy of the One. This One "is identical with the mind as the principle which enables the mind to posit itself. Yet, the mind cannot be said to be the One since it labours under a subject-object opposition. The One is present in the minds striving, not in its realization. Only a total adherence to this absolute unity will allow the mind to terminate its striving."[62]

To describe the passage of the mind to God Duméry borrows from Husserl and Plotinus. He uses Plotinus' stages of conversion of the mind to the One but he presents them as the reductions of Husserl's phenomenology. The first stage is what he calls *eidetic* reduction. In this stage, "The mind eliminates all factual, contingent elements from the phenomena of consciousness in order to grasp their universal essences."[63] The second stage is called *transcendental* or *phenomenological* reduction. This reduction "brackets all reference to existential reality in order to concentrate exclusively on the phenomena in their relatedness to the transcendental subject."[64] The third stage is an *egological* reduction which "views the phenomena of consciousness as not merely related to, but also *produced* by the transcendental subject."[65] An examination of these three reductions reveals that this method of studying what constitutes mental phenomena turns out to be a study of the transcendental ego. Yet while they are necessary for philosophical analysis these reductions cannot lead us to the ultimate absolute and so Duméry adds a fourth stage, *henological* reduction which involves "grounding the transcendental ego itself in the absolute One."[66] It is this final reduction which provides the foundation for the mind's striving for unity and so consciousness and the world of objects have to be seen as one ideal unity of meaning. This theory of

---

[62] Dupré, *Dubious Heritage,* 115.

[63] Dupré, *Dubious Heritage,* 116.

[64] Dupré, *Dubious Heritage,* 116.

[65] Dupré, *Dubious Heritage,* 116.

[66] Dupré, *Dubious Heritage,* 116.

transcendental reduction provides the epistemological basis for Duméry's theory of the creative self.[67] Yet at the same time, Duméry "repeatedly asserts that the transition to the One must not be considered a mere effect of human freedom."[68]

5.1.3.3 Autonomy, Act-Law and the Creative Self

Man is aware of his freedom and the choice that allows him to choose from the possibilities before him. Hence even if there are fixed values and ideas man can still choose. Sartre denies God because he feels that God's presence would deny the freedom of man. But his concept of freedom is negative and has no ulterior foundation thus ending up as a useless passion. Duméry agrees with Sartre, that a pre-existing realm of truth and value would restrict man's autonomy, but he disagrees that the existence of God implies a pre-established order of values. Duméry follows the neo-platonic tradition that God is without determinations. All values are created by the finite spirit. Yet while God does not create any values he is at the origin of man's value creating activity because he does not impose values but makes man capable of creating values himself. Thus, man's dependence is the source of his autonomy and his createdness is the root of his creativity. At the same time, God is active in creation without imposing any finite determination. A faith that obstructs the freedom of conscience is in conflict with the nature of true religion. Such an erroneous notion of God makes him out to be the supreme object containing all values and ideas, and thus demanding total obedience. In such a context, the non-believer is held to be in error. The believer while being intolerant towards the non-believer avoids assuming his responsibilities and pushes responsibility on to God by thinking that all he has to do is accept things on faith. In faith he believes that he possesses the truth in its completeness. Actual religious truth is communicated through revelation and is guaranteed by divine authority, but this truth is a 'way', a path to salvation. It presupposes values and norms which are expressed in human experience and in a human relation to God. They are created and posited within man's relationship with God.[69]

Consciousness creates meaning and value, but the meaning-giving ego is not the empirical self, but the transcendental *ego*. This transcendental ego constitutes both the self and the world. Duméry refers to this creative ego as *act-law*. He says:

> It is an *act* because it creates, produces and regulates. The ego acts autonomously but not independently: it receives its active impulse from the One which is above all determinations. This One is the object of the fourth *henological* reduction ... The self, then, is not an original creative principle as the One is: it is an act which is *pre-ordained* to determine being according to its immanent necessity, and which therefore rightly may be called *law*.

[67] Cf. Dupré, *Dubious Heritage*, 115-116.

[68] Dupré, "The Problem of a Philosophy of Christianity," 162.

[69] Cf. Dupré, *Dubious Heritage*, 117-119.

> The determination of all being is a necessary condition (Hegel would say a *mediation*) for the self's conversion to the One.[70]

In creating meaning the self is not a law unto itself because it is in creating meaning and value that it expresses its relation to the One. Man's creative activity reveals his inclination or pre-disposition towards the One and thus eliminates the possibility of any arbitrariness. So while there is a determination it is the self's determination. It comes from within and is not imposed from outside. When God is posited as the denominator of being, man is dependent on God thus challenging the autonomy of the act-law. For this reason Duméry does not accept the traditional notion of participation. "Being and the source of being cannot share in the same being. As to the principle of determination, Plotinus's *intelligible*, it *proceeds* from the One, but does not participate in the One. Henology and participation exclude each other."[71] The advantage of the henological reduction is that it guarantees the radical productivity of the One as the source principle and the creativity of the intelligible.[72]

5.1.3.4 Revelation

In this light we need to ask the question, "If God is above all categories, how can we know about him?" In looking for an explanation Duméry makes use of the notion of revelation. Due to his spiritual nature man naturally makes a movement towards God, yet this movement by itself is insufficient to know God. For man to know God, God has to reveal himself. He does admit that because God is beyond the determinations of language it appears that he is silent. Yet God is able to reveal himself as the source of our speaking. As he says:

> God is beyond our grasp, our categories, but he appears through them. He is the high point of our aims, he is their soul. Nevertheless, we must increasingly purify our ideas and our schemes. For instance, he cannot be called *personal*—personal as we are; but he is more. It is possible, it is normal to address ourselves to him as to a person, provided we preserve the mystery.[73]

Duméry held that a revelation of God through nature was not possible because nature could help man to reach God but it could not teach man *about* God. Revelation is essentially human, it is man who gives it meaning and expression. When God speaks he does so through man who alone is the image of God. In this sense, how can revelation be called God's Word, when its content and form is an expression of man? Duméry agrees that religious language is

---

[70] Dupré, *Dubious Heritage*, 119-120.

[71] Dupré, *Dubious Heritage*, 121.

[72] Cf. Dupré, *Dubious Heritage*, 121-122.

[73] Henry Duméry, *La foi n'est pas un cri* (Paris, 1959), 216, as quoted in Dupré, *Dubious Heritage*, 122-123.

relative since they are largely intermediate stages in the ascent of the mind to the One. Yet in spite of this relativity we cannot deny the absolute element and the objective aspect of revelation. The subjective structures that are used are unavoidable, but they are the means by which objective essences are obtained by the subject on different levels of consciousness. In fact it is because of the way in which they are received that particular facts are transformed into *religious* facts.[74] As Duméry writes, "The religious reality objectively contains the meaning which the believer recognizes in it; yet, this meaning is perceived only when the believer discerns this reality as religious. In technical terms: the religious object exists but we still must 'constitute' it as religious."[75]

The religious object has to be given a religious meaning and so it has to be received in a religious manner. It requires a personal commitment on the part of the person delivering the message. It also requires a religious acceptance on the part of the receivers. With regard to biblical scholarship Duméry holds that since sacred writers found their inspiration within a particular religious tradition, it is necessary that they be read in that tradition. It is from this point of view that religious meaning is attributed to historical events. But this acceptance in faith of a particular tradition does not mean that it is a merely subjective experience. Christianity is strongly historical but faith goes much beyond the historical facts. Faith needs to be founded upon historical facts but it is the dialectic between seeing and believing that leads to the experience of the transcendence. While the subjective acceptance is important, the original and basic meaning is equally important. The experience cannot be fabricated from nothing. There has to be some indication of a divine authority and some religious meaning must be transmitted and so this allows some room for religious interpretation. There has to be an appeal and a response. Duméry seems to say that the appeal as well as the response are fully immanent. Usually the concrete religious expressions are contingent and human. There is the impulse and the expression of the act, so either both are transcendent as well as immanent, or neither of them is. According to Duméry the determinations of the religious act are "structures created by the mind's own impulse toward a mystery which is neither determined nor determining. He thus separates the religious expression from the religious intentionality which inspired it."[76] What he is saying is that it is only the religious impulse that has its origin in the transcendent ground of consciousness. The concrete determinations in which this impulse is expressed are completely immanent and have no transcendent meaning of their own. These determinations and expressions are posited by the mind.[77]

[74] Cf. Dupré, *Dubious Heritage*, 123-124.

[75] Duméry, *La foi n'est pas un cri*, 258, as quoted in Dupré, *Dubious Heritage*, 124.

[76] Dupré, *Dubious Heritage*, 127.

[77] Cf. Dupré, *Dubious Heritage*, 124-127.

Duméry's seems to be a disincarnated concept of religion which seems to make demythologization a necessity. And Duméry rejects demythologization. But such an understanding is contrary to revelation as a positive communication from the transcendent. The eternal object of revelation is not a mere result of the striving of the mind to the ground of all being.[78]

5.1.3.5 The Dialectic of Givenness and Projection

There is a unique dialectic at work between the essential receptivity of the religious act. There is the transcendent revelation on one hand and on the other there is the active role of the believer in creating symbols and norms within which he receives that revelation. To study this dialectic we need to do something similar to Husserl's transcendental reduction which relates phenomena to a transcendental subject. The active role of the meaning-giving subject is undeniable. Some philosophers say that human projection is completely responsible for religious symbolization, but these fail to pay attention to the transcendent revelation. And if this irreducible transcendence and givenness within the *noema* and the *noesis* of the religious act is ignored we miss the specifically religious quality of the act.[79]

Henry Duméry paid careful attention to this dialectic of givenness and projection in the religious act. For him, meaning originates under the intentional glance of consciousness. The *ego* constitutes meaning and the meaning-giving subject projects this meaning to the imaginative, rational and spiritual levels of consciousness. Projection is not an autonomous activity of the mind, but "refers to the *mediation* by means of which the transcendental subject forms and distributes a *received* impulse within the various psycho-empirical strata of the mind. It transfers the received impulse over the entire field of consciousness."[80] The incarnated mind 'gives' religious meaning to a given and pre-existing transcendence, much like a projection. There is a receptivity and a projection or transference of the meaning. To explain why the religious act is considered as a response to a transcendent revelation, Duméry formulated his theory of the act-law. It states that "The subject's projective activity obeys a transcendent law that directs its hierophanic creativity."[81] It is the act-law which unites the self to its transcendent source and is the ground of personhood and freedom. It is similar to Plotinus' *Nous* and guides the projection of meanings and values. It is for the Absolute that the subject draws its projective impulse and this relation is expressed in different categories and schemata such as divine names, symbols and

[78] Cf. Dupré, *Dubious Heritage*, 127.

[79] Cf. Dupré, *Religious Mystery*, 9-10.

[80] Dupré, *Religious Mystery*, 10.

[81] Louis Dupré, "Phenomenology of Religion: Limits and Possibilities," *The American Catholic Philosophical Quarterly* 66 (1992), 184.

representations. The presence of the Absolute is at the heart of the creative power of the projective activity.[82]

The meaning-intention of the religious act focuses on the ultimate givenness of the real. The individual usually receives this transcendent intentionality from a particular religious tradition which has constructed a particular conception of transcendence. As the individual is born into this culture it takes on this same conception of transcendence. Our thinking is always within a tradition so religious intentionality always expresses itself in newer concepts and symbols while always dependent on the earlier ones and in many ways identical with them. The founding facts of religion become meaningful when they are interpreted. It is when historical facts take on symbolical meaning that they become objects of religious faith. Many people see the same things and the same facts but not every one sees them as signs. This ability to 'see' is transcendentally given as part of the manifestation. And yet this presupposes a human act of conveying meaning. So, the manifestation of transcendence is projected through its interpretive expressions on various levels of consciousness.[83]

5.1.3.6 Dupré's Evaluation of Duméry

Religion is much more than a mere speculative relation to the transcendent. It involves man's total existence in the world and his attempt to transcend the world. Religious consciousness projects its intentionality on the world and the philosopher shows how these projections originate in the religious impulse. We realize that religion is never pure interiority and involves man's total existence in the world. Religion discovers the transcendent in the immanent. It integrates all levels of human existence into one intentionality towards the transcendent. To this end Duméry's philosophy of religion shows that the religious experience is a total experience and need not be reducible to reason alone. While he escapes the rationalism of his predecessors he does not escape their gnosticism. He reduces the religious activity to the immanent dynamism of consciousness as a totality. In order that he can balance the absolute transcendence of the religious object with the autonomy of the subject he interprets all determinations of the religious act as structures created by the mind. His efforts to preserve the transcendence of the religious object are of no avail since he sacrifices the transcendent aspect of the act itself. Such a conception leaves out the notion of revelation as a positive communication from the transcendent. Besides, historical events of religion remain subordinate to the universal meaning which is bestowed by the religious mind.[84]

---

[82] Cf. Dupré, *Religious Mystery*, 10-12.

[83] Cf. Dupré, *Religious Mystery*, 12-13.

[84] Cf. Louis Dupré, "Philosophy of Religion and Revelation: Autonomous Reflection versus Theophany," *International Philosophical Quarterly* 4 (December 1964), 509-511.

According to Dupré, "Duméry assumes the presence of the Absolute in these projective expressions, but he fails to clarify how exactly that presence determines the projective activity."[85] On the positive side Duméry did address the creative role of the transcendental subject. He also insisted on the need to move from general concepts applicable to all religion to specific categories and representations proper to each religion. Another important aspect is that Duméry insisted on the need of studying religion as the believer lives it rather than as the philosopher decides that it ought to be lived. As he says, "The sole duty of the philosopher is to examine the meaning and value that the idea of God bears for living spirituality."[86]

5.1.4 Conclusion

Therefore when we speak about religion naturally the emphasis is on revelation and on experience. The interpretation of our experience of revelation and our expressions of this experience play a key role, an aspect that we shall explore in the next chapter. The important thing as Dupré points out borrowing from Schillebeeckx's theory is that without experience revelation does not make sense, and also that in all experiences there is an element of interpretation. Experience and interpretation cannot be separated because the expression of the experience is interpreted and often culturally determined. Reflecting on the Christian experience Dupré says that there is a continuing process of interpreted experience rather than only one privileged Jesus experience. The first stage of experience was codified and made into a canonical text. The process of newer experiences and interpretations still continues but is always dependent on the original interpreted experience.[87] Taking our cue from this observation let us make a study about truth in the context of religion which undergoes constantly newer experiences and newer interpretations.

5.2 On Religious Truth

While considering the various issues connected with transcendence and experience we cannot avoid examining the claims for legitimacy made by religious truth and examine these claims in the light of a general theory of truth. Before studying the phenomenological approach for religious truth Dupré presents briefly Husserl's position on truth. Husserl held that truth consisted in bringing the object of cognition to such a state of givenness that it is evident to the knower. This is achieved by fulfilling meaning-intentions. Evidence has to be experiential since it is of the contingent psycho-empirical order and differs from ideal meaning-fulfilment. The ideal concept of truth contrasts with the traditional theory

[85] Dupré, *Religious Mystery*, 13.

[86] Cf. Henry Duméry, *Le probleme de Dieu* (Paris-Bruges: Desclee de Brouwer, 1957), 33-34, as quoted in Dupré, *Religious Mystery*, 14.

[87] Cf. Dupre, *Religious Mystery*, 107-117.

according to which ideas correspond to reality. When applied to religion, the requirements of a theory of truth could not be reduced to a mere conformity to 'facts'. The 'truth' of a faith cannot be derived from historical facts but its meaning is derived from a transcendent intentionality. While the correspondence theory is adequate, according to Husserl it does not mean that automatically the coherence and consistency of meaning and intentions is sufficient. A coherent system must also be in agreement with other areas of meaning.[88]

To define the specific nature of religious truths Husserl revives the ancient idea of truth as disclosure. The idea of divine illumination spells out an idea that some compelling inner evidence spurs us on to a continuous search for more understanding. Modern philosophy instead stresses the role of the subject, but the fundamental assumption is of a real that discloses itself. "The road to the evidential intuition may be paved by the transcendental subject, but in the final intuition, reality genuinely discloses *itself*."[89] Religious knowledge rests on 'revelation'. That is to say the insight is received from a transcendent source rather than made up by the transcendental ego in its confrontation with the world. It is not a mere self-induced givenness, but a 'revealed givenness'. It lends what Gadamer calls *ein Seinzuwachs*, 'an increment of Being'. The religious mind is necessary, but is always limited to merely allowing the transcendent meaning to penetrate all of reality.[90]

5.2.1 Some Conceptions of Truth

The traditional religious conceptions of truth are strikingly different from the modern conceptions of truth because of the secondary role that is assigned to epistemological concerns, or occasionally for the complete lack of these epistemological concerns. Nearly all the religious traditions give more importance to the ontological and moral qualities of truth than to its purely cognitive qualities. In general we can say that for religion, truth has more to do with being rather than knowledge. In this light Dupré refers to Mahatma Gandhi—whose lifelong quest for truth is well known and documented—who said, "Nothing is or exists in reality except Truth. That is why *Sat* or Truth is perhaps the more important name of God. In fact, it is more correct to say that 'Truth is God' than to say that 'God is Truth.'"[91] He called this way of truth-being *satyagraha*, which meant remaining firmly faithful to the truth of being. For Gandhi truth implied a single-minded devotion to authenticity and it was this moral pursuit which would ultimately lead truth to reveal itself cognitively. Hence, with respect to ontological truth we

---

[88] Cf. Dupre, *Religious Mystery*, 15-17.

[89] Dupre, *Religious Mystery*, 17.

[90] Cf. Dupre, *Religious Mystery*, 17-18.

[91] M. K. Gandhi, "Yeravda Mandir" in *Gandhi Selected Writings* (New York: Harper, 1972), 41, as quoted in Dupré, *Religious Mystery*, 19.

need an attitude of devotion and fidelity because the path of truth that leads to God is the path of devotion.[92]

Dupré believes that the origin of the so-called correspondence theory which would later become exclusively cognitive, lies in such a religious vision which insists on a consistency between *what is* and one's conduct. "Not to be 'true' to one's self means in fact, to descend to a lesser mode of being. Only when we are fully connected with Being shall we be able to *know*."[93] The importance assigned to being is quite different from the modern trend which gives primacy to consciousness. The innate quality of religious truth is its ontological state by which the relation to God defines the definitive link with Being, and this allows also for the possibility of ultimate meaning. True *knowing* depends on *being* in the truth. Ultimately it is the transcendent pole that establishes the relation as well as human awareness of the relation. "Truth, then, consists in the right relation to the ultimately real, and only that transcendent reality can enlighten us concerning the nature and even the existence of that relation. This principle... marks the constant factor in religious truth."[94] This according to Dupré is the fundamental belief of truth in most religions. The Judeo-Christian tradition while accepting the above principle emphasizes the need of a divine disclosure, a revelation. The Absolute is described as self-expressive and so God speaks because it is his nature to reveal himself. The Christian doctrine that God became the Word established that reality was grounded in God's Being and so was an expression of his Being. Thus Being as such was considered to be self-illuminating and self-manifesting.[95] This concept became the basis for all truth. Later in the modern age truth was seen as grounded in the subject rather than in a divinely established reality.

5.2.2 The Truth in Religion

When we speak about a religious view of truth it is not possible to have one single view that is common to all the religions because truth is too broad a concept for one religion to be able to contain all of its diverse aspects. Besides each religion has its own concerns and these cannot be imposed upon other religions. What we shall deal with in this section is based on the notion of truth as founded upon the basic principles of the New Testament. Early Christian thinkers were surprisingly quick in accepting the Greek *gnosis*. By the third century theologians like Clement and Origen had already begun to see faith as the fulfilment of philosophical insight. But this understanding of *gnosis* was not a philosophical rationalization of faith, nor was it an extension of philosophical understanding.

---

[92] Cf. Dupré, *Religious Mystery*, 19. See also D.M. Datta, *The Philosophy of Mahatma Gandhi* (Madison: University of Wisconsin Press, 1953), 128.

[93] Dupré, *Religious Mystery*, 20.

[94] Dupré, *Religious Mystery*, 20.

[95] Cf. Dupré, *Religious Mystery*, 20.

Rather, the new *gnosis* was the self-understanding of faith. The Gnostic Christian appropriated what he believed. By accepting that the act of faith contained its own understanding, the Alexandrian and Cappadocian fathers avoided the opposition between faith and understanding that is seen in much of modern thought.[96]

5.2.2.1 Augustine

In the early years the Latin West was careful about merging worldly wisdom and the revealed truth. The change was initiated by Augustine. In his later years he judged the search for truth to be intrinsically good and salvific. Augustine did brand the search of some subjects for truth as mere *curiositas* implying that not all search for truth was virtuous, but by and large he attributed a divine and revelatory quality to truth *as such*. Perhaps, the most important contribution of Augustine vis-à-vis religious truth was the stress he laid on its interior quality. Originally, understanding was achieved through the faithful acceptance of the gospel. But according to Augustine, "God teaches each individual soul, though always *in consonance with* the objective testimony of Scripture and ecclesiastical tradition."[97] This divine light or interior voice informs the mind. Thus the believer is enlightened about Scripture as well as profane learning and the source and condition of truth thereby becomes sacred. It is through this concept of a so-called interior Master, that Augustine achieves a new synthesis between faith and understanding. The early Fathers had understood religious truth as a process of explication, while now it was seen as a simultaneous illumination that is derived from objective as well as subjective sources. Well aware of the danger that the transcendent message be reduced to a conclusion arrived at through a process of reason, Augustine always insisted on the *intellectus quaerens fidem*, that faith was ultimately the decisive argument.[98]

5.2.2.2 Anselm

Anselm represented another turning point in the quest for truth. His idea reflected a bit of the 'faith seeking understanding' of Augustine yet it moved in a different direction. Echoing the words of Augustine, Anselm writes, "Right order requires that we believe the deep matters of the Christian faith before we presume to discuss them rationally."[99] The revelation we receive prompts us to reflect on its implications and to draw further conclusions. One conclusion thus reached is the necessary character of God's Being, which in turn influences God's relation to his creation. Hence, "Anselm develops a logic of immanence and transcendence that encompasses even the historical event of Christ's incarnation. In as much as God

---

[96] Cf. Dupré, *Religious Mystery*, 21.

[97] Dupré, *Religious Mystery*, 22.

[98] Cf. Dupré, *Religious Mystery*, 22-23.

[99] Anselm, *De diversis quaestionibus*, 83, 48, as quoted in Dupré, *Religious Mystery*, 23.

is necessary in his very Being, divine redemptive activity must also result from an inner necessity."[100] Anselm deduces the inner necessity of God's dealings from the historical contingencies of human decisions and so he goes beyond the data of revelation and his conclusions are much more than a mere explication of the text. It was this aspect perhaps that gave rise to a religious rationalism and exceeded the limits of what reason could say about God's disposition to the world. Yet in spite of this tendency, the rationality that Anselm followed was always a devout rationality and for him faith always remained the basic presupposition for all genuine understanding. His example though initiated a trend of a rationalism of a less pious style, as for instance that of Abelard who held that no theological knowledge of Scripture was needed at all and that only logic was enough to understand even the dogmas. Also with Aristotle's works gaining publicity the study of theology gradually turned into a science and this led to an epistemic distinction between the philosophical and the theological order of knowledge.[101]

5.2.2.3 Thomas Aquinas

In reply to the question, "Is sacred doctrine a science?" Thomas Aquinas answers in the affirmative and to corroborate his answer he refers to the Aristotelian definition that 'science' progresses from self-evident principles. Principles which are known by the 'natural light of reason' as well as those which are established by the light of the science of God and the blessed, are put on the same level. It appears Thomas is proving by means of that which has to be proved. He does agree that they are articles of faith when he says, "As other sciences do not argue in proof of their principles but argue from their principles to demonstrate other truths in these sciences, so this doctrine does not argue in proof of its principles, which are the articles of faith, but from them it goes on to prove something else."[102] This higher science that he is talking of turns out to be revelation. Aquinas himself is not concerned about certifying the first principles but his main concern is about the formal procedure from the principles to the conclusions.[103]

Aquinas' so-called scientific definition of religious truth was a lot different from the emphasis on faith in Augustine and the Greek *gnosis*. According to Dupré, Thomas' scientific presentation may not be very much different from that which Augustine held. The articles of faith when examined closely are only 'external' principles. For them to make sense they have to be seen in an 'interior' light which enables the mind to assent to these principles. So these principles are like sense data which needs the mind to illumine them. "The light of faith provides the

[100] Dupré, *Religious Mystery*, 23.

[101] Cf. Dupré, *Religious Mystery*, 23-24.

[102] Thomas Aquinas, *Summa Theologia*, I,q.1,a.8, as quoted in Dupré, *Religious Mystery*, 24-25.

[103] Cf. Dupré, *Religious Mystery*, 24-25.

formal element that converts the objective data of faith into religious truth... The truth about God can come only from God, and in faith human beings respond to God's self-witness."[104] Faith and reason are closely linked.

5.2.2.4 After Aquinas—Nominalism

The synthesis between faith and reason that had been arrived at by Thomas and his followers was undone by Nominalism. Religious truth could not always be certain of the support of reason and so there were now two conceptions of truth. Truth of reason which was based on the presumed harmony between nature and mind, and truth of theology which was founded on an authority that was beyond nature. As a result the truth of religion as understood by philosophy was different from that as established by faith. Philosophy attempted to prove the existence of God by arguments that were purely rational. Even Anselm and Augustine did this. Yet the medieval writers while they did the same thing always attempted to do so in conjunction with the religious sources from which the idea of God had originated. "They wanted to show that this idea, far from conflicting with reason, fully agreed with that of an infinite Being that they considered to be necessary for supporting the finite."[105] On the other hand the focus of attention in the modern age is to prove the existence of God but without the aid of evidence that is intrinsically religious. Hence, the truth of religion should be arrived at by a process of reasoning that leads from the finite to the necessity of an infinite principle. The problem is that even if by a proof we are able to arrive at the existence of such a principle beyond the world, the challenge would be to show that this principle is the same as the God of religion. Thinkers like Aquinas, Maimonides and Avicenna did not face this problem in a way because of their acceptance of the God of faith. What they did was to show that it was not irrational to accept this God of faith. When the need of the infinite was established this infinite was equated with their religious idea of God. Because of their theological reflection they knew that God was infinite and necessary. The only problem was that because they knew the conclusion beforehand they were over anxious to reach their goal and sometimes were careless in their reflection.[106]

As compared to the way of faith, the way of reasoning too claims to arrive at full-fledged religious conclusions. Their method is based on the belief that the phenomenal world is capable of providing enough information about that which transcends it. If in order to make the real intelligible a transcendent ground is postulated, it is not the same as the idea of God as conceived in religious faiths. Whether the absolutely intelligible is identical with the perfect Being intended in the religious act is still questionable. Karl Jaspers holds that while

---

[104] Dupré, *Religious Mystery*, 25.

[105] Dupré, *Religious Mystery*, 26.

[106] Cf. Dupré, *Religious Mystery*, 25-26.

the philosophical idea of transcendence is an aid towards a deeper reflection, it is not able to reach conclusions that are specifically religious in content. It is only when transcendence is confronted from a religious angle that it is able to reveal the religious content. Modern thought assumes that there is no truth that is specifically religious. While religion is seen as a special field of consciousness, the final word is decided upon by criteria that are largely epistemic. Since 'revelation' is accepted as being capable of adding to that which we know by natural means, it is still subject to the general rules of truth and credibility. Hence, when it speaks of the truth of religious assertions the modern mind sees truth not from within faith, but as something extrinsically conveyed to faith. Earlier religious truth meant that there was a participation in the revealed mystery of divine Being and so the human subject was a receptacle with a divine potential for apprehending the truth as divinely revealed. But now when truth was seen as separated from faith, it led consequently to a separation between experience and faith.[107]

5.2.3 The Truth of Religion

If religion provides the foundation for its own truth, once we move beyond the domain of faith it would be questionable whether we can make a fair evaluation of religious truth. And so Dupré raises the question, "Can any statement be made about the truth *of* religion that does not coincide with the truth *in* religion itself?"[108] Traditionally, truth is accepted as consisting in an *ideal* presence and an objective quality which goes beyond the subjective experience of *certainty*.[109] Psychology and sociology began to challenge this especially in the nineteenth century and today there are more challenges to the objective quality of truth.[110] A critical examination that is made solely on the basis of pure reason and without taking into account religious experience will lead to a distorted view about the truth of religion. What Dupré aims at doing is to make a brief examination of some of the existing models of truth in order to investigate their aptitude for clarifying the religious fact. This is necessary since if the truth of religion is incompatible with these models then whether it would be valid to believe the truth in that religion would be a legitimate question. Religious truth if it is legitimate must be able to integrate with other concepts of truth. As Dupré writes, "Religion

[107] Cf. Dupré, *Religious Mystery*, 26-27.

[108] Dupré, *Religious Mystery*, 27.

[109] Louis Dupré makes a distinction between truth 'in' Religion and truth 'of' Religion. When he speaks about 'truth in religion,' he refers to religious truth *within* a particular tradition, as for instance within the Judeo-Christian tradition. These truths deal with theology, particular articles of faith, etc. When he speaks of 'truth of religion', Dupré refers to the truth *about* faith. He is talking of *religion as a whole* and how valid or true it is to speak about and believe in a religion.

[110] Louis Dupré, "The Truth of Religion," in *Morality within the Life and Social World: Interdisciplinary Phenomenology of the Authentic Life in the "Moral Sense,"* ed. Anna-Teresa Tymieniecka. Holland: D. Reidel, *Analecta Husserliana* 22 (1985), 457.

unfolds its own truth, yet it is forced to do so within the available categories of general discourse… However sublime and unique a message may be, in order to be expressed, it must adopt an *existing* language and thereby integrate itself within a *praxis* of discourse."[111]

5.2.3.1 Religious Truth as Correspondence

In the earliest traditions, when speaking of religious truth, the correspondence between the word and reality appears to have been one of its essential components. Words or concepts had to conform to things as they were in themselves. Philosophy made a crucial epistemic turn when it made a clear division between the purely 'mental' concept and a purely 'real' object.[112] This division was very naïve because it assumed the mental to be personal and private, while the real was that which is universal and extramental. Yet the so-called 'real' world is the result of an experience that is individual, mental and even cultural. The mental factor which is personal is also communicable and universal. Hence, both the poles have to be seen in combination. Still from this principle it does not necessarily follow that truth is merely a product of a mind that is determined by the real world.[113]

According to Dupré, it was the unsurmountable difficulties that were inherent in the unproven and assumed harmony between the mind and the world that led to Kant's radical reversal of the correspondence theory. After his 'Copernican revolution' the distinction between the correspondence and the coherence theory was hazy. "The relation between the mind and its intentional object came to be interpreted as one of immanent objectivity. The intuition of truth in the end, then, is the outcome of a process in which we bring the object to givenness."[114] It was such an immanent interpretation that made it difficult to draw the line between the correspondence and the coherence theory. Simply appealing to facts is not possible because there is always a process of interpretation that allows the conversion of data into facts. The perception of data always includes an interpretation. If this is so for data in general then when we speak about religion the role of the interpretation is especially significant and consequently it is also controversial. The same observable data could be seen as religious by one person and non-religious by another. Yet believers and non-believers could still collaborate on social and scientific projects. Nevertheless, while some are satisfied with partial interpretations due to the nature of their work, for the religious person religious interpretations can shed a unique light on all aspects of the real and can also affect attitudes on a deeper level. Thus, when we evaluate the 'truth of religion' on the basis of a correspondence theory of truth we have to keep in mind that on

[111] Dupré, *Religious Mystery*, 29.

[112] Cf. Dupré, *Religious Mystery*, 29.

[113] Cf. Dupré, "The Truth of Religion," 457-458.

[114] Dupré, *Religious Mystery*, 29.

different levels, different interpretations are possible and so these could possibly lead to conflict. Truth in religion claims to correspond to what ultimately is, and so must follow the rules of correspondence. The separation between the mind and ultimate reality is bridged by religious truth which as *revealed* is given to the mind by a principle of being that is beyond the mind's own reality.[115] "The *process* of truth overcomes an initial duality between the mind and the 'inner word' of revelation."[116]

5.2.3.2 Religious Truth as Coherence

Coherence cannot be restricted to logical consistency because then with respect to religion we would be able to establish a religious coherence, but then truth would be restricted to a mere exercise in logical creativity. Besides mere coherence signifies a cohesion of elements, but truth implies a truth that is intrinsic to the whole as such. Coherence can be translated into a theory and thus incorporated into a system of rational reflection which integrates the separate elements into a unity of meaning. Yet each particular element while being independent does not break all relations with other systems of experience. This does not mean that there will never be conflicts, but there is no outright contradiction.[117] When applied to religion the coherence theory needs to be qualified because coherence can easily end up in 'closedness.' To make genuine truth-claims, coherence should not only be internal but also external. It has to enter into dialogue with other realms and so at least there should not be a contradiction of the basic interpretations of experience. Because, religion has its own realm of discourse does not mean that it does not have to enter into dialogue with other realms. It should be compatible with the basic interpretations of common sense and the physical sciences because if not it is totally meaningless. Religious truth is distinct, yet while being distinct it should relate to all aspects of life because it cannot afford to remain in isolation. One of the problems faced by the modern believer is his inability to integrate social, psychological and scientific developments with their religious faith. Unexamined religious beliefs are isolated from the modern culture as an island of truth. What Dupré wants to point out is that the theory of coherence does not do enough to defend the claim of religious truth that its truth comes from outside the system.[118] Religious truth implies a transcendent revelation. Yet even though by itself it is insufficient, it is still appropriate "for legitimating the relative *autonomy* and distinct identity of religious discourse."[119]

---

[115] Cf. Dupré, *Religious Mystery*, 29-30.

[116] Dupré, *Religious Mystery*, 30.

[117] Cf. Dupré, "The Truth of Religion," 458-459.

[118] Cf. Dupré, *Religious Mystery*, 31-33.

[119] Dupré, *Religious Mystery*, 33.

5.2.3.3 Truth as Disclosure

While the correspondence and coherence models are important in order to understand the truth of religion, with the modern emphasis on the subject they lost their importance. According to Dupré the disclosure theory seems to be better adapted for the specific nature of religious truth. The roots of this system are seen in the beginnings of Western thought and especially in Plato, Plotinus and Parmenides. The modern understanding of the Disclosure Theory emphasises the priority of the ontological aspect over the epistemic aspect of truth. Heidegger writes that truth does not lie first in the proposition, but rather in the disclosure "through which an openness essentially unfolds."[120] While it is true that this disclosure takes place in freedom, the focus of truth "is not on the subject, but on the openness within which Being itself appears."[121] This theory appears well suited for religious truth but we need to examine how it justifies itself especially from the point of view of philosophy.

5.2.3.3.1 Gadamer

Hermeneutic philosophy has attempted to justify the disclosure theory not by the critical method but rather "by a careful analysis of modes of cognition that illuminate Being without being restricted by the epistemic criteria of the positive sciences."[122] The critical norms for the positive sciences do not apply to the aesthetic and historical consciousness of truth. Gadamer describes the 'critical' justification as a "'mode of philosophizing', a retracing in *actu reflecto* of what we are actually doing in *actu exercito*, rather than in establishing the kind of critical foundation that philosophy provides for the sciences."[123] This immanent reflection sheds light on Being and the human existence within Being. The ontological significance is of prime importance. According to Gadamer this is best seen in a fundamental reflection on language. In speaking of the image he uses the term *seinszumachs*—augmentation of Being—to refer to the ontological quality of the iconic symbol, and this refers in a special way to the truth disclosed in religious symbols. It is in this ontological nature of religious disclosure that we discover the truth of religion.[124] Yet, Dupré says that we cannot assume as Gadamer does that "language justifies its own disclosure. For the disclosure of language by itself provides no adequate criterion for distinguishing truth from falsehood—an essential task in the traditional justification of truth."[125]

[120] Heidegger, "On the Essence of Truth," trans. John Sallis in *Basic Writings*, ed. David F. Krell (New York: Harper and Row, 1976), 129-133, as quoted in Dupré, *Religious Mystery*, 34.

[121] Dupré, *Religious Mystery*, 34.

[122] Dupré, *Religious Mystery*, 34.

[123] Dupré, *Religious Mystery*, 35.

[124] Cf. Dupré, *Religious Mystery*, 34-35.

[125] Dupré, *Religious Mystery*, 36.

5.2.3.3.2 Hegel

Dupré believes that when Hegel declared the Christian religion to be essentially 'true' in the sense that it expresses the deepest dimension of Being, he had the same idea as Gadamer. Hegel holds that Christian Doctrine is not merely subjective but also has an absolute, objective content that is in and for itself. Besides he considers philosophy itself as being dependent on religious disclosure which is prior to philosophy. As Hegel says, "[The stand point of religion] is the affirmation that the truth with which consciousness is actively related *embraces all content within itself.* Hence, this relation of this consciousness to this truth is itself the highest level of consciousness, its absolute standpoint."[126] To this Hegel adds that the full disclosure of the truth of religion takes place only when "Religion itself reinterprets its representational form through philosophy."[127] So in the final analysis the justification of religious truth does not lie in the critical reflection upon an already established truth, but now it constitutes itself as truth. Thus the disclosure of religious truth has an ontological richness and ultimacy.[128]

This task of giving a justification for the ontological manifestation was difficult especially without having recourse to a supernatural revelation. Most people were content with merely giving a description of the unique disclosure that takes place in the religious act. They felt that in the religious act previous content and relations were seen in a new light because "Religious disclosure conveys to ordinary reality a symbolic and metaphorical quality."[129] For the religious believer the ontological disclosure takes place within the context of revelation. Yet far from providing the justifying evidence required by disclosure, the idea of a divine revelation itself is in need of support. For the believer revelation justifies itself, but it is not the same for the non-believer. Religious disclosure is not accepted universally. It needs an involved participation and a personal commitment. Some phenomenologists would follow the line of Gerardus van der Leeuw who concluded that, "The religious act and its intentional object cannot be understood unless one shares the faith that conditions them—that is, unless one accepts the transcendence of its object."[130] Extremely interpreted, this would mean that philosophy would have to be converted into faith, while on a milder level it would imply a general religious sensitivity. But in either case religious disclosure would not be universally accessible. So, if truth cannot be universally accessible can it be considered to be philosophically justifiable?[131]

---

[126] Hegel, *Vorlesungen*, 219. Lectures, Part 1, 315, as quoted in Dupré, *Religious Mystery*, 35.

[127] Dupré, *Religious Mystery*, 35.

[128] Cf. Dupré, *Religious Mystery*, 35-36.

[129] Dupré, *Religious Mystery*, 36.

[130] Dupré, *Religious Mystery*, 37.

[131] Cf. Dupré, *Religious Mystery*, 36-37.

5.2.3.3.3 Religious Truth as Disclosure

In reply to this query regarding the philosophical justifiability of truth, Dupré points out that the truth of disclosure with regard to religion is different from the truth of disclosure when considered in connection with scientific or historical truth. There may be some rules that are shared in common, but there are also other rules specifically for religion which cannot be measured by any extrinsic or universal norms. Some see religious disclosure in terms of Heidegger's existential interpretation. Rudolf Bultmann for example saw Christian revelation as disclosing a new dimension in existence. But then in assuming that transcendent revelation can be fully translated into existential terms, the unique nature of religious disclosure is not understood. Kierkegaard was aware of this sharp difference between transcendent meaning and immanent experience and hence he held that genuinely religious truth is permanently hidden from direct communication. It is interiorly disclosed, but the disclosure is never direct because it is passively received and then has to be dialectically interiorized. The translation into existence involves a never ending process of mediation.[132]

The self-manifestation of the transcendent is not the same as self-understanding, nor is it equivalent to the understanding of Being. Self-manifestation contributes to an understanding of the self and of being, but it also goes beyond both of them in referring to the inexpressible. This is a paradox that is accepted by mystical writers because such knowledge cannot be put into words. This ineffable knowledge is described as sublime because as John of the Cross writes, it is "transcending what is naturally attainable."[133] It discloses the presence of a reality that cannot be disclosed itself, and so religious disclosure is truth that refuses to submit to external criteria. A reflection on the notion of experience as understood in religion makes this clear. Disclosure always takes place in experience. An experience that is only a mental process has no relation to truth but if experience yields an insight that could lead to some sort of universality then it is on the way to truth. Experience defines its own meaning but it is in the process of experiencing that we learn that which we are experiencing. The truth lies in the knowledge and in the process itself because it is my own experience. Religious disclosure is a personal and communal experience, and in a way discloses more about the believer than of God because in it a transcendent message interacts with an immanent experience. Due to this connection religious disclosure does not become purely subjective since it is the reality that we experience which determines the nature of the experience. Not that through the immanence of the experience the believer gains direct access to the transcendent object, but "faith carries an evidence of its own that, without the manifest presence of its object, illuminates

[132] Cf. Dupré, *Religious Mystery*, 37-38.

[133] John of the Cross, *Ascent of Mount Carmel*, trans. Allison Peers (Garden City, New York: Doubleday-Image, 1958), II, 26, 8, as quoted in Dupré, *Religious Mystery*, 38.

the believer's relation to it as vital to the understanding of him—or herself and of all reality."[134] So this sort of evidence might not be able to give a scientific proof for its truth or may not even increase our theoretical knowledge of the world. But then what it does accomplish is that it enables a different perspective, so that metaphysical insight and empirical investigation can be seen in a new light, and according to Dupré this enables a personal justification of its own truth.[135]

5.2.4 Religious Truth

In general when we think about truth we think of it as a new correspondence or as a new disclosure. But then truth could also be a new way of correspondence, a different way of integrating a whole or as a new dimension of disclosure. Hence, in this case we are concerned not so much with a new content as with a new 'space'. And within this new space existing content and relations are seen in a different light. In this sense religion enables us to perceive this *other dimension*. We are not referring to merely going beyond the physical but "beyond this 'intramundane transcendence', the religious mind perceives another beyondness that ordains all other infinitudes. In its light these others suddenly turn into deficient symbols and metaphors of a more intensive reality."[136] Religious truth is not universally accepted. But even so it does not mean that it is invalid. One important aspect about it is the personal involvement on the part of the believer. A person may do detailed research and have a more scholarly knowledge of religion than most believers, but yet he cannot decide about its truth or falsity. Still, religious truth is not a mere subjective decision. Some principles such as a *transcendent reality* have to be universally accepted. The uncertainty is about the specific content of the religious act.[137]

Religious consciousness is unique yet that does not mean that the believer does not have to justify his faith. There may be no decisive reason against a particular faith, but it may contain so many uncertainties that an admission of that faith may be a completely irrational attitude. That which lies beyond the intelligible realm is accepted only if there are compelling reasons to make the acceptance reasonable. The issue of verifiability is a significant one for the believer and the believer knows that his belief—in principle—is falsifiable, and also that what may be acceptable today might fail the test tomorrow. Yet, it is not possible to define this test in universal terms. There is no universal criterion for verifiability or falsifiability, but the test of probability of a religion depends on the axioms and promises of each religion.[138] In this area there are no full-fledged empirical proofs

---

[134] Dupré, *Religious Mystery*, 39-40.

[135] Cf. Dupré, *Religious Mystery*, 38-40.

[136] Dupré, "The Truth of Religion," 460.

[137] Cf. Dupré, "The Truth of Religion," 460-461.

[138] Cf. Dupré, "The Truth of Religion," 461-462.

of faith. What we have are some starting points of reference. No objective facts can verify by themselves the truth or falsity of religious assertions. At most we have "pointers which, *when integrated within a religious context and only then*, become convincing."[139]

In conclusion we can say that the fundamental evidence that serious truth claims can be made, lies neither in any objective fact, nor in external information, but rather it lies in the basic tendency of all acts of consciousness. This is the foundational argument for any proof that deals with the existence and nature of a transcendent reality and its manifestation in any religion. Therefore, we have to distinguish the cognitive act from its conceptual expression. The expression never does justice to the implicit affirmation of the act which signifies and co-affirms infinite Being. Joseph Maréchal initiated a systematic exploration of this implicit presence and he speaks of it as the dynamism of the mind and the desire for what lies beyond that which is immediately asserted. He therefore presupposes that the indefinite pursuit for ever higher values such as truth, happiness and beauty makes sense only when seen in the background of a real infinite. It is because the mind is open to the 'unlimited' but 'never known' reality, that indefinite progress is possible. Karl Rahner in his turn refers to the *Vorgriff* by which we comprehend, but which itself remains incomprehensible. "The reality of this ultimate aim remains the condition of the possibility of every act of knowledge. The significant distinction here is between the act and its content."[140] Some like Henry Bouillard would completely separate faith from its representations. In any case this implicit presence cannot be separated from the affirming act as an independent object. Hence, truth with regard to religion, what Dupré refers to as the truth of religion cannot be objective.[141]

5.3 Conclusion

The religious act as we have seen has two important aspects. The first aspect is that of experience and consequently the second aspect is that of the symbolization of this experience. In this chapter we have spoken about religion and Dupré's analysis of three facets of religion, namely, feeling, freedom and representation. These three facets have enabled us to understand religion especially from the perspective of human autonomy. With the study that Dupré has made on Schleiermacher especially through the dialectic of consciousness between feeling and intuition, we realize that religion is subjective as well as objective and that through the feeling of dependence man is able to surrender to a totality which transcends the self, a movement in which feeling unites consciousness and being. Kierkegaard's analysis of the dialectic between human autonomy and theonomy

---

[139] Dupré, *The Other Dimension*, 71.

[140] Dupré, "The Truth of Religion," 463.

[141] Cf. Dupré, "The Truth of Religion," 462-463.

expresses the facet of the self as free choice. When the self is accepted as dependent then the self is able to confront the transcendent and for this what is needed is an attitude of faith. Through faith freedom is not lost rather it is recovered. What is essential is the honesty and sincerity of the relationship and the choices it entails. Thirdly, when speaking of religion we cannot avoid the representation that it entails. While we have briefly examined this topic, the next chapter will be a more detailed examination of religious representation especially in symbols, language, rituals and art which enables the self-manifestation of God.

We realize that this is a unique endeavour to understand the religious act but as we have set out to better understand it through experience it is through phenomenology that we are able to have a clearer view of the transcendent intentionality, especially of the *telos*. Husserl's 'intentions' is what, in a way, helps us to understand the need of faith and belief because no theoretical explanation will really make this possible. But Blondel's 'reflection' on experience, through the Dialectic of Action, enables us to reflect on religious consciousness as it actually exists. And finally to complete his analysis of experience Dupré refers to Henry Duméry who through the 'reductions' of experience, the act-law and the creative self is able to present this experience as a balance between givenness and projection. This enables us to work out a method about how to proceed in the religious experience.

Finally, the issue about religious truth and how best to arrive at an acceptance and discovery of the religious truth is also necessary. All these facets are necessary to make our experience of religion relevant and understandable. Having analyzed our experience and having come to a better vision of what religion is, and the method we need to follow in order to make this experience fruitful, the religious truth and its significance in our life is what will lead us to the movement of transcendence.

Truth with regard to religion is of special significance because on it is based the credibility of religion. While the coherence theory and the correspondence theory are significant, it is the disclosure theory that perhaps is the most relevant in connection with the 'truth of religion'. It is through disclosure that transcendence and immanence are able to come together and be of significance to man. Yet religious truth has to deal with the other aspects of cognition too and cannot remain isolated. Ultimately it is the personal involvement of the believer and his openness, together with the self-manifestation of that which is beyond and supported by the coherence and correspondence theory, which make the disclosure meaningful. Yet even though theoretically this experience is meaningful, ultimately what religion means for man is seen in the symbolization of this experience. The experience is a lived experience, and so the expressions that are meaningful and significant to man have to be examined.

Chapter 6

The Path to Transcendence

6.1 Introduction

Having made a fairly comprehensive study of religion which covered the religious subject and the religious object, we now need to examine how these are seen in relation to each other since Louis Dupré holds them as being part of the synthesis and as necessary for the concept of transcendence. While he has not written a specific treatise on this topic, we could say that many of Dupré's writings deal with this subject and hence in the light of what we have said we attempt to put together the various building blocks to form the bigger picture and this will put us on the track toward a concept of transcendence.

6.1.1 The Self and Consciousness

In our attempts to understand the nature of the self we generally concentrate on consciousness and its objective content. The general notion of selfhood is insufficient when we deal with experiences that lie beyond the range of ordinary object intentionality, as for instance when dealing with immortality. We are not so much concerned about whether man survives after death, but rather our concern is the origin of the idea of immortality and the experiences that lead to it. The belief in immortality is not just the conclusion of a rational argument but it seems to have grown out of actual experiences. Experiences of this nature may be rare for modern man, yet we are not fully deprived of intimations of permanence. When we speak of religious immortality the stress is not so much on an expectation to continue one's present life for a prolonged period of time, but rather we speak of immortality as a call for a total change of one's life. What is desired is not just survival, or more of the same life, but a higher and altogether better life and a qualitatively different form of existence. The major difficulty in this regard is the continuance of one's personal identity.[1]

If we consider the after-life to be similar to our present existence it would necessitate a corporeal orientation that has the possibility of continuing even after death. Dupré makes a reference to Joseph Maréchal's analysis of mystical states in which he shows how it is possible for the mystic to attain a vivid awareness of a bodily presence even without sense perception. While some would refer to this as mere hallucinations it still does not explain the transition that is made from an internal representation seen as a modification of the subject to the awareness of an external object. This 'feeling of presence' can occur even in the absence of perceptions that would normally be required to produce such a feeling. Dupré says the same could be the case in memory without the support of the body.[2]

According to Dupré the states of consciousness cannot dispense with the body altogether because even the mystic is bodily oriented. When his experiences take the mystic to the beyond it is the body that provides a vantage point. It is the body that keeps the mind from being totally disoriented. Memory by itself is not sufficient. It is the body that helps retain a continuity with the past. The body is not a mere instrument of the mind but helps one to define one's relation to oneself and to the world. This indissoluble union of mind and body is held by Spinoza and echoed recently by Klages and Merleau-Ponty.[3] This involves a certain dualism since the mind cannot completely do away with the body. There has to be an operative union of mind and body. In this light one's personal identity is connected to a particular mind-body relation. A different body would give rise to a different identity. My present body gives rise to my view point of the world which creates my personal identity. So a person cannot have a personal identity without his or her body.[4]

When we look at the self we look at it from two points of view. One aspect is that of bodily identity, and the other aspect is the continuity of memory. Hence to have a complete notion of the self we need an understanding that is capable of going beyond the actual boundaries of experience. The concept of the self cannot be completely *apriori* and must be supported by actual experiences. Besides the self cannot be identified with self-consciousness, because sometimes it has prolonged periods of loss of awareness but still retains its selfhood. W. Ernest Hocking posits a reflective self which is beyond the object-oriented self. "This reflective self

[1] Cf. Dupré, *Transcendent Selfhood*, 79-81.

[2] Cf. Dupré, *Transcendent Selfhood*, 82-84.

[3] Dupré refers to Klages who writes, "The soul is the meaning of the body and the body is the manifestation of the soul; neither of the two acts on the other because neither of the two belongs to the world of things." Klages, *Nom Wesen des Bewusstseins* (Leipzig, 1921) cited in Maurice Merleau-Ponty, *The Structure of Behaviour*, trans. Alden Fisher (Boston: Beacon Press, 1963) as quoted in Dupré, *Transcendent Selfhood*, 85.

[4] Cf. Dupré, *Transcendent Selfhood*, 84-86.

alone secures personal identity throughout variety and discontinuity. Steadfastly it maintains itself through the blackouts of consciousness and connects the intermittent stretches of consciousness."[5] Still the body while being indispensable is not the ultimate foundation because the self is much more than the sum total of physical phenomena and so must have a sub-phenomenal source. In artistic creativity as in day dreams the self goes beyond the ordinary world and even escapes the laws that rule the world. This deeper self is not as dependent on its bodily situation as the ordinary self. As Dupré says:

> ...at least *some* functions are both individualized and not *directly* dependent upon the actual presence of the body beyond the general physiological conditions (brain, nervous system, blood supply) of all conscious activity in the present life. This relative independence opens at least the possibility of states of consciousness that would require no actually present body. Yet ... even those states require some connection with an actual body.[6]

So we can say that the mind is not dependent on the senses for all of its functions and in some instances it functions independent of the senses.[7]

6.1.2 The Mystical Experience of the Self

When speaking about the self and the concept of transcendence one of the ideas that is a help in our study is the inward turn of religious recollection and the belief in immortality or as some would refer to it, the resurrection. Naturally this understanding differs from that of the self in terms of common states of awareness and so we refer to the mystics and the mystical experience in this section because as Dupré writes, "Those who aim at the most intensive experience of the self have at all times believed that they would attain in the end a self no longer circumscribed by the bounds of ordinary consciousness. The very purpose of the mystical journey is to move beyond this consciousness into the dark source of selfhood."[8] We realize that there is a completely different layer of selfhood that lies beneath the external succession of outward-oriented phenomena. Hence, the general rules that govern ordinary consciousness are suspended. Space and time are transformed and ordinary rational consciousness which earlier was thought to be the only type of consciousness is confronted with imagination, visions, dream consciousness and other potential forms of consciousness.[9]

Due to its special character the mystical experience is seen as an isolated experience, but yet it makes us aware that the soul rests on a divine basis. "To the religious mind the soul is always more than it is: it transcends itself, so that the way

[5] Dupré, *Transcendent Selfhood*, 89.

[6] Dupré, *Transcendent Selfhood*, 91.

[7] Cf. Dupré, *Transcendent Selfhood*, 88-91.

[8] Dupré, *Transcendent Selfhood*, 92.

[9] Cf. Dupré, *Transcendent Selfhood*, 92-93.

inward must eventually become the way upward or downward (depending on the schema one adopts)."[10] When the ordinary consciousness starts loosening its grip the transcendence of the soul becomes manifest in the mind's self-understanding. In that instant we enter that place where God and the soul touch, which is the very core of the self. True freedom is linked to this capacity for transcendence. According to Dupré the concept of the soul is a religious concept.[11] Like Dupré we restrict ourselves to Christian theology which regards the soul as an image of God, a concept that determines much of the development of Christian mysticism. The 'redeemed' soul is perceived to have a divine character and this structure of the soul can only be understood from a transcendent perspective. All this only goes to point out that the ordinary self is different from the mystical self.[12]

Jan Ruusbroec holds that in mystical awareness reason is suspended and the mind is emptied of all objects. This difference is also seen in the various metaphors that are used for this awareness such as isolation, secrecy, height and depth. The soul is often referred to as ascending beyond images and understanding which leads to a qualitative distinctness. It is also interesting to note different descriptions of the state of contemplation. In the *Brhad-Aranyaka Upanishad* we read, "As a man, when in the embrace of a beloved wife, knows nothing within or without, so this person, when in the embrace of the intelligent soul, knows nothing within or without."[13] Or again as Dionysius expresses, "Into this Dark beyond all light, we pray to come and, unseeing and unknowing, to see and to know Him that is beyond seeing and beyond knowing precisely by not seeing, by not knowing."[14] Saint Teresa of Avila also speaks of this paralysis of the ordinary psychic functions when she writes, "As to the memory, my belief is that the soul has none, and cannot think at all; the senses too, in my opinion, are no longer awake, but are, as it were, lost, so that the soul may be more fully occupied in fruition."[15]

This does not mean that all faculties stop functioning but rather that they do not function in the way they normally would. The Spanish mystics held that the will always functions even though there is no free choice. Mystical states always remain states of awareness and so are cognitive states. The imagination and senses receive new powers as a result of which mystics 'see' visions and 'hear' voices

---

[10] Dupré, *Transcendent Selfhood*, 93.

[11] Dupré refers to E. B. Tylor's theory, to Plato, to North American Indian and also Australian natives in this regard. Cf. Aake Hultkranz, *Conceptions of the Soul among North American Indians* (Stockholm, 1954), 412-424, as quoted in Dupré, *Transcendent Selfhood*, 94.

[12] Cf. Dupré, *Transcendent Selfhood*, 93-95.

[13] *Brhad-Aranyaka Upanishad*, 4,3,21. R. E. Hume, *Thirteen Principal Upanishads* (New York: Oxford University Press, 1931), 136, as quoted in Dupré, *Transcendent Selfhood*, 96.

[14] Dionysius, *Mystical Theology*, in Migne, PG, III, 1000; trans. Elmer O'Brien, *Varieties of Mystical Experience,* 83, as quoted in Dupré, *Transcendent Selfhood*, 97.

[15] Teresa of Avila, *Relations* V, in *The Collected Works of St. Teresa*, trans. E. Allison Peers (London, 1934-35), vol. 1. 328, as quoted in Dupré, *Transcendent Selfhood*, 97.

that others are not able to perceive. We cannot pass a judgement on whether these are illusions or hallucinations and so we need to be careful in interpreting mystical sensations. Dupré refers for instance to John of the Cross who describes the 'touch' of God. Dupré says, "... those touches occur 'in the substance' of the soul, not in its faculties, and consequently, that they have neither form nor figure. He seems to use the term 'touches' to denote an experience unrelated to sensation but analogous to it by its directly intuitive character."[16] Perhaps, the same holds true even for mystical visions which often are accompanied by intellectual visions.[17] We have to be careful about the external trappings and the haze of uncertainty that surrounds the spiritual and blurs our understanding because spiritual communication takes place on a much deeper level. At this stage we do not intend to make a profound study on this topic since it would lead to a psychology of mysticism. We restrict ourselves to the mystical experience that contributes toward the knowledge of the self as such.[18]

6.1.3 Dupré on Transcendence

We focus our attention on the purely spiritual content of the experience and so we realize that visions of this nature are often short, ecstatic and obscure. We are dealing here with "unified states of consciousness which allow the soul to contact its own core."[19] According to Dupré the unified stages of consciousness have a *noetic* quality because of which they are called intellectual. Still, the thought is not something different from the thinker. John of the Cross even claims that intellectual visions take place in the substance of the soul. The important thing is that the coincidence of being and knowing involves a unique and direct awareness of the self, especially the knowledge of ultimate selfhood, an immediate awareness of presence to oneself and a presence to the transcendent source of the self. Because it is immediate, this awareness avoids the usual channels of sensation and judgement by which the awareness of the self is usually attained. And so fully conscious being-with-oneself cannot be accounted for by using the categories of ordinary consciousness. As Dupré explains, "The ordinary awareness of the self is achieved through a reflection upon its operations. Yet in mystical states we attain a direct, explicit awareness of the self *as such*."[20] John of the Cross also spells out this difficulty when he writes, "It is like one who sees something never seen before,

---

[16] Dupré, *Transcendent Selfhood*, 98-99.

[17] We have to keep in mind that intellectual visions are not visions properly, in the sense that they are seen with the eyes, because they are not made up of perceptions or images. They are also not intellectual in so far as they do not follow from reasoning. Their main purpose is to give an insight perhaps even an all understanding insight as happened to Teresa of Avila and Ignatius of Loyola.

[18] Cf. Dupré, *Transcendent Selfhood*, 98-100.

[19] Dupré, *Transcendent Selfhood*, 101.

[20] Dupré, *Transcendent Selfhood*, 102.

whereof he has not even seen the like... How much less, then, could he describe a thing that has not entered through the senses."[21]

Dupré also refers to the *Vedantic* tradition which accepts a mystical knowledge of the self. This self is hidden from ordinary sense awareness an aspect that is highlighted by the fact that there is no duality between Brahman and man. This fundamental self is the ultimate reality and is unknowable yet attainable. Sankara speaks of the 'ground' of the soul. This 'ground' is the locus of mystical truth and is hidden and also transcendent. The soul in this reference is more than the individual soul and this deeper self is the core of all that is and goes much beyond the boundaries of individual personhood. Christians sometimes claim this to be pantheism, but even Christian mystics assert the transcendence of the mystical self. Even they hold that at a certain moment the soul and God are not two but one. Jan Ruusbroec held that man's true essence is his super-essence. Before a soul is created in the world it is present in God as pure image. Once the soul is created and has an essence this pure image becomes its super essence. So, mystical conversion is to regain one's pure image, that is to say the super essence, by surpassing the createdness of the soul and actively participating in God's uncreated life. For Ruusbroec from all eternity the soul is an archetype within God. So in its actual existence in time the soul dwells in God, depends on God, flows from God and returns to God. Its nobility is seen in its leading a virtuous, God-seeking life that is directed toward the Image, but total identification can be attained only through the graces of the God-seeing life. In this state the mind lives above nature and in the essential unity of God's own being.[22] Hence:

> The ultimate message of the mystic about the nature of selfhood is that the self is *essentially* more than a mere self, that transcendence belongs to its nature as much as the act through which it is immanent to itself, and that a total failure on the mind's part to realize this transcendence reduces the self to *less* than itself. The general trend of our civilization... has been to reduce the self to its most immediate and lowest common experiences. But for this restriction we pay the price of an all pervading feeling of unfulfilment and, indeed, of dehumanization. Deprived of its transcendent dimension selfhood lacks the very space it needs for full self-realization... Within such a restricted vision any possibility of meaning beyond the directly experienced is excluded.[23]

Louis Dupré's thinking and writing has a direct connection and relevance to life. More than providing the reader with a finished product, he provides the raw material in his various books and articles, and then invites the reader to build his own edifice. Apart from the depth of his writings we are also impressed by

---

[21] John of the Cross, *Dark Night of the Soul* II, 17, 3, trans. E. Allison Peers (New York: Doubleday, 1959), 34, as quoted in Dupré, *Transcendent Selfhood*, 103.

[22] Cf. Dupré, *Transcendent Selfhood*, 103-104.

[23] Dupré, *Transcendent Selfhood*, 104.

the diversity of his writings which delve into philosophy, theology, spirituality and ethics. Yet it is this brilliance of Dupré that has also added to the complexity of our endeavour in this study. Our main challenge has been the difficulty in clearly separating his writings. It is not possible to say that any particular book of Dupré is only philosophy or only theology or only spirituality. The author has been working toward a recovery of the lost synthesis of God, man and the world, and so in working out a harmony it is inevitable that the lines of separation between his philosophy, theology and spirituality get blurred and hence difficult to separate due to their interdependence. Dupré writes about life and especially about the religious dimension of human life. His concern is about the crisis in the world and he writes about the existential self that is in peril of alienation. When he writes about religion he tackles the situation of man-in-the-world who has lost all or most sense of transcendence. These are themes that concern the day to day existence of ordinary man, but more importantly they are the concerns that man has to confront in order that he might find the harmony that he seeks in existence.

Since his concern is about the philosophy of religion we have restricted our comments to what Dupré has written about the self, transcendence and the mediation in religion and also how this experience is given expression in symbols, language and art. His approach is from religious experience. Dupré's writings reflect a strong drive towards fighting the negative step that religious life seemed to be taking. This effort that he made towards correcting this dangerous drifting towards extreme secularism and subjectivity is seen in the direction that he indicated towards a meaning in life and existence. In *The Other Dimension* his approach to God and to religion is very clear and at the same time critical. This desire to approach God and religion is done in a systematic and detailed manner. His willingness to approach the question and also his awareness that the endeavour is always a tentative attempt towards synthesis is good, but at the same time it does not arrive at a final synthesis that we would expect of him. In this light Dupré has not developed a special or unique concept of transcendence and so if we were to search for this concept as a fully developed treatise we do not find it. But Dupré has nearly all the building blocks that would be necessary for constructing such a treatise. Yet as he says it is an ongoing endeavour and a constant dialectic of which we are all participants.

6.2 The Genesis of the Reunion

By and large nature and grace were considered separate entities. In order to overcome the theological dualism that was inherited with the medieval thought there were three main efforts made, namely, that of humanist religion, the early reformation and Jansenist theology. Let us then make a deeper study of these three responses which began the movement towards a reunion.

6.2.1 Humanist Religion and Renaissance Theology

There are different reactions to humanist theology. Some saw it as a return to paganism. Others saw the Renaissance as an anti-religious anticipation of eighteenth century French rationalism, while Burckhardt regarded it as totally void of every moral and religious ideal. Early humanism was a rhetorical movement that attached religious meaning to the poetic word and even developed a *theologia rhetorica*. They used figurative speech and a lot of ritualistic language. Hence, classical literature which revealed a type of polytheism also concealed a rigorous monotheism. The whole complex of gods actually had a single essence and each god represented one mode in which the One God manifested himself. Christian humanists such as Valla, Erasmus and Ficino held that a universal divine attraction sanctifies the natural order and draws it back to its source.[24]

6.2.1.1 Lorenzo Valla

Lorenzo Valla began a trend that was referred to as alternative theology. He initiated a systematic philological study of Scripture, of the fathers and other documents which were considered symbols of the Christian faith. In doing this he set new standards for historical criticism. He also tried to examine how the Christian world view stood up to the ancient literature that had been recently discovered. He attempted to make place for Epicureanism in Christianity. Human beings are naturally inclined to pleasure but society prohibits most of these pleasures. This prohibition is not normal because according to him our sense of moral values has been perverted by philosophy, especially Stoic philosophy. Christianity instead is an invitation to forgo the lower pleasures in order to attain the highest pleasure. While accepting that nature without grace is insufficient, Valla tried to move religious thought in the direction of a theology of the Word. Yet even though he did prepare the ground for a theological renewal we are unable to say that he achieved a new synthesis.[25]

6.2.1.2 Erasmus

Dupré also makes reference to Erasmus who aimed at reforming culture especially theology which was the heart of culture. He had a cosmic vision of culture ruled by the message of Christ and so he aimed at a religious renovation of entire culture. This required a good knowledge of its origins and hence the interpretation of ancient literature was important. In this connection he is called the father of biblical criticism. He advocates a spiritual reading of scripture and of the need to penetrate beyond "the flesh" of the letter to the hidden mystery of the spirit. For him, the study of theology began with piety and aimed at a spiritual transformation. He did not like scholasticism because he believed it obscured

[24] Cf. Dupré, *Passage to Modernity*, 191-193.

[25] Cf. Dupré, *Passage to Modernity*, 193-194.

the message by the use of dense language. He held that the essence of Christian piety was to move from the visible to the invisible. In Christ the two realms are united, since in Christ the visible becomes fully symbolic of the invisible, and through his word as recorded in Scripture he enables humans to move from one to the other. Erasmus did not support popular devotions and also refused to allow Christian truth to be equated with dogmatic formulations because they are not able to express fully the divine mystery which they intended. He also held that grace required our co-operation. While his theology was a great improvement on earlier theologies there was an overall decline since it was not comprehensive enough to deal with the problems of existence. His writings are vast but since they are not deep enough they are not sufficiently comprehensive to be able to deal with problems of existence and consequently are too fragmented to be used for a probable synthesis.[26]

6.2.1.3 Ficino

Another significant thinker was Marsilio Ficino. He did not share the humanist ideal of rhetorical elegance and for him words served only as a means for conveying ideas. He explored the relation between God's expression in the divine Word and human expressiveness. He made an effort to reconcile Plato's idea of God and that of Christian doctrine. According to him Plato assumed a kind of transcendent openness. So he felt that Plato's philosophy could help us to overcome the separation between nature which was the object of philosophy and grace which was the object of theology. He held that if revelation is true it has to be accessible to all and hence the truth of revelation acquires the full depth of its meaning only in the light of other faiths. Religion too is a natural instinct that is divinely inspired and is shared by all peoples. Hence, there is a common divine impulse that induces all toward worshipping the same one God. If God is totally ineffable then his nature remains totally unknown and cannot be revealed. So, Ficino held that God as perfect form unites in himself all forms. He is the supreme form and also the source of all forms which includes all forms without being completely contained in any form. Perfect form is a divine light that enables the mind to see and at the same time it also enables the mind to see the light reflected in what it sees. Yet God is not this light. The divine form is unknowable to the intellect and like the transcendent light is invisible, but the warmth of this light makes itself felt. While this theory of invisible form seems to be paradoxical yet this is what enables painters, poets, architects and sculptors to give expression and natural form through their work which is seen as a reflection of the invisible one.[27]

Ficino constantly appealed to Scripture. While God reveals himself in nature, scripture interprets that which nature accomplishes. But it is the human person

[26] Cf. Dupré, *Passage to Modernity*, 194-198.

[27] Cf. Dupré, *Passage to Modernity*, 199-202.

who mediates the presence of God in nature. The soul is a direct emanation from God and is naturally attracted to God yet only divine grace can reunite the soul to God. This natural desire for God legitimates the existence of other religions. Still he did not succeed in reintegrating nature and grace because basically Ficino's was a naturalist theology using Christian terminology.[28]

6.2.2 The Reformation

Humanism offered an alternative to scholastic theology, but the Reformation confronted the questions head on. Luther and Calvin held that grace—understood as an addition to nature—deprived culture of its transcendent dimension. They stressed the difference between the stages of nature before and after the fall.

6.2.2.1 Luther

The reformation was an effort to overcome the dualism of the modern age. Luther's work seems to be a continuity of medieval spirituality and theology. It is linked to the nominalist theology of the middle ages and has inherited both the mystical piety and the theological nominalism of the earlier period. The impact is clear when we see that in the *Theologia Germanica* which he was familiar with, the internal sanctification through grace, a direct inhabitation by God himself is far from a mere forensic justification. This sheds light on his principle that justice which justifies the believer remains God's own, and the justifying God is present in the soul. His concept of intrinsic justification sees justice not as an added gift separate from human nature but as something natural to man. God's will is sovereign, autonomous and inscrutable and divine justice is a substitute for our inability to attain inner sanctification. Neither good works nor our natural capacity for good can prepare us to receive grace according to Luther. In Catholic understanding redemption had two aspects, the judicial aspect of justification wherein God declares the sinner as justified, and the mystical aspect which sanctifies the person and actually unites the person with God. Justification and sanctification were therefore seen in conjunction. For nominalist theology justification meant that guilt was no longer attributed and grace was largely an external addition. Luther separated extrinsic justification from sanctification so that "God justifies the sinner by disregarding his sinfulness but without internally sanctifying him."[29] That God alone justifies and sanctifies also supports the assertion of God's uncreated presence in the soul.[30]

Luther debated with Erasmus on the topic of personal freedom within the context of redemption. Erasmus argued that if personal freedom did not play an active role in redemption then it was not worthy of being called freedom. Luther

[28] Cf. Dupré, *Passage to Modernity*, 202.

[29] Dupré, *Passage to Modernity*, 205.

[30] Cf. Dupré, *Passage to Modernity*, 205-206.

felt that Erasmus has missed the point of the New Testament freedom. While he felt that mere personal freedom underestimated the natural religious aspirations and capacities of man we also have to realize that salvation cannot be attained through personal freedom alone. In brief the Renaissance idea of unlimited human creativity could not be compatible with the Christian doctrine of justification, and a purely natural freedom is powerless in the area of justification. In this light the Christian concept of morality as a voice of conscience is actually the concept of natural morality which has been transformed from within and codified into divine commands. The difference is that for a Christian it becomes a matter of inner obligation. Yet ultimately it is a question of accepting God's redemption and trusting his mercy.[31] While all that Luther says is significant yet according to Dupré:

> A theology that fails to overcome the dialectical opposition between a totally corrupt nature and a divine justification must fall short of solving the particular problem afflicting the religious consciousness of the modern age, namely, the separation of nature from grace... The unresolved tension between Luther's mysticism and his nominalist dualism leaves the answer ambiguous.[32]

Calvin has a different response to the same issue.

6.2.2.2 Calvin

Dupré holds that Calvin can be seen more clearly as belonging to the modern age. He was concerned about the radical incompleteness of a nature that requires a transcendent dimension yet somehow appears to be deprived of it. He held that this incompleteness was due to the 'fall.' God's presence is still manifest in the natural order, and it is grace that enables nature to overcome its existential insufficiency and attain its final destiny. While God is immanent in his works, the works cannot be mistaken for the Deity. The universe mirrors an invisible God, but the best reflection of God's glory is the human person who is an image of God especially when he possesses right understanding, when his affections are regulated by reason and when all his senses are governed in the proper order.[33]

God's image in the human person gets disfigured because of the fall. But then through divine justification the believer is transformed from within and has an experience of salvation which depends completely on divine election. The natural order provides no basis for grace. In faith God presents himself to persons of his choice. This faith is more than just a mental reception of the word of Scripture. There is a personal encounter with God and through participation the believer is mystically united with God. Calvin stresses the need for a subjective

---

[31] Cf. Dupré, *Passage to Modernity*, 207-209.

[32] Dupré, *Passage to Modernity*, 209.

[33] Cf. Dupré, *Passage to Modernity*, 209-210.

certainty without which faith loses its support. This undoubting confidence in one's personal election forms an essential part of the election. This subjective certainty is itself a grace granted by God and so has to be received in trust. Our belief in the promises of God gives us confidence, and with this receptive attitude of faith we are able to receive grace. The problem here is that faith appears to be a self-authenticating act. And this ambiguity affects his view of human nature because on the one hand man is seen as an image of God while on the other hand this same man is seen as a moral degenerate. Naturally this also affects his view of the cosmos and of social order because then all power derives from God. Natural sovereignty rests with the people and the exercise of this sovereignty requires a secular authority, yet this authority is subject to religious restrictions. Calvin distinguishes two realms in the political order namely the spiritual and the temporal, and while the civil order enjoys a certain amount of autonomy, on the whole it is subordinate to the spiritual order.[34]

In its Calvinist and Lutheran forms the Reformation attacked the theological dualism of nature and grace. Seeing nature as totally corrupt they were not in a strong position to counter naturalism. In claiming that God alone is holy they attributed redemption to a God who sanctifies and divinizes whomsoever he chooses. Nature provides the assistance but it requires divine revelation for guidance.[35] Jansenius in turn held that human nature was intrinsically redeemed but historical redemption was insufficient. True redemption involved an election and this impeded a true integration of nature and grace.

6.2.3 The Jansenist Attempt

A fateful dualism had separated nature from its transcendent dimension, and the catholic distinction between nature and the supernatural seemed to consolidate them as two separate orders of being. The earlier concept of pure nature was challenged by Michel du Bay also called Baius who tried to restore an integrated concept of nature and grace. He held that at the moment of its coming into existence human nature was not yet fully formed. Its formation was complete only when human nature received the *forma filiorum Dei.* This *forma filiorum Dei* was what scholasticism refers to as 'supernatural', and is a status that is totally gratuitous, a grace given by God. Still it was a grace given in response to the demand of human nature and so the question arose, if this grace was received due to a demand of human nature then could it still be referred to as gratuitous? Augustine had declared that nature was a divine gift which was endowed with a trans-natural destiny right from the start. Baius said the situation was reversed

[34] Cf. Dupré, *Passage to Modernity*, 211-215.

[35] Cf. Dupré, *Passage to Modernity*, 215.

after the fall. With grace, nature veered toward the good but nature deprived of grace inevitably moved toward evil. This results in two separate orders of reality.[36]

Jansenius' main aim was to revive Augustine's theology of grace. The Jesuits under Molina had emphasized the need for free cooperation with a divine grace which is granted to all while the Dominicans under Banez had stressed the need for a special divine election to receive efficacious grace. According to Jansenius Adam's state was not exactly a state of grace but still he did not need grace in order to have a disposition for union with God. In his state he already had the disposition, but he only needed some divine help to act in a correct manner toward attaining divine union. But after the fall man requires grace both for the disposition as well as for the ability to act. He held that most humans were damned and only a few who were chosen would be saved but those elected needed to actively cooperate through good works in order to complete the redemption process. Grace does not just heal human nature but becomes a substitute for it. Unlike the scholastics for whom grace was a *habitus* that was implanted in nature and ennobled it, for Jansenius grace was "a conscious intention—the *motivum caritatis*—that needs to be actualized ever anew."[37] Grace for him was separate from nature and it was meant to heal and redeem nature.[38]

Christian humanists like Valla, Erasmus and Ficino held that there was a universal divine attraction which sanctified natural order and drew it back to its source. Most religions responded to this divine impulse. Luther and Calvin on the other hand rejected any theologically neutral concept of nature. They held that grace, which they saw as an addition to nature, deprived culture of its transcendent dimension. The difference in nature before and after the fall[39] seemed to cause a historical dualism within nature. Jansenius and his early disciples held that human nature was intrinsically redeemed but objective, historical redemption was not sufficient, and actual redemption requires a personal election which is not granted to all. But this prevented a genuine reintegration of nature and grace.[40] These three attempts to overcome the theological dualism of modern culture marked the steps made towards a reunion of nature and grace.

6.3 A Provisional Synthesis

In this section we look at three responses to the religious predicament which according to Dupré seem to have met with some success in reuniting modern

---

[36] Cf. Dupré, *Passage to Modernity*, 216-217.

[37] Dupré, *Passage to Modernity*, 220.

[38] Cf. Dupré, *Passage to Modernity*, 217- 220.

[39] The 'fall' refers to the fall from grace of Adam and Eve as a result of having committed the first 'original sin' of eating the forbidden fruit in search of immortality and the desire to be like God. It is a term of Christian theology.

[40] Cf. Dupré, *Passage to Modernity*, 190-191.

culture with its transcendent component. It is difficult to think of one single movement because different individuals and groups worked toward the goal of restoring an all-inclusive religious vision to the world. The whole pursuit gave rise to a new Christian humanism. According to Dupré, "in differing degrees and by different methods they accomplished in spiritual, moral, and aesthetic practice what theologians had failed to attain in theory."[41] In this transition from cosmological, anthropological and theological conceptions of the modern age to the devout life as it was lived reveals a striking continuity with the past. Modern spirituality seems to have remote roots in the twelfth century Christian humanism. As Dupré points out:

> Scholars who defend a total originality of Renaissance culture fail to account for its spiritual continuity, a continuity that does not consist in returning theological patterns thinly disguised under a secular surface... but rather in the persistence of a spiritual tradition... The mystical currents of the twelfth century were the very sources of that early humanism that marked the birth of the modern culture.[42]

The influence of Medieval Humanism on modern day spirituality is undeniable.[43]

Cultural changes were taking place but the spiritual attitudes did not change at the same pace and so "... in the fourteenth and fifteenth centuries, when men were finding new ideas and mental attitudes in the works of classical antiquity, their religious sentiments remained true to medieval themes and were nourished by traditional works of spirituality, especially those written in the twelfth century."[44] This is pretty clear in Ignatius of Loyola who had a strong influence on the direction of the early Modern Church and who himself was inspired by the medieval humanism introduced by the early Franciscans. The new spirituality was rooted in the clear cut separation that was made between spiritual doctrine and scholastic theology. The separation which was fatal to both enabled the spiritual life to free itself from the chains of an incompatible theology. It gained an independence that resulted in the spiritual life coining a language of its own. This enabled spiritual men and women however traditional in their piety to be able to dialogue with and collaborate with their contemporaries. Later on the language would be the cause for separation from the main concerns of modern life and it would give a certain amount of autonomy with regard to cultural and even ecclesiastical structures. The degeneration would come later but the new

---

41 Dupré, *Passage to Modernity*, 221.

42 Dupré, *Passage to Modernity*, 222.

43 Cf. Dupré, *Passage to Modernity*, 221-222.

44 Giles Constable, "The Popularity of Twelfth Century Spiritual Writers in the Late Middle Ages," in *Renaissance Studies in Honor of Hans Baron*, ed. Anthony Molho and John A. Tedeschi (DeKalb: Northern Illinois University Press, 1971), 5, as quoted in Dupré, *Passage to Modernity*, 222.

spirituality enabled a religious renewal and also contributed toward the cultural reintegration of the Baroque by restoring the transcendent orientation to human nature.[45]

6.3.1 Devout Humanism

The term Christian humanism is of ambiguous meaning. While some refer to it as the religious quality of Renaissance culture, it has been defined by others "as an exclusively spiritual movement that, with or without connections with humanism proper, combined a traditional religious piety with a modern commitment to secular duties."[46] When we speak of devout humanism we refer to the school of Francis de Sales as a kind of Christian humanism which believed in the powers of redeemed nature. Two thinkers who are significant in this connection are Ignatius of Loyola and Francis of Sales.[47]

6.3.1.1 Ignatius of Loyola

Perhaps the most original Catholic response to the challenge was given by Ignatius of Loyola. He placed the person at the centre of the universe. They shape themselves under the guidance of God's spirit. Persons ought to control their own lives, a skill that is acquired by methodical and systematic training of their will power. Hence, spiritual discernment is important to distinguish effective strategies from those that are ineffective. According to him grace must first liberate nature from a state of slavery and then it is able to help nature to reach its own natural potential. Freedom for him is not just a capacity for self-realization but is a divinely inspired surrender. The choice of life is between freedom that has been elevated and can help to transcend the self, or a freedom that is enclosed within the range of self-centred objectives between a good that liberates fully or one that only partially liberates. Freedom then is a motion of grace and results in an attitude of passivity which nonetheless requires that persons are able to distinguish these motions of grace. Ignatius' spirituality of action changed from a first vision which saw creation as proceeding from God the Father via the Son and returning to its divine origin and thus emphasizing contemplation, to a second vision that stressed the outgoing movement of God's Trinitarian life and thus laying the emphasis on apostolic action. Humans are called upon to descend with the Son into the created world and to sanctify it. This required an asceticism that was different from monastic piety and so Ignatius spoke of self denial that is attained through total devotion to their work and submission to those who are in authority. Thus Dupré says, "a contemplative spirituality based on medieval sources results in a typically modern worldliness. Ignatius transforms the anthropocentric ideal of creative self-

[45] Cf. Dupré, *Passage to Modernity*, 222-223.

[46] Dupré, *Passage to Modernity*, 223.

[47] Cf, Dupré, *Passage to Modernity*, 223-224.

development by placing it within a radically theocentric perspective."[48] He strove to fill the modern worldview with a traditional spiritual content. Similar to the Reformation option Ignatius opted for the primacy of grace, but in opposition to the Protestant trend he stressed the intrinsic restoration of nature in grace. As in early Christian humanism he accepted the divine presence in nature, but then for him this presence was a result of divine descent and not because of a self-directed human ascent.[49]

6.3.1.2 Francis de Sales

There was a move in the Counter-Reformation to express spiritual nobility through grace in demeanour and manners. Baldassare Castiglione drew up an aristocratic code that was based on a religious ideal. He presented a transition from a graceful appearance to the inner condition which was divine grace. On the other hand Francis de Sales sought the graciousness of manners only as an outward expression of inner grace. Like the other devout humanists Francis sought to reintegrate the divine and human components of culture. He describes human nature as being dynamically oriented toward the love of God. It is grace that transforms from within resulting in a reality that is single yet human and also divine. True charity is a result of human nature that cooperates with the love of God. So grace rules the spiritual life but not with force but rather by attraction since supernatural grace appeals to natural inclination. Francis was more concerned about practical piety than being caught up in the complications of theology. While he speaks of God's love as supernatural he holds that the love that is practised by humans is natural. Still there is no idea of 'pure nature' in Francis's writings because nature never appears to be self-sufficient for him. He advocated an internal withdrawal from the world and his synthesis is largely an interior synthesis between God and the soul. He does accept the physical world but has not integrated it into his synthesis. According to Dupré, "Salesian humanism succeeded in incorporating the new image of the person within its spiritual vision but failed to accommodate the new cosmology."[50] His 'theological unworldliness' as Dupré terms it, would have an effect on Jansenists and Quietists who took that aspect from him while not inheriting his warmth. It also had an effect on Catholic spirituality which was never closely linked with cosmos or society. Not that this aspect was totally absent but spirituality was largely seen as an affair between God and the soul and as a consequence spiritual life was separated from culture and also from much of scientific and social renewal.[51]

---

[48] Dupré, *Passage to Modernity*, 226.

[49] Cf. Dupré, *Passage to Modernity*, 224-227.

[50] Dupré, *Passage to Modernity*, 229.

[51] Cf. Dupré, *Passage to Modernity*, 227-230.

6.3.2 The Religion of the Heart in the Reformation

While early reformers did not allow fallen nature to play any active part in the process of salvation, later on they would allow for some need of cooperation. So together with grace there was the need to make an effort to respond to God's salvific will. There was gradually a leaning toward the thinking that the devout life originates within the heart and that within the heart God's grace meets the human will. As this trend developed, reason which was internally enlightened by faith had the final word on piety and conduct. Still while the Protestants continued to stress upon justification by faith, the Catholics insisted on the intrinsic sanctification of human nature. It was this search for inwardness that led the Lutherans of Germany to a 'religion of the heart'. Gradually, Lutheran pastors began speaking of God's inner presence which instructs and sanctifies from within. So Dupré says, "The Reformation held an objective message—to return to the word of Scripture—as well as a subjective one—to restore the direct contact of the soul with God through Christ."[52] This difference of orientation did lead to tensions because religious inwardness held that God's image in the soul had been preserved, while the New Testament Pauline doctrine of sin and justification laid the stress on the corruption of human nature. The religion of the heart naturally stressed religious inwardness and the preservation of the image of God in the soul. According to Luther fallen nature could not attain genuine goodness. Fallen nature and grace were juxtaposed rather than seen as going back to the original unity. Yet, while the religion of the heart always saw God as present in the soul even after the fall, it always had an acosmic character.[53]

Jacob Boehme spoke of a radical reunion of nature with its transcendent source. According to him the powers that interact in nature are of divine origin because God animates nature like the soul animates the body but nature is not God. God creates freely and in creating he gives full expression to his nature. Through his being he manifests his essence because without this manifestation he would not be the living God spoken of in Scripture. Boehme's attempt to reunify God and nature was challenged in the event of the fall. He explained it initially by referring to it as Lucifer's fall and as being unforeseen by God because of which Lucifer was held responsible for the disturbance in the universe. Later he attributed the responsibility to Adam and so indirectly to God who created beings as capable of committing evil was responsible and hence as the ultimate source of evil. To explain the union between God and creation Boehme refers to the dialectical opposition within the divine nature. God's mercy is balanced by his wrath and his love is balanced with his anger. These contrasts are the same as the distinctions within the trinity and the task of the mystic is to reduce these oppositions to their original unity and hence to the ultimate harmony of the

[52] Dupré, *Passage to Modernity*, 233.

[53] Cf. Dupré, *Passage to Modernity*, 230-233.

universe. The created world is an image of God and so he attributes all good to God and all evil to creation. In this setup redemption is added or imputed to a corrupt nature. His primary aim always seems to be to preserve the initial union between the transcendent and the immanent factors.[54]

By the middle of the seventeenth century Lutheran and Catholic spirituality began to be estranged from the social and scientific revolutions of the modern age. Spiritual life was more and more separated from culture and we see the Baroque attempt to develop a cultural synthesis. To be 'worldly' had a largely negative connotation and spiritual persons tried to reunite the fragments of a divided world within a purely internal synthesis. According to Dupré, the Baroque culture attempted but did not succeed in reuniting the three components of the ancient synthesis.[55]

6.3.3 The Baroque: The Last Synthesis

The Baroque was far from religious and so it cannot be presented as having achieved the ideal of an integral Christian humanism because the values it demonstrated are far from those generally associated with religious virtue. The reason why Dupré supports the Baroque as a model of an integrated culture is that:

> Despite tensions and inconsistencies, a comprehensive spiritual vision united Baroque culture. At the center of it stands the person, confident in the ability to give form and structure to a nascent world. But ... that center remains vertically linked to a transcendent source from which, via a descending scale of mediating bodies, the human creator draws his power. This dual center—human and divine—distinguishes the Baroque world picture from the vertical one of the Middle Ages, in which reality descends from a single transcendent point, as well as from the unproblematically horizontal one of later modern culture, prefigured in some features of the Renaissance.[56]

It was the presence of the dual centre that made the Baroque a dynamic entity. It was this dynamic impulse that also in part contributed to the expansionist drive of the Baroque mind. For them religion and politics were usually seen together. As a result political and military leaders were convinced that they served a higher cause. This dynamic aspect of a movement that is difficult to describe is seen also in the history of art. The Baroque does not refer to one style of art but to many different styles which are united by a complex aesthetic vision. Baroque art continued the Renaissance quest for form but the ideal of form shifted from simple harmony to dramatic tension. Artists were not satisfied with the aesthetics of self-enclosed form but sought a more intense spiritual expressiveness in an open-

[54] Cf. Dupré, *Passage to Modernity*, 234-236.

[55] Cf. Dupré, *Passage to Modernity*, 236-237.

[56] Dupré, *Passage to Modernity*, 237.

ended dynamic representation. As Dupré describes it, "Baroque art symbolizes an expanding world permanently in a state of being created and refusing to be confined within established forms. The endless openness of its style—more than the nature of its subjects or the feelings that inspired them—conveys a spiritual quality to Baroque art."[57] Baroque art turned toward the mysterious and the cryptic and a more comprehensive synthesis. It also used language to convey a complex spiritual message which often could not be grasped at once. They avoided a direct representation of the divine but always aimed for symbolization through earthly mediations. Another aspect of the Baroque art is that each part or aspect actively prepares for the position of the next and painting and sculpture mediate an enclosed space with the unlimited space. Because of this mediating quality Baroque culture is essentially representational and refers to a higher spiritual reality. When it is successful it is able to merge the horizons of immanence and transcendence.[58]

Creation according to the Baroque culture was pervaded by a natural desire for God and so it strove to bring the world to its sacred destiny. This goal of religious restoration was similar to the catholic concept of redemption. Catholic Baroque was extroverted and perceived presence in the cosmos while Protestant Baroque which was more inwardly oriented held the presence to be more manifest in history. And even though Protestant piety separated corrupt nature from divine grace it also revealed an intensity of religious feeling. But the religious culture of the Baroque also created many religious conflicts and caused political upheaval. The high ideals that they stood for gradually disintegrated and led to a sadness of life and a feeling of being abandoned by God and consequently the uncertainty of ultimate salvation. Still this was not true of everybody. Some poets and artists did manage to sublimate their religious anxiety into a deeper and more comprehensive harmony. There was always the danger of doctrinal discipline taking priority over living faith and especially of theology being regimented into a single form of orthodoxy, but it was the tragic conflicts that gave the Baroque a depth and complexity of culture. These internal tensions led to the discovery of a deeper meaning of existence. Such contrasts were well expressed in Baroque drama where often chaos was gradually woven into a pattern of order. Besides, "drama projected those contrasts onto a higher ground where they might be viewed as patterns of a providential design. It resolved no conflicts but showed how a transcendent power controls those conflicting forces and reconciles them on a higher level."[59] And it was this all embracing transcendence that according to Dupré held the Baroque synthesis together.[60]

---

[57] Dupré, *Passage to Modernity*, 239.

[58] Cf, Dupré, *Passage to Modernity*, 237-240.

[59] Dupré, *Passage to Modernity*, 247.

[60] Cf, Dupré, *Passage to Modernity*, 243-247.

It is interesting to note that in all this change theology proper had no major role in establishing or maintaining this religious synthesis. Theology had been unable to incorporate the modern scientific world view into its understanding and so gradually withdrew because dogmatically it was unable to deal with the modern cosmology that was emerging. Thus it was no longer seen as necessary in developing a culture. The situation called for an extraordinary effort on the part of theology to assimilate the new creations and discoveries of science, art, poetry, education and even of spiritual life. But no significant effort was made in this direction. Just when action was necessary theology drifted into a deep slumber. Partly due to this lack of a theological basis the Baroque synthesis gradually began to unravel and without the theological base the transcendent component lost its capacity to act as the integrating power. The transcendent dimension gradually withdrew from modern western culture. Baroque art degenerated into mere formalism and became ordinary decoration. It was like a body without a soul, mere parts without a centre. With the demise of the Baroque, western culture lost its creative impulse and a vital element went out of western civilization.[61]

6.4 Arriving at the Synthesis

While the previous attempts were not successful, neither were they complete failures. Keeping in mind the earlier attempts we look to mysticism which can help us arrive at a synthesis. The term mystical for the early Fathers meant a special way of reading the Scriptures so that the Gospel of Christ was seen as revealing a deeper meaning of the Old Testament. This biblical meaning later on would lead to a sacramental meaning. The hidden mystical element came to refer to the sacramental symbol. As Christ was hidden in the Scripture he was also hidden in the Eucharist. Access to this mystical knowledge of God was through the reading of Scripture and through the reception of the sacraments. It was an experience of the entire Christian community. Hence, the experience of God's grace is in and through union with the Church. The shared experience has to be seen together with other aspects of religion. As Dupré says, religion is never only pure subjective experience, but "is always primarily a response to a calling. To the extent that that response is active, we call it an attitude. But this active response would not have been given if some part of ourselves didn't resonate to the transcendent appeal."[62] In a very broad sense this passively infused experience which enables the religious attitude is mysticism.

[61] Cf. Dupré, *Passage to Modernity*, 247-248.

[62] Louis Dupré, *The Deeper Life: An Introduction to Christian Mysticism* (New York: Crossroad, 1981), 20.

6.4.1 Mysticism and the Deeper Life

Mysticism does not refer exclusively to the religious experience but according to a modern definition, "Mysticism consists in an expansion of the conscious self beyond its ordinary boundaries to a point where it achieves a union with a 'greater' reality. The experience is accompanied by a new feeling of integration, both with oneself and with that reality."[63] It is a spiritual awareness of an absolute that is beyond words. In this light we can talk of nature mysticism which deals with the self that is able to expand into a union with its physical environment.

Nature mysticism generally refers to a sort of intense experience in which the subject feels himself merging with the cosmic totality. Such a mystical experience of the cosmos may also be religious but as Dupré suggests, "In the religious experience a sense of transcendence persists throughout the experience of cosmic union either with regard to nature as a whole or to its underlying principle."[64] While being in union with nature the individual is also aware that he is taking part in something that infinitely surpasses himself. It is a union of the self, of one's environment and the transcendent, and at the same time an awareness of distance especially with regard to the transcendent. In Dupré's view when one is aware of the distance then it is religious mysticism. Yet this awareness of the distance is not absent in non-religious mysticism. The name of the mystical reality is not so important because mysticism can be extroverted in the sense that it is outward oriented. On the other hand when due to a turning into the self, the self expands within itself and achieves a wholly new state of consciousness leading to a new integration within the individual self, mysticism is referred to as being introverted.[65] This way inward can help us bridge the distance.

6.4.1.1 The Way Inward

Religious mysticism of the self is well articulated in Indian mysticism of the deeper self which gives us a good spiritual understanding of man. According to Dupré, Marxist literature too starts from the basic assumption that the human person constantly surpasses himself and is always on the way toward an ideal self that goes much beyond the present reality. But Marx does not recognize that this process of transcendence takes place passively as well as actively. The ideal self lies not just beyond the person's present state but also beyond his future potential. Even though it is beyond, this ideal self affects his present reality. He cannot control this deeper being which in some mysterious way forms the ground of himself. Mystical consciousness assumes a more permanent inward self for which space and time have a different rhythm and perspective. As Dupré writes, "The preliminary condition for regaining transcendence in our lives is the rediscovery of inwardness.

---

[63] Dupré, *The Deeper Life*, 20.

[64] Louis Dupré, "Mysticism," *The Encyclopedia of Religion,* Vol. 10, 1987, 247.

[65] Cf. Dupré, *The Deeper Life*, 19-22.

Until we succeed in creating the inner space in which true transcendence can be recognized, we are not ready for authentic religion."[66] Hence, full self-knowledge must reach this deeper dimension hidden below the ordinary consciousness and access to this deeper self is achieved through mystical experience. For Christians this is the point where God and the soul touch, a secret dwelling place where God resides and where the centre of the created being is united with God's creative act. According to Dupré the mystics want to tell us that:

> Self is in its deepest nature more than itself. To move into myself means to move beyond myself into that which is 'higher' than the self or 'deeper' than the self. The mystic knows all the time that man is that particular being that is *more than man*. In the language of modern philosophy, the person is a self-transcending being, yet not merely, or even mainly, through what he *does* but through what he *is* in his very nature.[67]

Hence, the mystical journey is an inward journey that is usually undertaken through memory and recollection. Through recollection we attain an interiorization.[68]

6.4.1.2 Recollection and Memory

In a certain sense this way inward and all of spiritual life is a re-reading of oneself and beyond the self it is a re-reading of all of history. It is a reviewing of my existence in its totality in an effort to grasp it in its unity. So it has to move in the direction of the primeval unity in which my existence originated. Dupré says, "Through the gate of memory I travel to the inner land where the core of my existence may be revealed. To know oneself religiously is to remember one's origin, to move to one's source. Here, the deepest immanence of being with myself becomes the highest transcendence of being with God."[69] As a person goes deeper into himself he transcends higher to God. For this endeavour, memory plays a significant role because the soul retreats to a level where other faculties are unable to operate and where only memory functions. But this memory is not just a mere remembering of the past because mere "recalling the past can paralyze the powers that enable us to act in the present and to plan for the future."[70] Mere remembering can become an obstacle for the functioning of the ordinary self.[71]

Dupré says that for Augustine God resides in my memory. While he does not say how this happens, Augustine shows how only through an inward movement

---

[66] Louis Dupré, "Secularism and the Crisis of our Culture: A Hermeneutic Perspective," *Thought* 51 (September 1976), 281.

[67] Dupré, *The Deeper Life*, 25.

[68] Cf, Dupré, *The Deeper Life*, 23-25.

[69] Dupré, *The Deeper Life*, 26.

[70] Dupré, *The Deeper Life*, 26.

[71] Cf, Dupré, *The Deeper Life*, 25-26.

recollection is able to encounter God in the mind. Mere accumulation of memory is not able to open the way inward. Memory gives access to the inner self when it is able, "to integrate the multiplicity of that past within a new, unifying pattern and to discover a different structure that changes my perspective upon myself."[72] In memory we must recollect our entire existence and go back to the ground of our being and the source of our existence. Only then we are fully present to ourselves. One important aspect of being present to oneself is to accept one's mistakes—even one's evil side—and consequently to accept guilt. It is when we are able to confess our past failings that we are able to be open to the future and begin the inward journey into the deeper self. The religious person does not seek the self as such but rather that which is revealed in and through the self. We are not content just with the self-conscious subject but we look for a deeper reality in which thinking and being are one. We need to overcome individual personhood and realize that the individual self is not an ultimate. We need to move beyond self consciousness to that deeper realm on which individual selfhood rests.[73]

6.4.2 The Being and Manifestation of God

What makes the West different from the East in the mystical path that is followed is not so much the 'nature' of the Absolute but rather the 'approach' to the Absolute. While the easterners in general look inward most westerners tend to look at the cosmos or the person for an encounter with the transcendent. Still this is only a generalization and is not true of every single easterner or westerner. Perhaps where all agree is that we cannot give a name to the Absolute. Christian tradition for instance lays emphasis on the difference between God and the human predicates that we use to name him. Pseudo-Dionysius speaks of the need to "abandon all sensation and intellection and all objects or sensed or seen and all being and all nonbeing and in unknowing, as much as may be, be one with the beyond being and knowing."[74] This extreme negation ends up in a divine darkness that does not allow for any divine revelation. Christian mystics hold that even though we are unable to describe God, he still continues to manifest himself. Gradually through a spiritual ascent that consists of negation and ascent, the dark turns into the light of divine self-manifestation. Meister Eckhart echoes Thomas' principle that God is Being. He refers to Exodus 3, 19 where God declares himself to be the one who is. Names define the limits of Being and so no name except that of pure Being can apply to God. Divine Being is not separated from the creature but constitutes the very core of the reality of the creature. Even though it has nothing in common

[72] Dupré, *The Deeper Life*, 27.

[73] Cf, Dupré, *The Deeper Life*, 27-29.

[74] Pseudo-Dionysius, *The Mystical Theology*, Migne P. G. 3, 997, as quoted in Dupré, *The Deeper Life*, 32.

with God the creature's true Being is God. And in the man who has arrived at the end of the inward journey this true Being becomes manifest.[75]

6.4.2.1 God's Being

God *is*. His divine Being is a self-contained simplicity which is the principle from which all other 'otherness' proceeds and to which it must return. Even in the divine unity there can be a multiplicity. Within the trinity God's manifestation is the Father and he also manifests himself outwardly in his creation. In its core the creature shares the Being of God, but in its createdness it is distinct from that Being and part of an order of succession and exclusion. The separation that we make between God's temporal manifestation and his eternal manifestation is due to our world view in which finite reality has lost its religious symbolism. Without a divine image words are without their ultimate reference and the world no longer speaks of God. As Eckhart describes it, "In the Son all creatures possess their own archetypal image. The Eternal Word contains the entire outward explosion of the world in time. In their archetypal image they remain within the Trinity; in their temporal appearance they move outside the circle of God's unity."[76] So the archetypal image of creation is in the Son but while the Son is within the Trinity, creatures in time move outside the circle of God's unity.[77]

According to Dupré Eckhart's mystical doctrine is based on the essential union of the soul with God. He believes that there is something in the soul that is very similar to God and which is already one with him. In this sense it is already divine. This Being of the soul is not a creaturely existence but is eternal Being. It is through this Being that the creature remains in God. As Dupré phrases it, "God's is-ness is my is-ness. In my primary Being, in my true essence, I am the living idea of God that continues to dwell in God. In this essential Being God expresses himself in his Eternal Word and, in the Word, in every creature."[78] This true Being of the creature is eternal. In this connection Christianity speaks of how the Father generates the Son in an eternal 'now'. This is significant because in the 'now' the Father begets the Son, and in the same 'now' he begets creatures in the Son. The 'now' of creation and the 'now' of God's self-expression are identical according to Dupré. Like all creatures the soul lies outside the essential being. It is converted to that eternal Being when it becomes aware of its divine essence. And only when it turns into this divine essence can it claim to be reborn as the Son of God in the Eternal Word. In the words of Eckhart, "The Father ceaselessly begets his Son and what is more, he begets me as his Son—the self-same Son! Indeed, He begets me not only as his Son but as himself and himself as myself, begetting

[75] Cf. Dupré, *The Deeper Life*, 31-33.

[76] Dupré, *The Deeper Life*, 35.

[77] Cf, Dupré, *The Deeper Life*, 34-35.

[78] Dupré, *The Deeper Life*, 36.

me in his own nature, his own being."[79] He thus says that the spiritual person changes himself to the pure Being. We are not able to name this Being and so Eckhart refers to it as the Godhead. This Being is beyond manifestation and in the Godhead there is only unity and silence.[80]

6.4.2.2 The Poverty of God

Before we can speak of its existence we have to speak of the Godhead and not of God because Being as such can have no name. Even the creature in its essence is nameless in the core of its divine Being. In its ultimate identity Being is what it is and it is only in the creaturely existence that it is confronted by God. What Eckhart refers to as the Godhead is beyond what we refer to as God, because God belongs to the order of manifestation. Being surpasses all the divine names. So the goal of the mystical journey is to reach this primeval poverty which is also the poverty of God. This poverty is attained by the soul when it is able to abandon its possessions, its self-will, its creaturely identity and even God. It is total detachment, a letting go of the self. In this poverty the soul gives up all desire, even the desire to acquire knowledge of God.[81]

Ultimate poverty is true humility and an honest acceptance of one's imperfections. The main result is that in this way one makes way for God. In this light, many look at the monastic lifestyle as an austere and hard life full of sacrifices and lived in silence. The monks themselves do not look at their life as a sacrifice. But the silence they practise is an aid to reflectiveness, a spiritual abstinence that enhances the value of speech which contains a density of meaning because relative values vanish before absolute meaning. According to Dupré the most striking quality of monastic life is the humility and total openness to life due to which one is not controlled by private desires and ambitions. The monk fulfils his task not because he wants to justify his existence with his work and not even to fulfil his emotional needs or to do justice to his talents. He does it because it has been assigned to him and he does not take his work more seriously than it deserves. It does not matter that 'he' does it, as long as it is done. Career and personal advancement are not his concern, what he is concerned about is God alone. For a genuine spiritual life we need a trusting and self-forgetting humility.[82]

It is through this letting go of oneself that one is able to reach the uncreated core of one's Being which is God's own creating act. Part of this letting go is what Eckhart refers to as *Gelassenheit* which means a resignation or a waiting in expectation, an openness without demands. It is through this *Gelassenheit* that we

---

[79] *Meister Eckhart*, trans. R. B. Blakney (New York: Harper and Row, Torchbooks, 1957), 181, as quoted in Dupré, *The Deeper Life*, 37.

[80] Cf. Dupré, *The Deeper Life*, 36-37.

[81] Cf. Dupré, *The Deeper Life*, 39-40.

[82] Cf, Dupré, *The Deeper Life*, 41-43.

arrive at the point of nowhere in the midst of all movement and the nothingness at the heart of all being. This *Gelassenheit* cannot be actively sought because the moment we know that we are seeking it we will never be able to find it. Dupré quotes Thomas Merton who advises:

> Don't try too hard. Don't be too much concerned about your own perfection and progress from day to day. Once you become aware of yourself as seeker, you become a possessor. You're lost. But if you are content to be lost, you will be found without knowing it, precisely because you are lost. For you are at the last nowhere, which is where God is.[83]

Hence, what we realize is that we cannot have a universal and sure method of reaching God and so at most we can only be aware of the inadequacy of our personal powers for this endeavour. This goes contrary to the emphasis that is laid on self-achievement and self-fulfilment in the world today. We live in a culture of practical a-theism and the current of secularism blocks us from lifting our mind to God. But then deep down in ourselves we still have the aspiration to break through into transcendence. As a pre-condition we have to be ready to let go of our own radical profaneness.[84] In the words of Dupré what we need is an, "Unconditional trust without knowing what it is we trust, willingness to let go without knowing whether anyone will ever catch us, preparedness to wait without knowing whether we will be met. Total looseness and unconditional trust are the virtues negative theology teaches us to cultivate."[85]

6.4.2.3 From Poverty to a Second Negation

We realize that negative theology is not the last word on spiritual life because it leads the soul into the dark of unknowing and undoing and stops there. Yet God is not darkness, he is light. Eckhart teaches that God reveals himself in the light of the Eternal Word through a fertile process of self-communication. The divine emptiness constantly generates itself and in generating itself it also generates its other, namely the creature. To be able to see the light and then to become the light itself according to Ruusbroec is to become completely poor and genuinely humble. While negation is used to reach this point the person must not persist in negation and so the negation itself has to be denied. Hence negation itself does not have the last word. "If we ever reach the divine unity, we must move where God Himself moves, that is, from the principle of generation into the principle of manifestation and, completing the sacred circle, back to its origin in the principle of unity."[86] The spiritual person denies the creature and then denies

---

[83] Dupré, *The Deeper Life*, 44.

[84] Cf. Dupré, *The Deeper Life*, 44-46.

[85] Dupré, *The Deeper Life*, 46.

[86] Dupré, *The Deeper Life*, 48.

the denial itself. Buddhists are mystics of silence and do not name the Absolute. Christianity on the other hand is a religion of the word and is not satisfied with ultimate silence. After renouncing creaturely attachments and even creaturely concepts of God it proceeds to the awareness that the negative perspective is itself a created one. And so the spiritual traveller has to sacrifice his own perspective and follow the Absolute in its manifestation realizing that his own efforts alone are not sufficient and so he abandons himself to the divine love.[87] The spiritual person is called to a life in unity and so Dupré comments:

> The soul united to God as self-manifest also embraces all creatures in which He outwardly manifests Himself. Partaking of the love between Father and Son, it like-wise participates in God's creative love of all creatures. In a world of multiplicity it recognizes the God it has found in a multitude of His self-manifesting relationships. Those relationships between God and the creatures in which he manifests Himself the spiritual Christian calls *love*.[88]

6.4.2.4 Love

6.4.2.4.1 Christian Agape

Christians profess a special type of religious love. According to Anders Nygren the Christian love which is called *agape* is unique because of its transcendent origin. It is the centre of the Christian faith because God himself is love.[89] *Agape* descends from heaven to man and so one is able to find the infinite love of God in the finite reality of the person. The love for the person is what gives rise to the love for one's neighbour and which ultimately reaches its climax in the love for the enemy. It is a non-desiring love for the person whom we encounter and not a love for a person of our choice. It becomes a giving love. We realize that love in itself is not religious but it becomes religious when one is able to go beyond its desiring tendencies. Still love cannot be said to be the essence of the religious attitude unless God is identified as love as is the case in Christianity. The determining element is love, and so objects are not able to obstruct this love. In loving the person who is next to him, the Christian is able to love God. If God is love and if all creatures are the objects of his love then in every person that is encountered each one is a living presence of the divine. Christian love is not just a sentimental feeling which is often self-centred, but is also a volitional moment in which one gives of oneself. As the love grows deeper the giving is more important than the feeling. In the selfhood of the other the Christian recognizes a transcendent dimension which due to its nature lies beyond experience. In religious love where God in man is loved, a human subject does not merely feel its way, because feelings do not

---

[87] Cf. Dupré, *The Deeper Life*, 47-49.

[88] Dupré, *The Deeper Life*, 50.

[89] Cf. Dupré, *The Other Dimension*, 474.

determine the act of loving. Love is more than a mere feeling. Love is a giving of oneself.[90]

Christian love is not indifferent to the nature of social structures and is not inactive in the face of injustices. While it is detached, it is not resigned and never despairs. For the Christian, salvation is not just an individual process but it also involves the community. Hence attachment to a community, the Church is a necessity. It is this communal aspect of religion especially in Christianity that enables the community to expand into a true universality. Being a part of this community though does not lead to a loss of individuality. "True religion is never an 'additional' reality: it is the depth, the ultimate dimension *of what is there*. Christian love then neither competes with, nor replaces human love, but gives it a new depth and a further expansion."[91] Hence this love does not negate human affection because the openness to the human thou is the essence of being human. And if we speak of religion as the transcendent depth of what is, then love can be truly religious only when it is truly human. So by faith we can expand human love but we cannot replace human love. [92] When Christianity identifies religion with love it is because it recognizes that religion is the heart of life and so it is at the centre of the religious act. According to Dupré, "Precisely the fact that the disposition to love is essential to the structure of the human mind makes me believe that love will more and more become a central feature of every religious attitude."[93]

6.4.2.4.2 Christian Mystics and Agape

Christian mystics believe that true love—what they refer to as *agape*—descends from God to the creature and so man can take on this divine flow into his own being and even attempt to return to its origin. Participation in God's own love is also the basis for man's attitude towards his fellow creatures. Yet desire has to be purified before it can attain divine love. To love with God's love is to forsake one's own personal possessive love of the creature and to love the creature for its own sake. We generally try to possess, manipulate and control the other, but divine charity is to allow the creature to be what it is. This conversion to pure love is a painful process and is best described in the words of St. John of the Cross who writes, "In order to arrive at possessing everything, desire to possess nothing. In order to arrive at being everything, desire to be nothing. In order to arrive at knowing everything, desire to know nothing."[94] This radical renunciation is not

---

[90] Cf. Dupré, *The Other Dimension*, 473-480.

[91] Dupré, *The Other Dimension*, 483.

[92] Cf. Dupré, *The Other Dimension*, 480-483.

[93] Dupré, *The Other Dimension*, 483.

[94] John of the Cross, *The Ascent of Mount Carmel*, I, 13, as quoted in Dupré, *The Deeper Life*, 52.

a forsaking of the creature, but only a renunciation of the natural *possessiveness* of human love which does not leave the person free to be what he is and which makes love exclusive and self-centred.[95]

Christian mysticism aims at embracing all creatures in one act of divine love. So life is cherished for its own sake and God is perceived in the creature not just in the creature's divine core but also in its finite individuality, its imperfections and in its vulnerability which also possesses a divine meaning. Angelus Silesius said that without the creature God would not be God. He meant to say that without the creature God is He who is, but only for the creature he takes on the name of God. Each creature then is a unique part of God's manifestation so Christian mysticism also includes a spiritual love for the creature. This love is not just a mere love of creatures but it means to be deeply involved with creation and yet to remain detached, an attitude that demands virtue. Ignatius of Loyola referred to this as the 'third degree of humility.' The first degree was the readiness to forsake the whole world and even life itself. The second degree consisted in not showing any preference neither for joy nor for suffering, neither ease nor hardship. And the third degree of humility was to choose that which is more difficult and more painful and so prefer suffering, poverty and humiliation rather than ease, riches, and honour. Once one has reached the third degree of humility one is able to perceive and love God in all things. One has to go beyond mere indifference and resignation. When such humility is arrived at after having gained control over the previous two degrees of humility, it is protected from turning into masochism.[96]

6.4.2.5 The Second Negation

There is much more to love mysticism than only love. Even though we are not dealing with the entire essence of the mystical tradition, yet different groups such as Moslem Sufis, early Franciscans, Flemish laymen, Spanish saints of the Baroque and French Jesuits of the seventeenth and eighteenth centuries all speak of the union with God as a state of love. 'Negative theologians' while declaring that God was beyond predication and that the soul was in need of total abnegation, differed on the ultimate status of the finite. They reasserted the independence of the finite through a complex balance that allowed them to value the finite for its own sake while at the same time allowing it to assume an active role in the affairs of the world. This balance is arrived at through a second more radical negation by which the human viewpoint is overcome and a divine attitude toward creation is adopted. This second negation in fact is completely positive. John of the Cross one of the best interpreters of this type of mysticism says that the first

[95] Cf. Dupré, *The Deeper Life*, 51-53.

[96] Cf. Dupré, *The Deeper Life*, 53-56. A Christian makes this choice for suffering and pain out of his or her love for the suffering Christ and also in order to imitate Christ and become more like Him.

determinations are declared to be out of proportion with the divine reality. The mystic does not judge the finite on his own terms and instead of saying that the finite does not truly exist as finite, he asserts that the finite even in its finitude depends on the infinite. "After denying his own determinations in God, he adopts God's own viewpoint with respect to the finite… the radical negation of the finite is an attempt to gasp the divine as it is in itself; it therefore culminates in a divine reaffirmation of the finite."[97] In this reaffirmation the divine transcendence is no longer a mere negation of the creature and instead is now looked on as an elevation. As Dupré describes it, "Transcendence is no longer found *above* creation but *in* creation. The creature is *in* God and God is *in* the creature. It is *as creature* and not only as uncreated essence that the creature manifests transcendence: God is the ultimate dimension of the finite reality, the inaccessible in the accessible."[98] The mysticism of love does not consider the transcendence of God with regard to the creature as ultimate as would be the case in negative theology. The difference with negative theology is that it radically denies creaturely determinations but the creaturely stand point is never negated and so the reassertion of the finite is weaker. In the spiritual life the willingness to lose enables the possibility of getting back, and when one is willing to lose the whole world then one will be able to gain it back. It is only the complete renouncing of creaturely desire and creaturely knowledge that will lead to universal love. It is this purification of the soul that leads to total negation and subsequently leads to the reintegration which overcomes the negation.

Spiritual poverty then is total openness without any of our personal preferences. This involves going against our inclinations and is achieved through mortification and suffering but not suffering for the sake of suffering, but a suffering for the love of the suffering Christ. Travelling along this path will finally lead to union and the mystical vision. And this is what we shall deal with in the next section which speaks of the dialectic from the initial negation to the final union with God and in God with the whole of creation through a complex process which is described in the three stages of purgation, illumination and union with God.

6.5 The Three-Fold Path of Transcendence

When we speak of union with God there is a dialectic that follows from the initial negation up to the final union with God and in God with all of creation. This dialectic has been usually expressed in three stages. The beginning of all spiritual life is the purgation of the soul, the first stage of contemplation in which it loosens its attachments through exercises in abnegation and mortification and then moves on to illumination and union. These stages are not well defined phases which are

[97] Dupré, *The Other Dimension*, 524.

[98] Dupré, *The Other Dimension*, 525.

well divided, nor do they follow in rectilinear development in time, but rather they are "cyclic occurrences in the rhythmic movement of spiritual life."[99] Let us then consider each of these stages of the three-fold path.

6.5.1 The Way of Purgation

The way of purgation is the first step in the process of mystical life which is a gradual purification of the soul. This stage consists of a privation of every type of pleasure that can be desired and takes place first through awareness and then through awareness to detachment.

6.5.1.1 Awareness

John of the Cross refers to passive purgation which he says does not occur until the soul reaches a certain level of illumination through meditation and quiet contemplation. If we want to proceed to a higher level of illumination we require a higher level of purgation in order to arrive there. The active life in fact requires contemplation so that the soul is gradually introduced to meditation and reflection and thus becomes aware of its wretched state. This awareness and contemplation is necessary if the soul is to arrive at some level of religious perfection. Besides the active life is the ability to convert this contemplation into virtue and good deeds. When entering into this stage of purgation the soul is already awake to the love of God. The awakening to a higher state of spiritual awareness takes place gradually and generally begins with ordinary prayer and meditation, and then moves into an inward recollection which develops into a state of habitually dwelling in the presence of God. This process could take place gradually or suddenly but the important aspect is the awareness of God's presence. At the start of purgation the soul must be centred upon God rather than itself. When through awareness it is centred on God then purgation truly starts.[100]

6.5.1.2 Detachment

The next important aspect of this stage of purgation is that of detachment. Here, the soul aims at removing the obstacles that block its spiritual progress and so the detachment from desire especially with respect to thoughts and concepts is important. Detachment is one of the universal requirements for the spiritual life and more than the mortification of the body the detachment with respect to thoughts is important. The spiritual candidate must leave the world behind. "The purgation process empties the soul of a diminished reality in order to allow it to discover its deeper existence."[101] Hence while the soul must be purified of the desire for the creature, the motive is union in love. What has to be renounced is

---

[99] Dupré, *The Other Dimension*, 526.

[100] Cf. Dupré, *The Deeper Life*, 67-69.

[101] Dupré, *The Other Dimension*, 527.

not just the pleasure but *desire* which is the self-centred aspect of pleasure. So the purpose of purification should not be to attain a future good for oneself but rather to express one's love for God. It is the inner detachment that makes purgation an inevitable expression of love. Part of the detachment is also mortification, or the deliberate choice for that which is disagreeable, painful and humiliating. The goal of such mortification is to reverse the habitual patterns of affection and behaviour. Detachment and mortification may not directly purify the soul but they prepare a structure within which the soul can actively pursue its perfection.[102]

Purgation through detachment and mortification is an active purgation of the senses. There is also a passive purgation of the spirit that is best described in the notion of the 'dark night of the soul' which is a period of spiritual dryness where God seems to be absent and far away and so the soul is unable to advance to full contemplation and cannot withdraw into meditation. It is a period of dryness and even aversion to all things spiritual. In this 'purgatory' the soul is detached from its last attachment to the sensible and spiritual experience of the presence of God. It is forced to let go of its last support so that it can make place for God alone.[103]

Christian mystics would connect this love of God and the purgation of the soul with the notion of imitation of Christ. Here Christ is not seen just as an ideal of unitive love of God but he is also the object of that love. He is the model and the beloved at one and the same time. Thus the imitation of Christ is an act of love and only when it is a gratuitous act of love is the imitation able to achieve the breakthrough aimed at through purgation. One of the aspects of the imitation of Christ is that of suffering. Christ himself underwent suffering and the spiritual person too is ready for suffering and to an extent prefers hardship to pleasure. Suffering is seen as a positive value in Christianity. Buddhism and Hinduism demonstrate an attitude of resignation with respect to suffering but for the Christian suffering is seen as a positive value and an opportunity to be purified of all attachments, even that of divine love. Suffering is looked at as a personal call and so it is accepted as a God-given opportunity to be purified.[104]

6.5.2 The Way of Illumination

In the rhythm of the spiritual life the purgation of the senses is usually followed by the perception of a transcendent reality. This overwhelming awareness of the divine presence which is characteristic of this stage of illumination is taken by some to be the fundamental mystical experience, yet not all who experience the presence of God can be called mystics. What distinguishes religious mysticism is the so called 'negative' character of religious illumination. Religious mysticism

[102] Cf. Dupré, *The Other Dimension*, 526-530.

[103] Cf. Dupré, *The Deeper Life*, 71-72.

[104] Cf. Dupré, *The Deeper Life*, 69-73.

refers to this illumination as the 'night' of understanding, a reference that was often used by John of the Cross. The light that illuminates in faith affects the understanding as 'darkness' because when it shines it disables our visual faculty. Johannes Tauler speaks of the darkness of this light "which by its blinding clearness appears dark to human and even to angels' understanding, just as the resplendent orb of the sun appears dark to the weak eye."[105] Divine illumination does not shed light on ordinary matters, and so ordinary ways of understanding have to be suspended. In a way this could be described as a purgation of the mind through which a profound transformation takes place in the cognitive powers.[106]

Divine illumination can take place on different levels of sense perception, imagination, and understanding. Ignatius of Loyola for instance speaks of smelling the infinite fragrance and tasting the infinite sweetness of the divinity. While this may seem trivial, it is the fruit of deep illumination. But as John of the Cross would warn, one should refrain from staying with these sensations because then it blocks the spiritual development and journey. In this light one has to be aware of deception and imagination. Images are useful though to the beginner who then must progress to the prayer of quiet where from discursive acts one progresses to a total awareness of God's presence. In using these words of night and darkness with regard to illumination of the understanding, we are expressing here that the mind becomes fully aware of the inadequacy of its own powers. This self-negation is the turning point and would lead to pure and dark contemplation which deals with the pain of being purified and at the same time the joy of being illuminated.[107]

6.5.2.1 Visions

Mystical illumination generally takes place through visions. There are also other passively infused and incontrollable cognitive sates which John of the Cross refers to as revelations, voices and spiritual feelings but we shall refer to all of these under the name of visions. Due to the passive character of visions, there is no evidence of their divine origin and because of this they could easily be called hallucinations since the visionary sees and hears what others do not. We must separate the psychological status of mystical visions from that of their religious truth or falsity because a hallucinatory vision could well be religiously authentic. At the same time it is difficult to distinguish hallucinations that are religious from those that are non-religious. According to Dupré it is the subsequent interpretation of the subject that determines this especially with regard to ambiguous and indeterminate experiences. Not that all experiences of the mysterious presence

---

[105] Johannes Tauler, *Signposts to Perfection. A Selection from the Sermons of Johannes Tauler*, trans. and ed. Elizabeth Strakosch (St. Louis: B. Herder Book Co., 1958), 132, as quoted in Dupré, *The Other Dimension*, 533.

[106] Cf. Dupré, *The Other Dimension*, 532-533.

[107] Cf. Dupré, *The Other Dimension*, 533-535.

are neutral because a mystical experience of presence takes place within a context that is usually religious. They could even be hallucinatory and yet religious. This feeling of presence permeates all of mystical life.[108]

6.5.2.1.1 The Content of Visions

The significance of these visions lies in their content. As William James wrote, they are "the abode of everything that is latent and the reservoir of everything that passes unrecorded or unobserved."[109] They contain inactive memories, hidden passions and many subconscious elements which become active in dreams. It is the mystical presence that gives all of these a specific religious meaning. The imaginary and sensory visions hide as much as they reveal the transcendent presence. The hermeneutical problem arises when the mystic begins to interpret what was only a sign of the invisible. We need to remember that the language of God is far removed from human understanding and so we have to be careful in interpreting the meaning of prophecy and revelation. The problem arises in translating these visions into ordinary discourse. For this we have to return to the original experience but equally significant is the language that is used to give expression to the experience. There cannot be any direct conformity with the transcendent referent and so the interpretation of visions requires extra caution. Besides we must also remember what Dupré says about visions, when he says that they are "imperfect stages of mystical illumination, the main function of which is to carry the soul from the active into the passive."[110] So visions are passive but are sensations that are perceived due to a feeling and an awareness of presence.[111]

6.5.2.1.2 The Dark Illumination of Visions

Different from the passive illumination of visions is the passive illumination which John of the Cross refers to as 'dark illumination'. This dark illumination lacks the distinct physical features of visions. It possesses a negative simplicity which the Spanish mystics refer to as an intellectual quality, where intellectual merely refers to the absence of sensory elements and not to any form of active comprehension. Johann Tauler describes this contemplation as "the mysterious darkness wherein is concealed the limitless Good. To such an extent are we admitted and absorbed into something that is one, simple, divine, illimitable, that we seem no longer distinguishable from it… This obscurity is a light to which no created intelligence can arrive by its own nature."[112] John of the Cross speaks of this highest state of

[108] Cf. Dupré, *The Other Dimension*, 535-537.

[109] William James, *The Varieties of Religious Experience* (New York: Cromwell-Collier, 1961), 375, as quoted in Dupré, *The Other Dimension*, 537.

[110] Dupré, *The Other Dimension*, 538.

[111] Cf. Dupré, *The Other Dimension*, 537-538.

[112] Johann Tauler, *Signposts to Perfection*, 132, as quoted in Dupré, *The Other Dimension*, 539.

contemplation as "an inflowing of God into the soul."[113] At this stage the mind reaches a high level of awareness in which the normal powers of cognition are no longer operative. The term 'night' is used to demonstrate not only the darkness for the active powers of the mind but also to express the torment and affliction of the night. It is in this darkness and emptiness of the passive contemplation that the highest illumination can take place. These are intellectual visions which cannot be seen in this life but which can be felt only in the soul.[114] Ignatius of Loyola had one such intellectual vision near Manresa and he describes in his spiritual biography in the following words:

> Without having any vision he understood—knew—many matters both spiritual and pertaining to the realm of letters and that with such clearness that they seemed utterly new to him... The most that he can say is that he was given so great an enlightening of his mind that, if one were to put together all the helps he has received from God and all the things he has ever learned, they would not be the equal of what he received in that single illumination. He was left with his understanding so enlightened that he seemed to be another man with another mind than the one that was his before.[115]

6.5.2.1.3 Intellectual Vision

John of the Cross describes these intellectual visions as knowledge of naked truths. Perhaps this is the best description because they are neither intellectual nor are they visions. They no longer pertain to mundane matters but directly deal with the union between the soul and God. This illumination takes place in the mind rather than in a function of the mind but there is no break with the faculties. So, mystics at this stage would continue with their normal activities and even be capable of increasing them due to a higher level of concentration. To refer to these visions as intellectual visions is something of a misnomer because to use the term intellectual for an experience that is as much about knowing as it is about loving, is indeed insufficient. What we are clear about is that it is one of the purest forms of religious experience in which the mind remains with the single awareness of its own unity. The mind does not know more than before nor is there an increase in its ability of comprehension, but there is a new dimension of consciousness due to which all that was known earlier takes on a different meaning. Not that new ideas have been infused but only that there has been a total transformation of consciousness which has had unique repercussions on the cognitive power of the mind. We do not negate the intellectual aspect of the visions completely because they are an intellectual insight and possess a certain amount of permanence which

---

[113] John of the Cross, *Dark Night*, II, 5,1, as quoted in Dupré, *The Other Dimension*, 539.

[114] Cf. Dupré, *The Other Dimension*, 539-540.

[115] *Acta Patris Ignatii Scripta a P. Ludovico Gonzalez da Camara, in Fontes Narrativi de S. Ignatio de Loyola*, Vol. I, Rome, 1943, 404-405, as quoted in Dupré, *The Other Dimension*, 540.

is much more than that of imaginary visions. As Dupré himself says the intellectual vision consists first of all in an increased awareness of God's presence due to which the soul sees itself as well as other creatures as existing in God. It is through the intellectual intuition of the intellectual vision that the mind knows directly its being in God. This intellectual vision does invite a Gnostic exploration, the problem being that since it is a spiritual gift and a mystical insight it may lack theological and philosophical accuracy and mystics would look with suspicion upon this sort of a systematic interpretation because it takes the cognitive element out of its context. The mystical experience of illumination is mainly one of union and if the mystic accepts a personal God, it is an experience of love.[116]

Illumination leads to understanding and an inflowing of God into the soul. So illumination leads to a union in love. The supreme illumination has an impact on the will because through volition the mind responds to the divine touch and this leads to union with God.

6.5.3 Union with God

When the Greeks spoke of God they did not speak of God in general nor in the Christian sense of three Persons together. For them God or what they referred to as *Theos* was the Father. This was in agreement with the New Testament in which for Jesus, God meant Father. What is striking is the difference between the attitude of the Greek fathers and the Latin tradition. For the Greeks the ascent to God takes place in the Logos through the Spirit. God has saved us in Christ through the Spirit. So our knowledge of God is through a revelation in Christ. The revelation is not something abstract but it reaches us through God's personal revelation, Christ. So God is the revealing one as well as the revealed. The three persons operate at once but in different modes on the soul. For the Latin west though, the starting point is the one God and the distinctions are added on later. So God's operation appears as one effect. According to Dupré, since the westerners begin with one God they virtually dismiss the Trinity as a mystery that is beyond comprehension and which consequently has lost its meaning. But because it is a mystery the theology of the Greek fathers is mystical. When the scriptures speak of man as an image of God, it is not saying that man appears like God in attitude, task or psychic structure, but "it refers to the indwelling of God's uncreated Image in the soul, which makes man himself into a divine image of God."[117] For Origen the soul is the image of God because the word, the *Logos*, which is itself the divine image of God resides in the soul. The Greek theory of the image begins with the identity of the image with that of which it is an image. Still the extrinsic resemblance is merely a reflection of the primordial identity which is

[116] Cf. Dupré, *The Other Dimension*, 540-543.

[117] Louis Dupré, *The Common Life: the Origins of Trinitarian Mysticism and its Development by Jan Ruusbroec* (New York: Crossroad, 1984), 13.

inherent in human nature itself. So the sinner is also an image of God. The ascent of the spiritual life would be "a 'living toward the Image,' that is, in an increasing awareness of, and growing toward, that divine Image which holds the center of my very self."[118] Dupré says that only the mind that is spiritual is able to reflect this Image in its own way and only the saint can let this image shine through. So spiritual life would begin from the conscious presence of the Word, the Image of the Father and it is through this awareness that the mind moves to that which the Image reflects and in what it participates, namely, the divine life of the Father.[119]

6.5.3.1 Divine ***Gnosis***

Dupré refers to Clement of Alexandria who speaks of the divine *gnosis* as the way to becoming aware of God's presence. *Gnosis* does not refer only to study and reflection but he says that what unites us to God is full awareness of Christ's presence in the soul. So, Christ is the key to *gnosis* because in him we receive a full revelation and knowledge of God's inhabitation in the soul and our participation in his nature. Also it is through the mystical reflection upon the revelation that man is transformed into what he seeks. In 'knowing' God man is able to possess him, and through knowledge we can be united to him. Such a *gnosis* is not just a matter of study, but a loving relationship with the *Logos*. Gregory of Nyssa too spoke of the union with the Word as one of love, asceticism and purification. It is through contemplation on the divine Image within himself that one is able to be united to the Father. And this is possible because essentially man is an image of God. He describes the growing toward the Image as an increase in cognition and a growing in love through a spiritual enlightenment that takes place in different stages. It is a movement from darkness to light, but as the soul goes deeper into the religious realm the light becomes dimmer and darkness overshadows it as it enters into the secret chamber of divine knowledge where it is encompassed by an awareness of an invisible and incomprehensible presence. Like many other theologians he too is struck by our inability to grasp the intricacies of God's presence in the soul through human cognition.[120]

6.5.3.2 The Image of God

It was Augustine with whom the spiritual development of western Christianity took on a psychological turn. For him the human mind is an image of the triune God since it consists of three elements the memory, intellect and the will. He draws attention to the spiritual impact that the presence of the triune God left on the soul. Augustine argues that the divine presence must have left a trace of the Trinity in the soul itself. He begins with God and seeks the divine-like quality

---

[118] Dupré, *The Common Life,* 13.

[119] Cf. Dupré, *The Common Life,* 10-16.

[120] Cf. Dupré, *The Common Life,* 14-21.

of the soul, so the union with God becomes the starting point. Direct contact of the soul with the Trinity must be reflected in the quality of the soul. Beyond the self the soul is seen not in its own appearance but in its divine reality. The direct contact with God will reveal the divine impression upon the soul. Dupré comments:

> The mind is able to move beyond itself and thus beyond all psychology, to attain a direct union with God. It is in the exercise itself, in the very process of actualizing the Trinitarian image in the soul that the union with God occurs. The more we know God, Augustine claims, the more we love him and the more we will be like him.[121]

As the self gets more united to God it gets transformed into an image of God. The soul is already united with the Trinity and so is an image of the divine Trinity. The mind remembers God and so by understanding and loving him it gradually transforms the external image of the Trinity in the soul into a real, intrinsic image. Though he is close to the Greek idea that the image is grounded in an identity, Augustine differs because he does not start from the soul's initial identity but he starts from its threefold function of remembrance, understanding and love because of which the soul gradually gets drawn into God's own life and thus becomes an ontological image of God. As the soul awakens to God's presence in itself it becomes alert to the traces and reflections of this mysterious inhabitation. Later on this thought would be developed into the insight that man is an image of God because in his deepest essence he is identical with God.[122]

6.5.3.3 Growing Toward the Image

The dialectical tension between the divine Image and the created likeness reached its climax in the writings of Meister Eckhart. He too accepted Trinitarian spiritual theology and held that the Father ceaselessly begets his Son in the soul in the same way as he does in eternity and so the divine self-expression in the Word contains all other expressions. All creatures retain their primordial being in the divine Image of God and in its innermost being the soul too coincides with the divine Image and so it must try to become what it already is in its uncreated core. According to Eckhart every image has two properties, one by which it participates in that of which it is an image and the second by which it is distinct from the original in so far as it is only an image. It is both the created image of God as well as God's uncreated Image. There is a difference and an identity and in this sense an image is a dynamic reality. Like the Greek Fathers Eckhart too felt that to refer to man as an image is to assert that in his innermost being he is already united with God and the purpose of the spiritual life is to journey toward complete

[121] Dupré, *The Common Life,* 18.

[122] Cf. Dupré, *The Common Life,* 16-19.

union. We arrive at this point by attempting to overcome the external likeness and move to something deeper. And so we move from dissimilarity as well as similarity to complete identity. The likeness should lead us to attain identity and this can be attained only when the likeness, that is, when the imprint and the image are abandoned. So in this sense we are unable to assert anything positive about God. Nothing remains of God but the barren Godhead of which the Trinity is only a revelation to the creature. In moving toward this identity the soul moves toward a state in which there is no more activity or form. It leaves us with a doubt about whether this identity is a total darkness or whether it is a spiritual ascent of the mind into a divine reality where there are no distinctions. Does the mystical darkness intend that human language is unable to express God's full reality or that there is no internal dynamism at work in God? What happens is that as we grow toward the Image and as God's immanence penetrates deeper into us we have to abandon our attachment to creation and enter into total darkness and silence. It is for this reason that Eckhart's understanding of silence appeals to those who are seriously engaged in the spiritual life since those who are closely related with God will not want to be superficial and banal in their usage of words about him.[123]

In Dupré's view one of the persons who best expressed this internal dynamism within God was Jan Ruusbroec. He never considered silence and darkness as the end of all spiritual life. There is an unceasing movement into the darkness, an abandoning of distinctions and a moving out again in the revelation of the Word. It is a continuous movement from God's rest to God's work and back into rest.[124] John Tauler a disciple of Eckhart holds that the Trinity inhabits the soul and so we must learn how to find the Trinity in ourselves and realize that we are formed according to its image. However, imperfect the soul is, in its natural state it still bears the divine image. It is a finite reflection of the perfect Image of God's self-expression and so it participates in the divine life of the Son. Spiritual progress is to recognize the blessed image in ourselves above all things. Tauler says that God is in this image and in fact is this image while also being imageless. So any one formed in this image of God will find all other images dim and unattractive. The only real image is my identity with God, and my being in the Son.[125] As Tauler says, "Once men are free of images, the divine sun shines into them and they are

[123] Cf. Dupré, *The Common Life*, 22-26.

[124] In terms of Trinitarian theology, according to Ruusbroec the realm of silence and darkness *is* the Father, that is to say, it is a silence that expresses itself in the eternal self-manifestation of the Word, a darkness in which the Light originates. Eckhart's theology placed the Absolute beyond the Trinity and the Godhead beyond the Father and this is where he went astray. So, while the Father is the principle of darkness and silence, it is a darkness that breaks out into the Light and a silence that is to speak the Word. This theology of the Image leads to what lies beyond images. Cf. Dupré, *The Common Life*, 26-27.

[125] Cf. Dupré, *The Common Life*, 27-28.

most marvellously drawn out of themselves and out of all earthly things."[126] And so Dupré concludes:

> Hence the real image of God in me consists of my super-essential being within the divine reality, that part of my being where God touches me in his creative activity. Spiritual life moves toward that point of identity. The movement of identification, never complete, results in darkness and silence as the expression returns to what it expresses. Yet darkness and silence are not final. For the God we reach has spoken and continues to speak his eternal Word. Only in the divine silence can we clearly hear God's Word, in the divine night see God's Light.[127]

6.5.3.4 The Union that Leads to Transcendence

6.5.3.4.1 Dynamism and Rest

Dupré holds that Ruusbroec presents a unique synthesis of Eastern and Western spirituality. Eastern spiritual knowledge as we have seen earlier was related to the specific identities of the Father, the Son and the Holy Spirit in the works of creation and salvation. The West on the other hand followed a more psychological approach and was more inclined toward the one God or the God-man and most often was not seen in relation to the other Persons. Ruusbroec strove for a union between the psychological and the objective Trinitarian approach. The soul takes part in the constant flowing out and turning in of the Trinity, that is to say, the perpetual generation of persons that accompanies the outward movement of the three Persons and the contraction in the unity of one nature. Man participates in this divine ebb and flow through the Son who is the divine Image. The creature who is a partial, finite expression of God has to grow toward the divine Image. He gives equal importance to divine unity and the Trinity. Spiritual life moves upwards but does not end in divine unity. There is a moment of unity without distinctions but the movement must continue beyond this static point. The dynamism knows no rest and goes on. The spiritual person seeks contemplation, but when union with God is arrived at in contemplation the soul partakes of the divine flowing and ebbing in which God can be found. It is not a remaining quiet without any inward or outward acts that is forgetful of God and blind to our neighbour's needs. Grace urges us on to works. As Ruusbroec writes:

> It is a sitting still, without either outward or inward acts, in vacancy, in order that rest may be found and may remain untroubled. But a rest which is practiced in this way is unlawful, for it brings with it in men a blindness and ignorance and a sinking down into themselves without activity. Such

[126] John Tauler, *Spiritual Conferences*, trans and ed. Eric Colledge and Sister M. Jane, O.P. (Rockford, Illinois: Tan Books, 1961), 128, as quoted in Dupré, *The Common Life*, 28.

[127] Dupré, *The Common Life*, 28.

> a rest is nought else than an idleness into which the man has fallen and in which he forgets himself and God and all things in all that has to do with activity… And in this natural rest one cannot find God but it certainly leads a man into a bare vacancy, which may be found by Pagans and Jews and all men—how wicked soever they may be, if they can live in their sins without reproach of their conscience and can empty themselves of every image and of all activity.[128]

He rejects the state of rest when understood as a state of quiet as the end of all spiritual life. In pursuing rest for its own sake one obstructs the work of God and does not allow him to operate.[129]

6.5.3.4.2 The Spiritual Life as Union

Dupré presents Ruusbroec's understanding of the spiritual life as a path that leads us to the unity and union that we seek through transcendence. Ruusbroec holds that spiritual life consists in a process of gradual unification and simplification. The first stage in this process is the 'virtuous life' which consists in leading a life of virtue and an active longing for God through good works. In the second stage which he calls the 'interior stage' the soul is purified and enlightened and it becomes unified in the higher faculties of intellect, memory and will. And this gradually leads to the third stage, the 'contemplative stage' where God alone is important, and is actually more important to the individual than even ones own self. It is not so much an intensity of feeling or a great show of virtue, but just an attitude of complete and total trust. In this third stage all of spiritual life makes sense.[130] In describing this union Ruusbroec writes, "This essential union of our spirit with God does not exist in itself, but it dwells in God, and it flows forth from God, and it depends upon God, and it returns to God as to its Eternal Origin."[131]

The divine ground of all createdness and the ontological basis of the mystical life is that:

> The spirit in its essence possesses God in the nakedness of its nature, as God does the spirit: for it lives in God and God in it. And it is able, in its highest part, to receive, without intermediary, the Brightness of God, and all that God can fulfil … And, in its created being, it incessantly receives the impress of its Eternal Archetype, like a flawless mirror, in which the image remains

---

[128] Jan Ruusbroec, *The Spiritual Marriage*, Bk II, Chp. 40, as quoted in Dupré, *The Common Life*, 32.

[129] Cf. Dupré, *The Common Life*, 29-32.

[130] Cf. Dupré, *The Common Life*, 38-40.

[131] Ruusbroec, *The Spiritual Marriage*, II, 57, as quoted in *The Common Life*, 40.

> steadfast, and in which the reflection is renewed without interruption by its ever-new reception in new light.[132]

It is for this reason that a genuinely religious person can lead a life that goes against most ordinary human aspirations since that person has God who is inviting him to total union at the core of his existence. The union between God and the soul is an intimate union, without intermediacy so that nothing stands between the soul and God. The mind forever bears the imprint of its eternal Archetype, or more accurately, the soul remains in that Archetype.[133]

6.5.3.4.3 God and the Soul

The theory of creation does not imply that God got things started with the act of creation and then left the whole of creation to manage by itself. He has not left us, nor have we gone away from him. Our entire being and existence is in him. God dwells in the space in which we live. Not many may realize or be aware of the divine presence in the soul, but he is there. Hence any concept of man must take this transcendent dimension into consideration. As Dupré writes:

> God's own being is the axis around which the self moves. Its super-essential unity places the self in God's constant presence... If God is able to visit the soul, it is because he is already there. It is not simply that he is present in me. I am in him, for he never leaves himself... The mind possesses God 'in the nakedness of its nature' only because God possesses the mind. Inseparably, my essence is joined to his essence.[134]

Ruusbroec too reflects the same thought and says that if in the nakedness of its nature the mind were to be separated from God then it would vanish into nothingness since the unity of our spirit is united to God according to nature. The divine presence in this sense is natural in all men but the awareness of the divine presence is not present in all persons. Truly spiritual persons grow toward the Image which would involve an active participation in the divine life but it could as well be passive and experiential.[135]

6.5.3.4.4 Union with God through Works

Having seen that the essence of the soul or the nature of the self is inclined toward mystical union we also realize that we have to grow toward the Image. And this requires that we work toward this goal. These works that correspond to the mystical union do not consist in works of virtue alone. They are part of the

---

[132] Dupré, *The Common Life*, 39-40.

[133] Cf. Dupré, *The Common Life*, 40-41.

[134] Dupré, *The Common Life*, 41.

[135] Cf. Dupré, *The Common Life*, 41-42. On the topic about growing toward the Image, see, Dupré, *The Deeper Life*, 87.

spiritual life.[136] What is important is that God invites the soul to union with him and it is the response of the soul to the invitation of God that really launches the journey toward supernatural union which makes us 'like' God through grace and virtue. This likeness while it is of the created order is not given by nature but is a result of the divine grace and the human response. As the human person responds to the call of divine grace it becomes more and more 'like' God. When grace is seen in virtue and good works then it is referred to as created grace, and in this created grace is manifested the uncreated union with the Trinity in the essence of the soul through which it maintains the essential unity with God. This unity is the source of strength and power which is witnessed to in works and virtue. In this way the soul resembles and also reflects God's uncreated Image while it is still on the level of 'likeness' and external resemblance, yet it is related to the dynamic Image of God and is always on the path toward fuller identity with God. Most often the uncreated Image remains hidden and most believers are content with the created image and likeness and so do not progress toward the union. We can never lose the Image of God within us, yet we often fail to attain our natural unity with him. Ruusbroec would say that this union with God, above all likeness and means can only happen on the level of the spirit because on the spiritual level there is only God, and the spirit united with God, and no intervening means.[137]

In the essential union all distinctions disappear from the experience. The spirit goes into its own essential depth and loses itself experiencing a total waylessness. It has let go of creation and is left with a feeling of nothingness and emptiness. For Ruusbroec this pure unity without determination is always within the Trinity. So while the effect of this contact with God is one of silence, it is a fertile silence which is always ready to break out into speech. But even at this early stage of contemplation the soul is unable to enjoy permanent rest without going out into works and into creation. Even when the soul rests in unity with God the contemplative moves out into the multiplicity of works. This outgoing is much more than merely continuing the practice of virtue and good works but is a participation in the motion within the Trinity. There can be no spiritual rest without spiritual motion and there can be no spiritual motion without rest. The ingoing into unity and the outflowing into multiplicity cannot appear apart from each other. Hardly has one reached God than one has to go out to meet him so that the union that has been achieved can be preserved. At the same time, this going out prevents the person from retreating back into a residual state of

---

[136] The spiritual life can be either 'essential' or 'active'. In the essential mode of being, the presence of God is without means and without interruption. Here, the soul has its being in God's eternal Image. In the active mode, we strive to reach God through the virtuous life and longing for God through good works.

[137] Cf. Dupré, *The Common Life*, 42-45.

consciousness. So there has to be a perpetual renewal whereby God gives ever-new gifts and the spirit in its turn continually grows into a higher life.[138]

6.5.3.4.5 The Rhythm that Leads to Transcendence

The world that the contemplative returns to is not the same world that he left. Due to his unity with God the world has been completely transformed. As Dupré says, "In the divine perspective creation emerges, within the Son, from the Father's generating act, in order to return within the Son to the Father. This new perspective, far from distorting the view, allows the contemplative to perceive creation as it is in its essence."[139] Creation fully manifests itself only to the spiritual person. And in this a new dimension is uncovered in the real. Through this life of the spirit the environment possesses a certain amount of completeness and nothing seems to be missing because the essential is present. In this movement of the spirit into itself and then out toward creation, God is always present, and this continuous drawing in and flowing out of the spiritual life follows the same rhythm as God's inner being. This expanding and contracting rhythm of all life gives an ultimate mystical foundation to life since the soul meets God through God rather than through itself. So, the soul is united and one with the Spirit of God and in him we possess our eternal bliss. In this attainment of the ideal of the God-like life God is more important to the person than he is to himself and God takes over his whole essential being and his essence now coincides with his super essence which is God's essence.[140]

This does not mark the end but is only the beginning of a new life for the contemplative. Ruusbroec is talking in Christian terms of the God-seeking life that has now led to the God-seeing life. Two characteristics stand out namely, the ongoing dialectic between the contemplative and the active life and secondly the relation between God's one nature and the distinct modes of being of the three Persons. In speaking about the life in union, Ruusbroec says that the inward man sinks himself in his essential being with the delights and riches of God. He explains this through the metaphors of darkness and light when he writes, "And from out the Divine Unity, there shines into him a simple light; and this light shows him Darkness and Nakedness and Nothingness."[141] Dupré gives it a Trinitarian interpretation and holds that the light refers to the Son's revelation of the Father. In this realm of the Father at the beginning of contemplative life is the realm of darkness and silence. The Light reveals this darkness and nothingness. As we progress in the contemplative life it changes so that finally the Light which is the Son, and Love which is the Holy Spirit will overcome the darkness. At this

[138] Cf. Dupré, *The Common Life*, 45-47.

[139] Dupré, *The Common Life*, 47.

[140] Cf. Dupré, *The Common Life*, 47-48.

[141] Ruusbroec, *The Spiritual Marriage*, II, 65, as quoted in Dupré, *The Common Life*, 49.

stage of the contemplative life Ruusbroec presents virtue not as something that is practised by novices, but rather that what results from wisdom which he holds as the ground and origin of all virtue. This passivity underlies even the active practice and is the basis of the contemplative life. This combination of action and fruition is such that one does not obstruct the other but always strengthens the other. On this level rest and work alternate and Ruusbroec holds that this mixture is the best for the true contemplative. Besides, this alternation is also helpful to revitalize the energy of life which otherwise would be depleted. This resting in unity and working in multiplicity is part of the divine life in which the contemplative partakes.[142] In this way by leading the 'common life' which is a unification of the virtuous life of the heart, the God-seeking life of the mind and the God-seeing life in the spirit, the just person "goes *toward* God with fervent love in eternal activity; and he goes *in* God with fruitive inclination in eternal rest."[143]

6.6 Conclusion

In this chapter we have seen the movement towards a synthesis as based on a concept of the self that allows for the inward turn of religious recollection. For this Dupré turns to mysticism for help because in the concept of transcendence we concentrate on spiritual content. It is when we go deepest into the self that we discover its transcendent dimension.

This rethinking of the self, the cosmos and of the concept of transcendence has not yet come to an end in our age. There is a constant and ongoing effort to redefine the meaning of contingency and necessity, of autonomy and dependence which has led to new ways of conceiving the ontological limits of the real. This change was not initiated just to include the heliocentric theory into the medieval theology but has led to a revision of the accepted concept of transcendence. The traditional concept of transcendence was that of a power that was hierarchically transmitted from *beyond*. This concept was changed to transcendence seen as a source of power *within* the universe. Hence, God's presence permeated all parts at once. For panentheistic philosophers like Cusanus, Bruno and others, the being of the cosmos is a disclosure of God's Being. Their ideas are slowly resurfacing in recent thinkers and so Dupré says the search for an adequate conception of transcendence continues. Some of the questions that remain unanswered are, how does the necessary allow genuine contingency, and how does the contingent affect the nature of necessity.[144] As Dupré writes at the end of his book Passage to Modernity, "While anxiously seeking a new wholeness we must nevertheless

---

[142] Cf. Dupré, *The Common Life*, 48-51.

[143] Ruusbroec, *The Spiritual Marriage*, II, 65, as quoted in Dupré, *The Common Life*, 51.

[144] Cf. Dupré, *Passage to Modernity*, 252-253.

carefully protect those fragments of meaning that we possess, knowing that they may be the bricks of a future synthesis."[145]

[145] Dupré, *Passage to Modernity*, 253.

Chapter 7

Critical Appraisal of Dupré's Concept of Transcendence

Louis Dupré's thinking and writing has a direct connection and relevance to life. More than providing the reader with a finished product, he provides the raw material and then invites the reader to build his own edifice. Apart from the depth of his writings we are also impressed by the diversity of his writings which delve into philosophy, theology, spirituality and ethics. Our main challenge has been the difficulty in clearly separating his writings. It is not possible to say that any particular book of Dupré is only philosophy or only theology or only spirituality. The author has been working toward a recovery of the lost synthesis of God, man and the world, and so in working out a harmony it is inevitable that the lines of separation between his philosophy, theology and spirituality get blurred and hence difficult to separate due to their interdependence. Dupré writes about life and especially about the religious dimension of human life. His concern is about the crisis in the world and he writes about the existential self that is in peril of alienation. When he writes about religion he tackles the situation of man-in-the-world who has lost all or most sense of transcendence. These are themes that concern the day-to-day existence of ordinary man, but more importantly they are the concerns that man has to confront in order that he might find the harmony that he seeks in existence.

Since his concern is about the philosophy of religion we have restricted our comments to what Dupré has written about the self, transcendence and the mediation in religion. His approach is from religious experience. Dupré's writings reflect a strong drive towards fighting the negative step that religious life seemed to be taking. This effort that he made towards correcting this dangerous drifting towards extreme secularism and subjectivity is seen in the direction that he indicated towards a meaning in life and existence. In *The Other Dimension* his approach to God and to religion is very clear and at the same time critical. This desire to approach God and religion is done in a systematic and detailed manner. His willingness to approach the question and also his awareness that the endeavour is always a tentative attempt towards synthesis is good, but at the same time it does not arrive at a final synthesis that we would expect of him. In this light Dupré has not developed a special or unique concept of transcendence and so if we were to search for this concept as a fully developed treatise we do not find it. But Dupré has nearly all the building blocks that would be necessary for constructing such a treatise. Yet as he says it is an ongoing endeavour and a constant dialectic of which we are all participants.

7.1 A Critique of Dupré's Thought

7.1.1 The Self

Dupré when speaking about reflection also speaks about man's reflection upon himself. In this process of reflection man becomes aware of himself as a subject, as an interiority distinct from the objective world of things.[1] Even though he also describes the self as a dialectical movement of freedom, this self is not completely free. Human freedom is practised in a situation where it is controlled because of its relation with the material world and with the spiritually transcendent. Dupré believes that existential phenomenology examines the 'situatedness' of the self. This situatedness is important because the subject constantly intends the object and the essence of the subject is to posit itself in the world. Hence when we speak of the freedom of the self, it has to be within the context of this situatedness that freedom can be exercised. The authentic self must recognize and accept its imperfection. It is in this affirmation of the self's dependence and the acceptance of this dependence that opens up a new sphere of existence. The self has to balance the tension between freedom and necessity and this leads to a transformation of the self to a higher level of existence. Kierkegaard holds that this can be resolved in the act of faith not by reconciling the two poles but rather through accepting the opposition between them as a sign of man's basic insufficiency.[2] The situation in the world today looks for homogeneity in reality but at the same time is confronted by the relative independence of the cosmos. Combined with these is the gradual receding of the transcendent which as Dupré points out leads to a detachment from nature and from the self. This has happened, says Dupré, in a gradual transformation of culture which began with man's wanting to assert himself over nature. This resulted in the subject as the sole source of rationality, a subjectivization that also led to his doom. This also initiated the gradual

---

[1] Cf. Dupré, "Philosophical Stages," 413.

[2] Cf. Louis Dupré "The Constitution of the Self in Kierkegaard's Philosophy," *International Philosophical Quarterly* 3 (1963), 526.

disappearance of transcendence due to a secular attitude that led to a major lack of inwardness and consequently the loss of transcendence.[3]

Dupré has a concept of the self which he speaks of in terms of subject and person. Yet at the same time he always speaks of the self in connection with experience. In this sense while he speaks of the subject as existing he tends to lay a strong emphasis on the self in terms of the body and the exteriority of the self. Yet he also speaks of reflection and so he does not speak 'only' of the self as object. Perhaps his concept of the self could have been strengthened if he had spoken and reflected a little more on the psychological aspect of the self. This would have given a basis to the need that he expresses of man who has been separated from an original synthesis of God, world and man, and now lives a fragmented existence and hence needs to rebuild the bridges so that he can connect once again with those spiritual traditions that once were an integral part of his being and his existence. This endeavour has been taken up by Dupré, but there does not seem to be a basis that is strong enough so that we can use it as our foundation to build up a concept of transcendence. Thanks to Dupré we have the building blocks, and he has done much of the ground-work. But the search for a coherent foundation continues.

7.1.2 God or the Absolute

7.1.2.1 On God

In my opinion, when Dupré speaks about God, he speaks of religious consciousness that is dialectical. There is a statement, a negation of the statement and then a negation of the negation. Yet while our thinking of God is dialectical in character, God himself is not dialectical. Religious consciousness in a first negation sees God as an absolute. Everything else is relative. In a second moment all oppositions are removed and God is not seen as opposite to all things, but as an integration of everything. This leads to an awareness of God who is absolutely incomprehensible and hence transcendent. God is infinity who from within consciousness manifests himself as transcendent to consciousness. Dupré's understanding of God especially in *The Other Dimension* is of a pure unnameable mystery who is in essence unknowable. What we do know of him is through a self-negating dialectic of religious consciousness. But then the problem that arises with Dupré's idea of such a divine is that it appears to be a hidden God. Such an absolute mystery would mean we can have no knowledge at all about God and so we need to have recourse to faith. Dupré's God seems to end up in an empty transcendence. His descriptions are indeterminate and purely in the realm of possibility. Most of what he speaks of God does not characterize God's own being.[4]

[3] Cf. Casarella and Schner, *Christian Spirituality*, 230-232.

[4] William J. Hill, "The God of the Other Dimension" in *The New Scholasticism* 50 (Spring 1976), 212-214.

We are of the opinion that Dupré has made a very significant exposition on God. But as we have said, his explanation of God does not leave us with a systematic exposition or understanding of God. While he writes a lot about God, we are given fragments. Perhaps we need a deeper study and a longer period of time to grasp his synthesis which seems incomplete. He does explain the discovery and the unravelling of God in a dialectical movement, but this movement seems to be unending. We need to have at least some idea or image of God which would serve as a motivating force to enable us to carry on the dialectical effort. Without these partial successes and small conquests the movement becomes frustrating and could well be a fruitless striving for the mythical 'pie in the sky'.

7.1.2.2 The Dialectical Movement Towards Transcendence

In my opinion the synthesis that Dupré seems to be moving towards is very much influenced by Hegel. He holds that genuine religiousness is dialectical in nature and in a dialectical movement progresses in negations. He follows this movement of negation to a certain moment but then to his credit Dupré moves away from Hegel. Dupré holds that this dialectical movement itself makes man aware that God in his own being is not dialectical. God is not dialectical, our thinking about God is dialectical in nature. In the first negation we are conscious that God is absolute and therefore in opposition to all else, which in contrast to God, is relative. But then this negation leads to a second negation which is what opens the way to God and this is what leads to integration. Hegel sees absolute Idea as immanent in rational thought. For Hegel the infinite determines itself in and as the finite idea of limited consciousness. Dupré instead sees the dialectical movement as leading to a conception of God and an awareness of God in his incomprehensibility. Dupré sees God as transcendent where for Hegel the infinite is only immanent to consciousness. For Dupré, the infinity, from within consciousness, manifests itself as transcendent to consciousness. Hence when Dupré speaks of the other dimension, God is seen as pure, unnameable mystery and revelation takes place as the self-negating dialectic of consciousness. Revelation in this sense is seen as self-revelation. In pointing towards infinity we are not sure if by the term infinity Dupré means merely the 'not finite' or whether he intends the Absolute as it is in itself. Dupré's understanding and description of God remains mysterious and yet we have to accept that Dupré has shown us a path. God as Absolute will always remain a mystery, and the nature of a mystery is that it remains unknown. But through the dialectical movement, man is able to continue this search for God who eludes him. He knows that he cannot possess the Absolute completely, but every step is a step forward and Dupré has enabled us to make many steps in the right direction. Hope and his religious belief, coupled with the intellectual capabilities of man gradually leads him towards his goal, but this method while being a help is not sufficient to reach the end.

7.1.2.3 On Causality in General

We can speak of the transcendent in terms of the principle of causality which, Dupré feels is of no use in this situation because causality demands a separation of God from the creature.[5] But then he explains that causality properly understood requires a presence of the cause to the effect. As he says in *The Other Dimension*, "My problem with causality is that…God's Being becomes separated from that of the creature."[6] Yet according to him, if we really look at the principle of causality a certain *presence* of the cause to the effect is necessary. Here we refer to the being of the creature, the effect, and so it would involve the presence of the cause. God is 'other than' his creatures, but this does not mean that therefore he is separated from his creatures. So when God is spoken of as the cause of the world, there is no separation but a presence. And yet there is also a distinction that is maintained as the distinction between the cause and the effect. So God is 'other than' but not 'apart.' In our opinion Dupré rightly accepts that God is beyond the range of our intelligibility. Hence to think about God we have to transcend the categories of being. This is something positive in Dupré because when we can speak of God, we can affirm him but we cannot grasp him completely. So God can be reached as intelligible in a movement of consciousness, but this movement must not end in a negation, but in an affirmation. Hence, God is not restrained by determinations but he transcends all these determinations in their finitude. An affirmation of God cannot end in a definite concept of divinity, but the striving towards a God who always remains unknown is itself an affirmation of God. This is what Dupré indicates is transcendence and hence while he may not describe God, this movement and dynamism towards the beyond is what makes the concept of transcendence meaningful.

Dupré seems to accept pan-entheism wherein creatures are able to retain their independence within God. God is absolute and fully independent and yet needs the relative realization of existence. But his dependence is not like creaturely dependence as a result of which the creature varies and has a relative existence. God's relation to creatures is entirely stable and has no subjective fluctuations. Hence, while not every finite is directly related to the infinite, Dupré holds that "finitude does exist and hence that it must have its function in and through infinity."[7]

The concept of transcendence is significant because God is the cause of all beings but he can be understood as the cause only transcendentally. He is beyond all determinations and so this situation leaves us with a constant striving for this beyond. Yet this beyond is infinite and therefore always remains unknown. Given the dynamism of the noetic capacity of men, this forever unknown and infinite can be grasped in an indirect and relational way.

---

[5] Cf. Dupré, *The Other Dimension*, 335.

[6] Dupré, *The Other Dimension*, 335.

[7] Dupré, *The Other Dimension*, 361.

7.1.2.4 Participation

Dupré's conception of transcendence is one in which the sacred and the profane are considered as mutually exclusive and yet share the same plane of reality. He agrees with Thomas Aquinas' position on participation by which he links the creature to God and thus allows for God's immanence.[8] The problem that arises is that Thomas describes the divine immanence through a relation of causal dependency. This according to Dupré is problematic because then God's "presence to the creature is reduced to the impact of one being upon another."[9] Further, such causal dependence does not allow for an intimate union. It also affects the intrinsic independence of a free agent because causal dependence is not compatible with genuine freedom according to Dupré. As he says:

> A genuine transcendence conceives the relation between creature and creator, between saved and savior as much more intimate than causal terminology can ever express. The causal concept entails a succession of active and passive roles on the part of God and man in which human autonomy and divine omnipotence are alternatively sacrificed.[10]

The concept of creation in the traditional causal sense is inadequate according to Dupré. However, we have not yet reached a solution where the creator and creature can be seen as interdependent. The answer Dupré points towards is the paradox of divine transcendence as described by the spiritual writers for whom God was most vitally present.[11] To this end Dupré holds that any reflection of an individual takes place against the background of one's beliefs and in the light of a living faith this is especially significant when we are talking about the philosophy of religion. We need to give importance to culture as well as religion especially in the shaping of one's thoughts and reasons. Dupré has raised significant questions regarding causality and has even given us partial answers. This is because he has not been able to give a strong foundation to the presence of the transcendent and the relation between immanence and transcendence. He speaks about creation as a total dependence on God and that is what causality is about. Dupré criticises the idea of causality that separates the cause from the effect. Such a separation between God and the creature is not possible. He speaks about transcendence and immanence as theological categories and in this he has indicated a correct direction. We agree with him that the solution lies in a relationship of participation.

---

[8] Cf. Dupré, "Transcendence and Immanence as Theological Categories," 3.

[9] Dupré, "Transcendence and Immanence as Theological Categories," 3.

[10] Dupré, "Transcendence and Immanence as Theological Categories," 9.

[11] Cf. Dupré, "Transcendence and Immanence as Theological Categories," 1-10.

7.1.3 Representation

When we speak of transcendence one of the questions that we need to answer is how do we have a consciousness of the transcendent, how do we know it. To approach this question Dupré speaks of religion as representation and he turns to Hegel's theory of symbolic representation. Hegel's explanation of philosophy holds good also for religion and indeed philosophical truth is arrived at through the development of religion. Also the preliminary stages of consciousness lead to religious awareness while at the same time Hegel speaks of religion as being not merely for its own sake but also as a help to educate the mind to become aware of its infinity. Representation is between subjective forms of consciousness and thought. He speaks of the role of imagination which has a de-temporalizing function, a creative force and a religious impact.

In the final moment of the subjective spirit the opposition between the mind and the object out there is overcome. The mind makes its own the object of consciousness, which is then projected on to an ontic reality and thus transcends a purely mental existence. In representation the intuitive content is freed from the temporal restrictions of the sense intuition. Besides since it is separated from its original setting, it takes on a certain universality and consequently a transcendence of the content. Hegel speaks of three stages, recollection, imagination and memory which lead to representation. The representation is interiorized when through a process of objectification a number of intuition images are united into a universalized totality. Hegel calls the concrete universal representations, symbols and these point beyond toward the object in itself. Representational consciousness invites a deeper reflection which leads to the realization that the representation represents something. He stresses this objective character of the representations while seeking an overarching unity.

A representation is not the same as an image. An image is a subordinate aspect of the representation. The image expresses directly, but considering the vastness of transcendence and the content of religion, it is only representation that through a process of abstraction is able to elevate the images to a universal level. Hence the representation transcends that which is merely sensible and to enable this process of attaining transcendence it makes use of language whereby it has a system of meaning that allows the spiritual content to go beyond natural symbolism. God's inner life is followed by an outward creation and the infinite spirit mediates itself through the otherness of the finite, an otherness that is re-integrated with the infinite spirit. This self mediation of God is presented as a manifestation which requires to be mediated with the divine self-identity. The appearance of the absolute is for itself, more than for us. Without the interiorization the idea has no otherness, and without the internalization of the spirit God's self manifestation is merely profane.

When we accept the Absolute as self revealing, the logic of manifestation is significant. Hegel held that since God is before the creation of the world, his reality is manifested in pure thought. So the science of pure thought is capable of expressing this reality. Hegel starts the discussion from the divine infinite reality. Religious representation takes place within essential reflection and so even the attributes of God need to be seen in their relatedness. Through the negative reflection of the notion into itself it posits itself as different, but a difference that is its own determination. Hence in the judgement the notion has a particularity which is arrived at due to a self-reflection. The notion mediates the singularity of the subject and the universality of the predicate. In the spirit the gap between thought and reality is bridged and it allows philosophy to move beyond and integrate the total otherness of nature. Hence the content of religion can go beyond its religious representation.

This explanation of Dupré is taken from Hegel. While the explanation of our knowledge of that which is the object of transcendence is reasonable, it does not satisfy our concerns regarding the concept of transcendence. Our concern about transcendence is connected with the Absolute. While he has presented a fair exposition on representation what is lacking is a justification of knowledge of the Absolute. This justification can be got through reflection and judgement, which through the complete return results in total reflection.

7.1.4 Religious Experience

Another significant issue in connection with transcendence concerns our experience of the transcendent. If the transcendent does not enter into experience then our study is limited to mere inner intentions and outer expressions, and remains separate from the transcendent Absolute. Through his analysis Dupré attempts to arrive at an essential intuition of an object that otherwise lies beyond experience. To do justice to our study we have to address the fullness of the religious act, that is to say, religion as experience as well as religion as transcendence. The experience has to be seen in relation to the revelation because the experience renders a transcendental object as intentionally immanent in some way. While mental acts have a transcendent intentionality, the object has an essential transcendence.

7.1.4.1 Intentions of Experience

Dupré refers back to Husserl's intentions of experience. The religious act cannot be reduced to a subjective experience. Psychology only deals with the empirical aspect of experience and does not specifically deal with the religious aspect. Still it is able to indicate the emotional component of the religious phenomena. Phenomenology largely deals with the ideal aspect of the religious act. Actions are never completely pure and so their intentionality also is never easily and clearly evident. The challenge is to maintain the transcendence of the religious object while also insisting on its real existence. It is through religion as experience that man looks for the meaning of life in its totality. Yet the ultimate meaning is 'beyond', but the 'beyond' itself is not attained merely in this reaching towards. To attain the beyond requires a believing attitude because there is only a partial immanence of the transcendent object in material things.

Husserl describes transcendence as a being which is intended by consciousness but whose reality falls outside consciousness. The ground of the factual world lies in consciousness, but consciousness itself is unable to explain the world completely. The contingency of the world is unavoidable and so it has to be founded on a necessary being. Intentionality is based on a trans-conscious universal drive. There is an open infinity and universal teleology is directed toward an infinite perfect and hence transcending the time-constituted consciousness. Without this infinite and transcendent *telos* intentionality has nowhere to go. Still he does not answer beyond all doubt the question as to whether this *telos* is purely transcendent or not. Husserl's was a genuine effort to understand true transcendence but he left too much contingency in the teleological process and as a result that transcendent which ought to have supported itself was unable to account for its own being. So the real issue is not so much one of teleology but more of contingency insofar as we need to examine whether the teleological process is grounded within itself or in another. In restricting it only to the teleological aspect Husserl does not address transcendence in its fullness.

7.1.4.2 Reflection and Experience

To have a better perspective of transcendence, Dupré refers to Blondel's explanation and speaks about reflections and experience. Subjectivity has a significant role to play in connection with the study of transcendence, and after Kant attempted to separate the subject from the object, Blondel attempted to define the nature and being of the subject through action because it is through acting that the subject realizes its own insufficiency and simultaneously the need for a transcendent fulfilment. The immanent in its openness to the transcendent makes revealed religion possible, and consequently transcendence is possible. Since, transcendence does not belong to the immanent structure, belief requires a transcendent order of reality. This is not to say that philosophy which deals with the immanent structure cannot discover the transcendent order but just that it cannot disown the transcendent order. If this was the case, then the transcendent order would lose its transcendence. As a transcendent reality, this transcendent order is beyond immanent reflection but as a necessary hypothesis it is an essential part of immanent philosophy.

For Blondel, cognition and volition are united in the intellect through the acting subject. The subjective element is still significant and is more than merely a sum of all the objective elements. Here, we also recognize the role of freedom which goes beyond all the determinations. There is a dialectic taking place in which freedom gradually progresses and transcends from one determination to another.

As it progresses it becomes aware of its insufficiency and yet its transcending movement postulates a trans-phenomenal reality thus revealing an infinity in the very heart of action. The discrepancy between the real and the ideal cannot be bridged completely and in this insufficiency of the human action man is able to find God. Yet while Blondel does go beyond the phenomenal order there is no ontological transition from an ideal structure to a living reality. Philosophy does not deal only with logical possibilities but it also aims at discovering the necessary in the real. While we are looking for the transcendent terminus in human action it is only a possibility that there is this transcendent fulfilment. For Blondel the transcendent is discovered exclusively in the existing insufficiency and not in the necessity of fulfilment. For religion this claim has already been actualized. Yet since it remains a hypothesis its realization need not be necessary. Again while we could experience transcendence in the insufficiency of action it could still be possible that the supernatural order cannot be experienced. What we experience is not the supernatural but only that through which the transcendent communicates with the immanent. Since the supernatural order lies beyond actual experience it cannot be dealt with in philosophy alone and its existence can only be implied. We experience the supernatural as reflected in conscious activity. We can experience transcendence insofar as the immanent points beyond itself. Of the supernatural we only experience the possibility. Blondel is concerned about this 'possibility'. He holds that through reflection on this possibility one can enter the supernatural realm which leads to faith through which more is affirmed than that which is experienced.

We can reflect on the supernatural order without being committed to it as an immanent necessity. Philosophy respects transcendence but refrains from speaking about it beyond its own scope. From within its scope therefore, for philosophy, the existence of the transcendent is always a possibility. Philosophy cannot fully grasp the supernatural because the human experience of the supernatural is limited and our reflection on the supernatural is restricted to this experience. Blondel bridges this gap between the immanent and the transcendent through action because for him through action the supernatural becomes a reality of experience through an internal conversion. The deficiency of reflection for Blondel is overcome by the experience of action. Yet according to Dupré if the supernatural is transcendent to thought it should also be transcendent to practice, and hence action alone is not enough for this conversion.

The reflection is made on religious consciousness as it actually exists. Religion is not reduced to merely immanent experience because it is both immanent and transcendent. Through symbols the data of revelation becomes a part of human consciousness and hence has an immanent aspect. In Blondel's analysis philosophy and the transcendent element are juxtaposed and in fact it is often influenced by religion and revelation. The supernatural does not contradict but rather completes human action. Religion has to be immanent for man and judgement is passed on religion and not on the ontological status of the religious object. Blondel left the religious object largely to faith. But to understand and grasp the logic, structure and intentionality of religion, we need to reflect on the experience.

Dupré has to be acknowledged for his study of experience in man and especially his examination of the religious experience of man. While he has made a detailed study of religion and the religious attitude in his book, *The Other Dimension*, he has also examined the external aspect of the religious experience, namely, its expression. He is also able to tell us that the religious experience is very much a part of our existence and cannot be separated from life and indeed is that which serves to make our life whole. Dupré's analysis of religion and the religious experience goes a long way towards enabling us to attain this wholeness.

7.1.5 Mysticism

Among the many areas that Louis Dupré has studied, undoubtedly mysticism held a special place. *The Deeper Life* and *The Common Life* dealt specifically with Christian mysticism, but he also co-edited *Light From Light: An Anthology of Christian Mysticism* with James Wiseman. His study is of special significance because he seeks to understand the largely modern situation of unbelief, despite the fact that a majority of persons claim to believe in God. Dupré believes that this unbelief is largely the result of the assumption that it is the human mind alone that gives meaning and purpose to the individual, and that nature is self-supporting and self-moving. Yet, Dupré addresses those persons who still seek the spiritual in this world and to these Dupré points out a way. This path, as we have shown earlier, is the classical path followed by most mystics, which goes through Purgation, Illumination and Union. This path is not original to Dupré. Dupré highlights the incomprehensibility of God and also the centrality of love, in Trinitarian mysticism. This is one of the positive aspects of Dupré's explanation of mysticism. I agree with Dupré on this because God makes himself present to us in mysticism.

In my opinion Dupré could have developed the aspect of divine revelation a little more. He does speak of man's self-transcendence, but together with man's effort and capability, Christian mysticism indicates a dependence on God who chooses to reveal himself to his subjects. Dupré does accept disclosure and revelation, but for him this revelation "cannot be rendered intelligible unless it still proves capable of being assumed within the modern pattern of speaking and thinking."[12] He seems to be allowing for divine revelation when he says, "The self-manifestation of the transcendent is, in the end, neither self-understanding nor understanding of Being. Though contributing to both, it also surpasses them in

[12] Louis Dupré, "Reflections on the Truth of Religion," *Faith and Philosophy* 6 (1989), 266.

referring to the inexpressible."[13] He says that mystical writings are the best suited for this because they are the best expressions that we can have of this paradox. Dupré accepts the transcendent origin of the divine disclosure. All in all the philosophy of Dupré on religion is acceptable even though it has its limitations because for him religion is Dialectical, Representational and Revelatory. As he says, his is not yet a synthesis that is finished, but he has laid down the ground plan and is working toward adding flesh to the structure and filling in the gaps. The Dialectic continues in hope.

7.1.6 The Methods used by Dupré

Dupré is well aware that there are different possible approaches to religion and hence to transcendence. All of these are approaches and therefore helps, but none by itself alone is able to arrive at a full understanding of transcendence. They are all methods that are helpful but none is exhaustive. Dupré himself spells out the various methods.

7.1.6.1 The Psychological Method

One method of reaching transcendence is through psychology. Not all of psychology can help us attain this end, but then the psychologist can help us to understand the conditions in which it could be possible or not possible. As Dupré says, "Psychology fulfills a positive function as well in analyzing the religious experience as it appears in the totality of the psychic structure. Provided such an analysis is not expected to yield the *entire* meaning of the act, the term 'psychological meaning' is fully justified."[14] We have to remember that the psychological method deals with the experience and that it concerns motivations. Psychology does play an important role in analyzing religious experience and yet we have to remember that while it does not provide the complete meaning of the religious act, it does provide a human meaning. The conclusions of the psychologist "bear only upon the *experience* and its motivation, not upon the act as such, that is, the experience insofar as it is directed beyond itself *toward a transcendent terminus*."[15] Hence, the psychological method is a help but it needs to be complemented by another method.

7.1.6.2 The Philosophical Method

The philosophical method according to Dupré is another path that could help us to explore transcendence. A philosophical reflection is capable of making us aware of a new dimension in being. Philosophy helps us to have an attitude by which we are conscious of the beyond, and our expectant attitude helps us to

[13] Dupré, "Reflections on the Truth of Religion," 271.

[14] Dupre, *The Other Dimension*, 98.

[15] Dupre, *The Other Dimension*, 99.

recognize this beyond when we encounter it. Its method of enquiry is a help to strengthen our faith. As Dupré says, "In an advanced culture faith naturally recurs to philosophical concepts to develop its ideas."[16] Yet while philosophy is crucial, at most it helps us to discover the transcendent horizon of reality. But then the philosopher is unable to say much about the content of this horizon. It can only establish the possibility of meaningful religious assertions. According to Dupré, "Philosophy in the final analysis is and has always been the ultimate reflection upon experience, it receives it subject matter from nonphilosphical sources."[17] In keeping with this the next step is that through mere reflection upon the real as such philosophy is not able to arrive at the existence of God. God's existence cannot be accepted at the end of a study as an established fact. Dupré says, "The philosopher may independently discover the transcendent horizon of reality, but of the content of this horizon he knows nothing."[18]

7.1.6.3 The Religious Method

One of the most significant ways to arrive at transcendence is the religious way. This method he says is dialectical and symbolical, because, "Sacred reality is grasped directly in the appearance of a relative being—not as the conclusion of a logical process. The absolute shines directly through the relative."[19] This method is dialectical because the sacred is looked at in opposition to non-sacred, profane reality. As a result the term 'transcendent' takes on a different significance in different contexts. It is always seen as transcendent in relation to its surroundings.[20] The religious method helps us to approach transcendence because, "The religious act is not a simple experience, but a complex movement by which the mind discovers a new reality which, although lying beyond the phenomenal and contrasting with it, ultimately integrates all reality in a higher synthesis."[21]

7.1.6.4 The Phenomenological Method

The method that Dupré prefers is the phenomenological method. While he acknowledges that he uses the phenomenological analysis in his most important work, *The Other Dimension*, he also acknowledges that phenomenology alone is not capable of yielding the entire meaning of the religious act. The phenomenological approach considers the religious experience not as a subjective state, but as an intentional act, that is to say, as "an experience which points

[16] Dupre, *The Other Dimension*, 141.

[17] Dupre, *The Other Dimension*, 7.

[18] Dupre, *The Other Dimension*, 8.

[19] Dupre, *The Other Dimension*, 14.

[20] Cf. Dupre, *The Other Dimension*, 14-16.

[21] Dupre, *The Other Dimension*, 10.

beyond itself toward a transcendent terminus. The terminus is considered only as *immanent in*, and *constituted by*, consciousness."[22] Hence, Dupré proceeds by examining the experience and the terminus that is intended by the experience. So, phenomenology is a possible methodology to investigate the religious act. Yet while phenomenology explains religion-as-experience, it describes the reaching toward but it cannot attain the transcendent object. That according to Dupré requires faith. And so the phenomenologist is not able to affirm the real existence of the religious object. The phenomenologist differs from the believer because "He is concerned with what *appears* in consciousness: the transcendent object of the revelation interests him only to the extent that it is intended by an immanent experience."[23] Phenomenology is not concerned about the transcendent object in itself, or whether God has really spoken to man. "The notion of transcendence is phenomenologically relevant only insofar as it enters into the immanent experience."[24]

Yet in spite of the fact that he follows the phenomenological method Dupré is well aware of its limitations too. He accepts that because the object of the religious act never becomes sufficiently immanent to allow a full analysis, phenomenology alone cannot adequately describe the religious act. This happens because "the immanence of the religious act is such that it constantly *transcends* itself in an intentionality which ultimately escapes the purely phenomenological analysis."[25] As he concludes, "Phenomenology presents a theory that preserves the specific nature of religious truth: one that envisions reality as entirely symbolic of a higher meaning and yet does not sacrifice such other levels of truth as that of historical facts."[26]

7.1.6.5 Dupré's use of the Phenomenological Method

Dupré's phenomenological analysis is to be appreciated because it helps us to understand the meaning of the religious act. In considering the religious experience not as a subjective state but as an intentional act this method points beyond itself to a transcendent terminus, and this terminus can be known only in and through the religious act. Hence the transcendent is attained only in faith, and this is beyond the scope of phenomenology. Dupré does accept this and says, "Phenomenology *alone* cannot reveal the full meaning of the religious act."[27] Dupré has helped us to go beyond the usual philosophy of God. As he says, "What the transcendent object is *in itself*... Has God *really* spoken to man? Does

---

22 Dupre, *The Other Dimension*, 104.

23 Dupré, "Philosophy of Religion and Revelation," 503.

24 Dupré, "Philosophy of Religion and Revelation," 503.

25 Dupré, "Philosophy of Religion and Revelation," 505.

26 Dupré, "Phenomenology of Religion: Limits and Possibilities," 188.

27 Dupre, *The Other Dimension*, 104.

the transcendent really communicate with the immanent being of consciousness? Those questions do not interest phenomenology."[28] Phenomenology can never give an apt description of the religious act because the terminus of the religious act is never sufficiently immanent in experience so as to be capable of being analyzed. This is not to say that the terminus is not at all immanent, just that it is not sufficiently immanent and phenomenology deals with immanent being. Hence some amount of faith of the believer is necessary, and Dupré admits this when he says, "Actual faith is not a necessary condition for phenomenological analysis. However, without at least some previous experience of faith the full meaning of the religious act must remain closed to the analyst."[29] We have to move from the traditional philosophy of God to a phenomenology and philosophy of religion which must always be complemented with a philosophy of God. Dupré accepts that philosophy alone is unable to reach the idea of God, an idea which is often taken from religious sources and spoken of with the background of religious experience. Arguments from reason cannot bring us to religious conclusions. And so philosophy has no option but to borrow the concept of God from religion. The existence of God cannot be proved because according to Dupré God cannot be reduced to an object. As Dupré says,

> Unless philosophy studies God from *within* the religious experience where his name was first heard, it will always fall into the error... of identifying two differently intended objects without proving that they are identical. The absolute of philosophy solves an intellectual problem. The God of religion brings salvation. The latter is revealed in the religious experience, the former is a product of speculative thinking which borrows the name God from religious language for its own purposes. The metaphysical idea of God is never a subject, while the God of faith is. It is not merely that we speak differently *about* a person (object) than *to* a person. In the case of God we cannot talk *about* him except in a context of talking *to* him.[30]

The brightest aspect of Dupré's works is that his writings cover a vast area and take into consideration the totality of life. He adopts a critical position regarding the different aspects of existence and for this he makes use of various thinkers and philosophers. He does not judge his findings only from one point of view, but he constantly strives to reach a harmony through a constantly developing a dialectic that aims at a final integration. At the same time, very often more than a philosopher of religion, he seems to be a philosopher-theologian. He encourages religion as dialectical, as never purely objective or purely subjective but constantly moving in a dynamic relation between mind and reality, which is influenced by many personal factors, but enables us to express a relationship

[28] Dupre, *The Other Dimension*, 107.

[29] Dupre, *The Other Dimension*, 110.

[30] Dupre, *The Other Dimension*, 130-131.

between the immanent and a transcendent dimension. Insofar as his works enable us to transform the awareness of God that is present in each one of us into an affirmation of transcendence, it leads to a union of creator and created. Dupré believes that this is possible in and through religion and the religious attitude. This concept of transcendence needs a personal commitment and with this the concept of transcendence becomes not just one of the aspects of life, but it becomes the meaning-giving factor of our existence.

7.2 The Justification of Transcendence

7.2.1 Man as a Thinking and Reflecting Being

We begin our reflection on the concept of transcendence with man and especially the being of man. There are different characteristics of man that are conducive to transcendence. One of the most important aspects of man is that he is a reflexive being. It is his capacity to reflect that makes man ask significant questions about the world, about others and more importantly about himself. These questions involve the whole man and are significant because it is the answers to these questions and the process of searching for the answers that gives meaning to man's existence. The questions are also significant because they concern the ultimate 'why' of his existence and hence the questions, the questioning and the search for answers touches man's ultimate being. Deep within man is this openness which is ontological as well as intentional. Man is open to the world and to the infinite. Hence man's capacity for reflection, especially the capacity for self-reflection enables him to go beyond the material confines of this world. He is able to transcend because of this capacity. Another reason for his ability to transcend is that his capacity for reflection is complemented by his intentional openness, as a result of which he is a being-in-the-world but with the capacity and the possibility of going beyond the boundaries of this world.[31]

Man's capacity to transcend is a vocation. It is a special calling that he receives to live a particular way of life. Every individual has a unique vocation that enables that person to live a significant life and at the same time contribute to the well being of the rest of humanity. We are beings immersed in this world but there are two aspects that enable us to live an authentic life. The first is that of 'reflection' and the second significant aspect of man is his freedom. Man has been described as a possibility and it is significant because this aspect highlights that man is able to choose his destiny. Man is able to make choices regarding the Absolute. He can choose to accept it or deny it. He is able to prepare a project for himself in complete freedom. Yet we are also aware that while freedom is a privilege, it comes together with a responsibility which could give rise to *angst*. Hence, man

---

[31] Cf. Giovanni Magnani, *Filosofia della Religione*, 9-10.

has to learn to make proper and responsible use of his freedom because it is only in freedom that man can experience who he really is.[32]

Hence we describe man as a Person and a Subject. As person he is placed in the world, and as being-in-the-world he has a certain personality and a personal identity which makes him unique and different from others. As person he is able to define and know himself, and as person he is recognized and also accepted by others. As person, we come from a particular culture and this background has a large role to play in shaping the person that we are. Our being a person gives us a sense of continuity in time and history, it gives unity and coherence to our lives while at the same time it also allows for diversity because our identity makes us different from the others and gives us a particular place and role in society. It is the diversity and uniqueness of the person that while creating a separation also allows for independence and the possibility to affirm oneself and not get lost in an anonymous existence by living as a non-entity despite being a part of a group. Being a person also allows for one's originality and gives one a personal identity which is given expression in personal acts and actions that express the person that he is, and more significantly it allows a person to give expression to his value system and hence give expression to a deeper and more profound aspect of his personhood.[33]

As person there is always the possibility of a personal relationship with the beyond in responsibility and freedom. As subject his being in history enables him to have an individual identity. As an individual and as part of the human race man experiences that to a large extent he is the result of things and processes outside of himself. Hence he has the possibility of shifting responsibility away from himself. To have a better understanding of man we say that he is made up of matter and spirit, a division that is sometimes referred to as body and soul. But whatever the separation, man is always one united whole. He is very much rooted in empirical reality but his destiny beckons him beyond his origins. The unique aspect of man which makes him a subject and a person is his capacity to know himself, to analyze himself and to ask questions about himself. This is the first step of transcendence, a step that opens up newer and vaster horizons. His questioning makes him realize that he is more than just a sum of the components that make up his external reality. It is this understanding of himself that gives him a knowledge that is within himself, but still gives him a vantage point that is much beyond his empirical reality. It is the spirit in man, his soul, which is very much a part of him yet which cannot be empirically separated from him, which leads him

---

[32] Cf. Magnani, *Filosofia della Religione*, 12.

[33] Cf. Magnani, *Filosofia della Religione*, 24-26.

to transcendence. Man's total presence to himself allows him to confront himself and consequently transcend himself.[34]

Man is part of the world and deals with transcendence in his everyday life. In a way he is under the control of the beyond but as a human being he can also assert himself in freedom and responsibility. When we speak about transcendence it does not make sense to speak of mere transcendence in the superficial sense of the word. Transcendence only makes sense when we look at it in connection with the person who is striving for the beyond and who undertakes the quest. When we understand the person better then we can understand the movement and the quest for transcendence that is part of his being human and being spiritual. Man in his humanness is historically constituted but this historicity is not his whole being. He is in need of the beyond to enable him to uncover and unravel the fullness of his being. It is in and through values that man reaches towards his fullness.

7.2.2 Values as Connected to the Absolute

We can have an intuition of the Absolute value, but we cannot have an immediate experience of the divine. The Absolute has to be received through symbols and acts of concrete beings. René Le Senne speaks of a psychological path of Value. The search for the soul of human existence which tends towards value proceeds in stages. The presence of value first of all is felt in its absence. The lack of something makes us aware of that which is lacking. The soul that is without God knows God in the emptiness it suffers without him. The soul that feels this absence, feels the need of the absolute value, and this presentiment makes it do all it can to receive and achieve the Absolute value. The response to the need is felt in the mediations that direct the search towards the single value. Our vocation to the Absolute Value, our response in hope brings about a spiritual conversion to attain the value. The mature spirit through a complex personal experience receives the revelation through illumination and contact with value. The value assumes our existence and is present in us. It is a presence that illuminates. The main modes of illumination are intellectual, moral, artistic and affective. The desire for the values is what motivates us, and in proportion to our union to value and to its dignity, we find the eternal in the temporal. We need to pass from the historicity in which the values are intuited, that is in their particularity, to the common traits. Things are generally valued because they are a means to an end. But values are treasured because they have a value in themselves and it is this that makes them absolute values. The value is either absolute, or it is not a value. It has significance in itself. The absoluteness of the value is given. The person is oriented towards value.[35]

---

[34] Cf. Karl Rahner, *Foundations of the Christian Faith: An Introduction to the Idea of Christianity*, trans. William V. Dych (London: Darton Longman & Todd, 1978), 26-31.

[35] Cf. Magnani, *Filosofia della Religione*, 105-107.

Another aspect of the Absolute seen in the value is its characteristic of infinity. In the axiological intuition of the value there is an inspiration that surpasses everything given, in which it is manifested, and which projects it towards the absolute. The value always goes beyond, animates and energizes us. It is always present as an infinite halo towards which we move and which we hope to gain in some way. This halo is present in the metaphysical movement and enables us to discover the presence of an Absolute value which is the foundation of all values. In every apprehension of a value there is a metaphysical movement which Le Senne refers to as trust. There is a dynamic participation in trust, and there cannot be trust without a transcendent that attracts us and who cannot betray us. We cannot reject the value, as also we cannot create it. We cannot doubt its reality because we live it continuously. It cannot be reduced to a mere empirical level nor a mere subjective desire. In the religious experience, the first level of participation in the Absolute, we see the connection between the value and the sacred.[36]

7.2.3 The Absolute as Present and Known

We consider the transcendent a mystery, and so because of its ineffability it is difficult to explain how the transcendent enters into our world. Yet the fact is that it does or else it would not preoccupy our minds. The question that arises is, "How are we able to experience transcendence?" "What is the foundation of religious experience?" "Our experience of God, which is an experience of going toward the beyond and trying to attain that beyond: where does it start?" These are questions that need to be confronted.

7.2.3.1 Transcendence in this World

Transcendence is described as the ground of all that has appearance but which cannot have an appearance all of its own. In order to make itself credible even though it is beyond this world, it is necessary that transcendence be a part of the created world. We generally explain this presence of the transcendent in the world through religion and in our religious beliefs. Yet it is difficult for that which is a mystery to have an immediate presence in this world. Its presence would have to be mediated at least in some way so that its presence can be perceived by human beings. The problem arises because the presence of the beyond is not self-evident. As the transcendental ground and horizon of all that has existence in this world, its presence is always in and through the existence of finite things. It is true that finite things are not able to adequately represent the transcendent in its fullness, but at least in their finitude they are able to give us a glimpse and foretaste of the beyond.

The human person searches history and nature for signs and expressions of the presence of the transcendent. The beyond is self-revealing while the person

---

[36] Cf. Magnani, *Filosofia della Religione*, 107-109.

is in search of a fuller subjectivity. This combination enables the relationship to become a reality. The human person is spirit and at the same time is a being who is placed in history. It is his historicity which is the basis of man's relationship with the beyond. Man's openness and questioning nature gives him the impetus to look for signs and explanations of that which is mysterious and beyond. By himself he is unable to comprehend everything and so man is dependent on something that is bigger than him and which is beyond him. But that which is described as beyond need not be apart from us, in the sense of being separate. It could be part of our being as the ultimate foundation, the one ground of all reality. We cannot know individual beings unless we first know being as such, a knowledge that most often is implicit. Our knowledge of finite being is not possible unless in some way we also have knowledge, or at least an awareness of being in its fullness and totality. We cannot speak about different beings until and unless we also have an idea of being in general. Hence in this sense, even before we set out to know being, we already know being.[37]

7.2.3.2 Transcendence and Immanence

When we speak about transcendence, we realize that in the world today we have to confront a major loss of the sense of transcendence among human beings. Transcendence is always connected with man for whom it has significance and hence is connected with immanence. All human beings, given their intelligence and emotions have an orientation towards the beyond. Transcendence generally plays a secondary role in the life of a person, but the acknowledgement of the presence of transcendence is manifested in different ways. Usually it is manifested in religion and in the ritual worship of the divine, but it is also manifested in our respect for the world of nature, and our respect for our fellow human beings who together with us are sharers of this transcendence. Our contact with this infinite reality which is an ineffable mystery would have to be through an experience of transcendence. Yet even in such an experience the contact with the beyond may not be immediate nor self evident. What is very much possible is that such an experience points toward transcendence. This is possible because the transcendent operates in secondary causes through which its presence is manifested. But the transcendent is not merely one in a chain of causes. It is the basis of the chain of causality and it is through the causes that it is present in the world. This presence as already mentioned is not a self-evident presence but it is a unique presence that is historically mediated and yet transcendental. This presence by which the infinite and mysterious beyond intervenes in concrete reality also requires a certain openness on the part of the subject so that it can be received and also perceived. This openness of the subject together with the self-communicating nature of

[37] Cf. Karl Rahner, *Hearer of the Word*, trans. Joseph Donceel (New York: Continuum, 1994), 9-13.

the infinite and mysterious beyond is what makes the relationship between the transcendent and this-worldly creation possible.

Hence, we realize that there has to be a balance between transcendence and immanence. We do not need to sacrifice one for the other. Both can be held simultaneously in a functional relationship which is necessary because in the awareness of its freedom and subjectivity, the person becomes aware of transcendence and is then capable of giving full expression to its personhood and subjectivity. And when the person becomes aware of the presence of the transcendent, its presence becomes meaningful. The freedom of the person in becoming aware of this presence and the self-communicating nature of the transcendent initiates and enables the relationship.[38]

7.2.3.3 A Presence that is Real

Many people tend to be preoccupied with other things and so are not aware of this transcendent presence within themselves, a presence which tends to be overwhelmed by the presence of many other things, and which sometimes is even denied. This could happen due to some misinformation or a defective interpretation of available data as a result of which the presence is wrongly attributed to something else. Hence, we realize that the beginning of the idea of the transcendent within the mind of the individual does not lie outside the individual, but is very much within. The presence is always there. What could be required may be an occasion or a particular phenomenon to trigger off the mind and rekindle the memory. This awareness of the transcendent is unique because while it is always present it is never self-evident, nor does it impose its presence by force. Its presence has to be discovered and has to be responded to. It is like a constant call that awaits a free response in love. It "is mysteriously present in us from the beginning, prior to our concepts, although beyond our grasp without their help, and prior to all our argumentation, in spite of being logically unjustifiable without them: it is the inspiration, the motive power and justification of them all."[39]

The transcendent has been described as the "Being present *par excellence*,"[40] and can be met and encountered everywhere because all things are filled with its unique presence. Sometimes, we are unable to perceive this presence because of our weak intelligence but transcendence always signifies a presence. Transcendence does not mean that the beyond is absent, but only that the presence has not been perceived. The transcendent is never distant from nature and creation,

---

[38] Cf. Rahner, *Foundations of Christian Faith*, 75-89.

[39] Henri De Lubac, *The Discovery of God*, trans. Alexander Dru (Chicago: Henry Regnery Company, 1960), 43.

[40] Pseudo-Dionysius, *Celestial Hierarchy*, iv, I (PG, iii, 177-178); John Scotus, *De divisione naturae*, I, n. 3(PL, cxxii, 443B); n. 72 (518A), as quoted in De Lubac, *The Discovery of God*, 92.

it is near. In this sense we also need to speak of immanence. Henri de Lubac says, "Those who uphold immanence deny transcendence, whereas those who believe in transcendence do not deny immanence. Indeed, they grasp the idea of transcendence sufficiently to understand that it necessarily implies immanence."[41] The transcendent being is wholly within and at the same time is also wholly without. It is completely beyond and yet deeply within. It is all around and at the same time present in us. In fact there is nothing above, outside or without the transcendent.[42]

7.2.4 The Absolute that can be Known

7.2.4.1 Transcendence and Knowledge of the Transcendent

Usually when we speak or write about the transcendent it is always in terms that are meaningful to us and to our fellow human beings. Therefore the question arises, "Are we describing the infinitely mysterious beyond in our terms and as we understand and grasp it, or are we describing it as it is in itself?" To a large extent we cannot avoid this because when talking and communicating we have to use terms and representations that are meaningful to others. If the representations do not make sense to others then we are unable to communicate. We experience this beyond, but our difficulty lies in recounting and representing that which we experience. And so we ask, "How can we know the beyond? How can we perceive transcendence? How does the transcendent become immanent?"

Our knowledge of the transcendent is knowledge that is acquired from the world. It is mediated through our encounter with the concrete reality of things and persons. This knowledge is not immediate but is usually the consequence of some degree of reflection which is necessary. It is in our thinking and reflecting on the absolute mystery that we affirm and become aware of transcendental structures. That we speak about and reflect upon the transcendent is an indicator of a greater knowledge of that transcendent. This is possible because as human beings who are free and intelligent, we are oriented towards that beyond. It is expressed either through the religious activity of prayer or through metaphysical reflection. It is through reflection that all that we know implicitly about our freedom, our subjectivity and our transcendence becomes clearer. Through reflection we are made aware of the mystery. The mystery will never be completely comprehended, but then the mystery takes hold of us and we are in its presence. Our orientation towards this mystery of the beyond is what fuels our quest and it is this orientation that keeps transcendence as a part of our existence.[43]

Our knowledge of the transcendent realm is not a result of our intellectual powers alone, but also depends on the self-disclosure of the transcendent. Because

[41] De Lubac, *The Discovery of God*, 97.

[42] Cf. De Lubac, *The Discovery of God*, 97-99.

[43] Cf. Rahner, *Foundations of the Christian Faith*, 35-39.

of this self-disclosure the subject is able to experience transcendence as a mystery. This mystery is not just something that escapes our comprehension, but it also has a sacredness about it which opens out into an infinite. For this reason it is difficult to define transcendence and give it a name that would do justice to that which it signifies. There is a unity between being and knowing because in its original nature knowing is the self-presence of being, the reflection of being upon itself. We also realize that this reflection and self-presence is not always perfect and so according to the level of self-presence and reflection, being is able to perceive and be aware of the mysterious and infinite beyond. Hence knowing is proportional to the being, in the sense that as a result of more being, more is known of being, and hence, there is more knowing. In pure being there is an identity between being and knowing.[44]

7.2.4.2 The Capacity for Knowing

The human being has the capacity to receive and make at least limited sense of the presence of the infinite mystery and in this is open to revelation from the beyond. In nature and in the world the presence of transcendence is not so clear. Being is intelligible and hence can be communicated and received. When we say that being can be communicated and received, it signifies that the receiver is capable of a judgement on that which is received. When an object or an individual being is grasped, it is grasped as an individual but is subsumed under some larger concept. It is in this sense that it subsists in the knowledge of the knowing subject. We are able to subsume this individual object under a concept which we grasp as a universal due to our power of abstraction. Abstraction enables us to grasp the universal in the singular. We grasp the 'whatness' of the individual object and realize that this 'whatness' that we have grasped is much larger than the individual object. The 'whatness' of this object extends much beyond this finite object and can be used to identify other objects that share the same 'whatness'. The 'whatness' in this sense is unlimited. But not only is it unlimited, in a sense it is prior even to the knowledge of this object and goes much beyond this individual object. This beyond cannot be just another individual object like the one from which we obtained the 'whatness', else we remain where we are. This beyond has to be the absolute horizon of the 'whatness' of that object and consequently would also lead us to the horizon of all objects that can be known. This is possible because human nature has this power which generates a dynamic movement of the spirit in man toward the ultimate horizon. As Rahner says:

> This grasping of all objects in the horizon of being as such is often misunderstood. It does not mean that, after we know the single objects, we combine them under a general point of view. It means rather that to be human is to be spirit because, from the start, in our dynamism toward being

[44] Cf. Rahner, *Foundations of the Christian Faith*, 51-61.

> as such, we grasp single objects as moments of this unending movement of the spirit... We see them right away under this horizon of being as such, on account of which we are always already open for the absolute being of God.[45]

Various thinkers look at this horizon differently. Some hold that this horizon is that of sense intuition and hence not capable of going beyond space and time, while others would see it as tending toward nothingness. Still others see this horizon as tending toward being as such, with no limits. All the same the capacity for abstraction indicates that human beings have a capacity to know transcendence.[46] This takes place through the process of reflection and judgement.

7.2.4.3 Reflection and Judgement

There are different moments in our experience and in the process of reflection and judgment. In a first moment of reflection the spiritual dimension remains implicit and is only the background of the act of intelligence. We begin to understand that it is material objects that occupy the explicit field of our knowledge. But a person who remains immersed in the materiality of objects and makes no effort toward an interior reflection is unable to have an experience of the spiritual dimension. This requires a certain philosophical discipline which enables us to penetrate into a deeper dimension. Yet while all our knowledge is through the senses, it is in the act of judgement that we realize that we are thinking beings and capable of interiority. Such reflection only gives us a vague concept of the spiritual dimension. This requires a second moment of reflection.[47]

The doctrine of St. Thomas on the human judgement is significant in this light and we refer to its exposition by Peter Hoenen.[48] The human judgement is generally an affirmation of a composite intellectual representation. Hence, the judgement is preceded by data that is received through a phantasm, that is to say, an internal sensible representation of a material thing through the external senses. This intellectual representation is a result of the sensible representation. The primary function of the senses is to make this 'presentation' of the object to the mind. The mind through apprehension, the first operation of the intellect, registers this presentation of the senses in a representation. This composite representation through a purely intellectual activity of the mind leads to judgement on the content of representation. The judgement adds nothing to the content but is merely an affirmation by which the mind discovers that the representation conforms to, or is proportionally like the thing.

---

[45] Rahner, *Hearer of the Word*, 52.

[46] Cf. Rahner, *Hearer of the Word*, 44-52.

[47] Cf. Magnani, *Filosofia della Religione*, 97.

[48] Peter Hoenen, *Reality and Judgement According to St. Thomas*, trans. Henry F. Tiblier (Chicago: Henry Regnery Company, 1952).

> Truth, as we have said, is, in its primary significance in the intellect. Now since a thing is true as having the form proper to its own nature, it must follow that the mind, in the act of knowing, is true as having the likeness of the thing known, which is the form of the intellect in the act of knowing. Accordingly truth is defined as conformity between intellect and thing.[49]

Hence, this second operation involves reflection or a 'return' on the first operation. This reflection is only a metaphorical movement and does not involve any change in the intellect. It involves a going forth and a return. There is the apprehension and it is followed by the reflection.[50] Reflection can be divided largely into two categories, one which leads "to the knowledge of the *nature* of the operation to which the mind returns... The other category of reflection leads to the knowledge of the actual presence of an operation."[51] The first category is reserved to the intellect alone while the second category is also found in purely sensible knowledge.[52]

Different reflections lead to different judgements so it is not necessary that philosophical reflection leads to judgement. Reflection is not merely a comparison of the content of the apprehension with the object. "It is only a return of the mind on the first operation itself, and it is in itself that the intellect finds the first justification of its judgement."[53] Thomas Aquinas gives his explanation and justification in *De veritate* Q.1, a.9. where he writes:

> Truth is known by the intellect inasmuch as the intellect reflects upon its act; not only inasmuch as it knows the relationship [proportion] of its act to the thing, which relationship cannot be known unless the nature of the act be [first] known; and this cannot be known unless [at the same time] there is known the nature of the active principle, which is the intellect itself, whose nature it is to be conformed to things; hence the intellect knows truth inasmuch as it reflects upon itself.[54]

Thomas makes a distinction between sense knowledge and intellectual knowledge. In both these cognitions, truth is found as a consequence of the act, insofar as this act has a relation to reality. But only the intellect can know this

---

[49] *S.Th.*, I, q.16, a.2.

[50] Hoenen, *Reality and Judgment*, 137-141.

[51] Hoenen, *Reality and Judgment*, 151.

[52] "In this reflection the intellect can know its own proper operation, the sense cannot. But the sense operation can be known by another sensitive faculty. Thus the 'common sense' (*sensus communis*) knows the operation of the external senses. This operation of the 'common sense' is also a reflection of the soul on the things within it. Note also that the human intellect, in reflecting on the actuality of its operation, knows this latter in its dependence on the object." Hoenen, *Reality and Judgment,* 141.

[53] Hoenen, *Reality and Judgment,* 151.

[54] As Quoted in Hoenen, *Reality and Judgment,* 295.

relationship or presence and it arrives at this knowledge only by a reflection on its first operation. There is a return in both faculties, but it is incomplete in the senses, while it is complete in the intellect.[55] It is incomplete in the senses since it gives knowledge of the act. The sense is able to sense itself sensing. But it is complete in the intellect because the intellect *knows* that its act is true and conformed to the thing. Such a reflection is needed in a judgement. A judgement "is a complete return, that is to say, one which reveals to the intellect the nature of its act, and through this its own nature. It is by reason of its knowledge of this nature that the intellect *knows* that in the preceding representation, it possessed the truth."[56] The judgement then is a result of a reflection of the intellect on its apprehension, that is to say, its relation to the thing. But the truth of the apprehension cannot be known unless the nature of the act is first known. Hence, the knowledge of the nature of the act must *precede* the knowledge of the relation to the thing, that is, it must precede the apprehension. And so we conclude, "the second knowledge is then, always and necessarily, simultaneous with the first, inseparable from it, but the first remains prior in nature (*natura prior*); and everywhere we get the knowledge of the intellect from its act… the first has only a priority of nature."[57] The principle is known by means of the act, or as Hoenen phrases it, "The noetic nature of the intellect is known necessarily and immediately from the knowledge of the noetic nature of the act."[58] The first reflection makes us aware of the noetic nature of the act. The intellect is not explicitly affirmed. The mind remains with the content of the apprehension. A further reflection allows us to arrive at the knowledge of the nature of the intellect.[59]

The transition from apprehension to judgement consists in reflection and is an activity of the mind. This reflection is a preparation that enables a judgement. It starts from the object but then takes on a noetic nature in the representation. The mind understands its own operation and then follows the judgement 'so it is' or 'it is not so'. According to Hoenen, "This operation intuitively contains its own justification; intuitively, by reason of an intuition of its object; and the *esse* with which it is concerned is the *esse* of realism."[60] These judgements arise from the intuition of a necessity. A nexus is intuited from the senses. Yet the motive of the affirmation is independent of the fact that the datum comes from the senses. The motive is intellectual but the representation is concrete. Hence, when we know the nature of the act by reason of the object, the 'act' and the 'object'

---

[55] Cf. *De Veritate*, q.1, a.9. c. (Thomas Aquinas, *Truth*, trans. Robert W. Mulligan (Chicago: Henry Regnery Company, 1952).

[56] Hoenen, *Reality and Judgment,* 152.

[57] Hoenen, *Reality and Judgment,* 159.

[58] Hoenen, *Reality and Judgment,* 159.

[59] Cf. Hoenen, *Reality and Judgment,* 152-159.

[60] Hoenen, *Reality and Judgment,* 288.

may be universal concepts, but they represent a determined proper object. Also, "From the characteristics of the apprehended object as apprehended [we] come to know the nature of this determined act of apprehending... intuitive knowledge of this abstract nature of the intellect can only follow (*natura post*) these first intuitions of the intelligibility of a determined object and of the nature of *this* act."[61] The intuitions are followed by the knowledge of and a judgement on the nature of the intellect. This becomes the object of another reflection which in turn can lead to judgements on the general noetic nature of the intellect. The object of these judgements is the relation of the activity of the intellect to being, and the relation of being to the activity of the intellect. In reflecting, the subject gains knowledge about himself by knowing something other than himself. In going toward the object in order to attain it he goes 'out of himself'. If he knows his act, that is to say, he knows he has 'gone out of himself' he has returned to himself, but this return is still incomplete.[62] "The complete return takes place when he knows a thing placed outside of himself, comes to know not only the act by which he knows the thing, but also himself, the principle of the act, in his proper nature. Only beings endowed with intelligence enjoy this faculty of perfect reflection on themselves."[63] We know and experience the beyond through our religious experience and through religion which gives us a religious attitude. Man's openness to the beyond and the fact that man is also spirit points towards this openness to the beyond. Therefore given man's openness, he experiences the things of this world which are all symbols of transcendence, and through a process of reflection and a complete return in a second reflection, man is able to arrive at and know this transcendence.

7.2.4.4 The Truth of Religion

We are now faced with the question about the truth of religion. We need to refer to the correspondence and the coherence models in order to grasp the truth of religion but the modern emphasis on the subject has made us look also in the direction of the disclosure theory. A philosophical examination of religion should not be reduced to either an objectivist or a subjectivist attitude. The transcendent is neither merely an object of knowledge nor is it a subjective construction. Truth refers to being rather than to knowledge alone, and so in this sense truth is not solely intellectual. Together with truth we also need to look at divine disclosure and revelation. This is necessary because we understand truth as the right relation to the ultimately real. Hence, we need to accept this relation with the ultimately real and also we have to accept that the awareness of this relation is given by the

---

[61] Hoenen, *Reality and Judgment,* 288.

[62] Cf. Hoenen, *Reality and Judgment,* 288-297.

[63] Hoenen, *Reality and Judgment,* 297.

transcendent. The self manifestation of the transcendent has a significant role to play in truth.[64]

The problem is that 'revelation' has to be intelligible and so consequently this revelation resorts to already existing discursive practices. Through symbols and symbolic form the transcendent is given expression and thus become available to the human being. These symbolic forms are generally beyond speech but at the same time are capable of being interpreted. Actually these symbols are not complete unless they are interpreted and so these forms need to be seen in conjunction with religious language. Religious truth therefore requires that there be a continuous and ongoing dialogue between the self-manifestation of the transcendent, and the way in which religion is able to speak about this transcendent. This requires that the message of the transcendent be first of all received, and then interiorized through a process of reflection. Religious disclosure needs to be translated into existence and this happens through an ongoing process of mediation that never comes to an end.

The self-disclosure of the transcendent makes use of discursive practices and this leads to a transformation of that which it inhabits as a symbol. This also initiates a process of interpretation of these symbols on the part of the human being. Hence it creates a response on the part of the human being to its presence within the symbol and this response sets in motion a transformation of the human being. Gradually, the self-manifestation of the transcendent goes beyond the understanding of the self and of Being because it is trying to refer to that which is inexpressible. For this we look to the mystics and their writings which are able to give expression to this paradox.[65]

7.2.5 Religious Experience

7.2.5.1 Our Experience of the Transcendent

A significant issue connected with transcendence would be our experience of transcendence. If the transcendent does not enter into experience then our study would merely be limited to inner intentions and empty expressions of our intentions and would have nothing to do with the transcendent Absolute. We aim at an essential intuition of an object that would in ordinary circumstances lie beyond our experience. To do justice to our study we have to address the fullness of the religious act, in the sense that we have to address religion as experience as well as religion as transcendence. The experience has to be seen in relation to the revelation because the experience renders a transcendental object as intentionally immanent in some way. Purely mental constructions only have a transcendent intentionality, there is no immanence. A religious act cannot be reduced to a mere subjective experience. Psychology does make an attempt, but it only deals

[64] Cf. Dupré, *Religious Mystery*, 20.

[65] Cf. Dupré, *Religious Mystery*, 38.

with the empirical aspect of the religious experience and does not deal with the religious aspect. Still it is able to indicate the emotional component of the religious phenomena. Phenomenology largely deals with the ideal aspect of the religious act. Actions are never completely pure and so their intentionality also is never clearly and easily evident. The challenge is to maintain the transcendence of the religious object while also affirming our experience of this object. It is through religion as experience that man looks for the meaning of life in its totality. Yet the ultimate meaning is 'beyond' but this beyond is not attained by a mere reaching towards. To attain the beyond requires a believing attitude because there is only partial immanence of the transcendent object in material things.

7.2.5.2 The Integral Experience

As person and especially as subject when man is present to himself he is able to recognize within himself a resonance of the divine. This is possible because man has an 'integral experience' as Magnani describes it. It is integral because it includes all aspects. It is personal, interpersonal and takes place within a global totality. It is passive and active and can be got in many ways. A special aspect of this integrality is man's option for freedom. In this option man reveals his choices but more significantly it reveals a hierarchy of values. There are some choices that condition others and choices that sometimes lead to conflict. But the deeper and more significant choices reveal a norm, and consequently the need of a God because the ultimate option is connected to the Absolute. Man not only tends towards God, but is open to him and discovers the presence of the Absolute within himself. This apprehension of a value on which all other values are based is the 'fundamental option' that man makes, and it is this fundamental option that makes man a person. Without this fundamental value man cannot be man. We might not be able to give a definite description of the Absolute, but we refer to it as the Ultimate Reality. More importantly we accept that we are open to this transcendent and given our personhood and subjectivity we have the capability to dialogue with the Ultimate Reality which we refer to as God. God is Spirit and person and not an abstract and empty idea. We enter into a relationship with God through a personal religious experience.[66]

Experience generally signifies an immediate apprehension of something individual, which could be an event, a thing, or a person which results in acquired knowledge. It is generally an external impression that results in internal knowledge. Our openness enables us to be receptive, but we are predisposed to certain experiences. This is significant especially when we speak about spiritual experience. There is a certain ambiguity regarding the spiritual because it is not immediately perceived. We do not experience our essence neither do we experience the spiritual directly, but we do experience our thinking and willing

[66] Cf. Magnani, *Filosofia della Religione*, 15-18.

acts. In accepting these acts we accept that profound dimension within us, without knowing perhaps that it is the 'spiritual'. We accept the spiritual insofar as we accept man's capacity for 'reflection' which indicates a deeper aspect to the self. Naturally this dimension is not evident and neither is it clear. So our knowledge has to pass from a global apprehension to a more determinate knowledge and this is possible through reflection.[67]

7.2.5.3 Religious Experience and the Essence of Religion

Religion is described by Mouroux as the relation to the sacred being as it is, object of adoration, object of love and the end of man. Full communion between man and God is an absolute gift. Religion is a personal relation to God who is the ultimate perfection and supreme act of the human being. Man's vocation is to attain this relation. Religious experience is an integrating experience. It also has an intellectual component namely the idea of God as Truth, a willing component whereby we accept our creaturely condition before the greatness and sanctity of God, an affective component and also an active component. Religion is an experience of the divine which puts man in relation with the totally other. The contact with God is a contact with an abyss which we might never discover. It is a relation with God as the end of man. To understand this and abandon oneself to God is religious experience. It calls for a personalization and an interiorization of the religious act. God is the first and has absolute priority in me. I cannot experience the act by which God creates me, but I can have the experience of having been created by him. In this I experience the divine truth that constitutes me.[68]

Religious experience is always a mediated experience. The presence of God cannot be a direct experience. It has to be an experience through signs. God is not given directly in the experience, but can be grasped in the religious act. Religious experience is the understanding of the mediation that the act realizes, the understanding of the relation it establishes between man and God, and the understanding of God as the end and goal of the relation. There is a great abyss between God and man but all our efforts are directed toward him. We are the image of God, but we are a mere sketch, and so every day we have to build up this image and become more complete. God cannot be possessed fully, we can only grasp his absence and be aware of him as the beyond. But we have hope, and hence we constantly strive to attain full communion. Our desire motivates us to continue our search and not give up even though the goal always seems to be out of our reach. The Absolute is like the supreme participating value. God presents himself to us as the foundational Being and Value. The human intellect is the faculty of the infinite within us and is the background against which personal values can

[67] Cf. Magnani, *Filosofia della Religione*, 95-96.

[68] Cf. Magnani, *Filosofia della Religione*, 113-116.

be accepted. God appears to us as the ultimate founding and participating value, a participation in which he, the infinite donor, makes himself available to us as a gift. The religious experience is the acceptance of the Absolute founding Value that is grasped as the transcendent presence in every value. The level to which it is grasped and accepted depends on our openness to the Divine and also on our capability to recognize that the human person and all human beings are gifts of love received from him. This 'religious' way matures according to a corresponding increase in the experience of the intimate presence which reveals and maintains its transcendence. This happens as man becomes increasingly aware of himself as person. And in this awareness of the Presence man moves towards the infinite richness of God for whom he is destined. This is the result of transmediated intuition of the Absolute Value in the religious signs and in the religious act itself. Religious Experience is a call to salvation as a relation with the divine, a relation to which the whole man is open to and which touches the intimate depths of his being. The analysis of the metaphysical structure of the act which makes one human, namely, freedom, thinking and willing, shows that this act is directed towards the ultimate value in an intentional openness to the Absolute.[69]

The object of religious experience is not an ideal value, but something real which belongs to the order of existence. God is not just a moral ideal of humanity, but is its real foundation. God respects human freedom and extends an invitation to man to discover the world beyond this world, an invitation that is in keeping with man's openness to the mystery. Transcendence does not alienate man, but is a condition for man to be able to attain his fullness. Man is made for the Absolute, the Ultimate reality, which while being beyond is also immersed in the world as the ultimate foundation of all values. It is through participation in the founding value that man is able to avoid falling into the nothingness of existence. Without the ultimate value man is a being unto death.[70]

7.2.6 From an Absolute that is Known to God

7.2.6.1 The Ineffability of God

The deeper we advance into our journey in the quest of the infinite, the more we realize that it is a mystery and cannot be fully understood. When confronted with the Being of God we are forced to confront our own nothingness. It is not that we cannot know 'anything' about God, but just that knowledge of God is unique. At every step of our search we uncover some truths about God. But every truth that we uncover is never the end, but always a beginning. The moment a truth about God is known it becomes insufficient in itself, and now becomes a necessary stepping stone to a further and a deeper truth that brings us one step closer to our goal. In this way our knowledge of the beyond can only increase, and yet since

[69] Cf. Magnani, *Filosofia della Religione*, 117-129.

[70] Cf. Magnani, *Filosofia della Religione*, 129-130.

our knowledge of the transcendent will never be complete, our journey will never end. The knowledge that our finite mind is capable of, would never be sufficient to comprehend the being of the infinite beyond. As St. Augustine would say, "If you have reached an end, then it is not God."[71] While the knowledge of God and the experience of God is so complex, describing this being is even more difficult and complicated. Hence we speak of God as being ineffable.

The ineffability of God does not mean that we should maintain a silence about God, nor does it imply our inability to speak about him at all. The poverty of language and the lack of proper words to describe God makes us only more aware of his ineffability and of our inability to speak about him. We use analogy and symbols to describe him. The description and language we use is always a conclusion we arrive at after having made an effort and so has some significance. Hence it is not an agnosticism that we arrive at, but rather we become aware of the greatness and immensity of that which lies beyond. We resort to negative theology because we realize that the qualities that we affirm of the beyond are affirmed with the knowledge that these do not do justice to him, but are our feeble efforts at describing that being which is above and beyond all that can ever be said of it. As Henri de Lubac says, "The ineffability of God is only another name for absolute transcendence. Silence comes at the end—not at the beginning."[72] Trying to understand God is difficult, but describing him appropriately is impossible.[73] Yet it is in striving to discover ways of experiencing the beyond and giving an expression to our experience so that we can share it with others that makes religion and the religious experience significant.

7.2.6.2 Human Knowledge of the Transcendental Dimension

In this field of the transcendental dimension and of the human knowledge of God there is a dialectical tension as Alfaro describes it.[74] We are torn between a 'yes' and a 'no' because all that we can know about God is to know that we do not know God. Our human intellect is not on the same level as the divine substance which far surpasses it. Hence all that we know of God is limited by our capacities. We know only as much as our limitations allow us to know of him. In himself God far surpasses all that we can ever know of him. In the proposition 'God is', the predicate is included in the essence of the subject because in God, his essence is necessarily identified with his existence. But this is not evident to us because we

[71] St. Augustine, *De civitate Dei*, XII, xviii (PL, xli, 368) as quoted in De Lubac, *The Discovery of God*, 121.

[72] De Lubac, *The Discovery of God*, 122.

[73] Cf. De Lubac, *The Discovery of God*, 119-122.

[74] For this section we refer to the article, J. Alfaro, "La dimensión transcendental en el conocimiento humano de Dios según S. Tomás" in *Gregorianum* 55 (1974), 639-675. We have referred to its Italian translation in Giorgia Salatiello (ed) *Il Soggetto Religioso: Introduzione alla ricerca Fenomenologico-Filosofica* (Roma: Editrice Pontificia Universitá Gregoriana, 1999), 99-138.

do not know the divine essence immediately. We know the existence of God in this world in a mediate way. Our starting point is the reality of the world and we strive to arrive at its ultimate foundation. It is aposteriori knowledge.[75] We are not capable of immediate knowledge of the divine being and hence we cannot have immediate knowledge of its existence.[76]

Divine truth is not accessible in itself because of the weakness of our intellect which is limited to sense experience, and also because of the creaturely condition of the human intellect. No created intelligence by its own natural dynamism can arrive at the vision of God. Based on the fact that man cannot know the existence of God except by starting from a previous knowledge of this world, Thomas Aquinas in the five ways shows that these realities are not intelligible unless they are founded in the divine being, that is to say, unless God exists. The five ways, through motion, efficient cause, contingency, participation and finality are not independent, but need to be understood together in order to arrive at the affirmation that God exists. Each by itself is only a partial aspect, but seen together they lead us to God.[77]

This is so because there is in man an anterior knowledge of God which is different from that which is acquired by reflection on the realities of the world, that is to say through intuition. There is a divine knowledge that is naturally imprinted in us. However this image is not immediate, but is a similarity to God. Thomas Aquinas speaks of an implicit knowledge in the natural desire of God. All that man desires and knows, he desires and knows insofar as he is the image of God. What makes man unique is the spirit within man. It is this spirit within that makes man the peak of the entire universe. Through his being spirit man is open to the infinite horizon of being. It is this same openness and dynamism that allows man to transcend all the beings of the world. The openness of man is due to the boundlessness of man's spirit, and this openness to the infinite meets the infinite horizon of being. This mutual correspondence leads to a perfect balance between man and the universe in which he lives. Besides, this perfect balance also allows for the 'complete return' because the conscience as lived self-presence of the subject in its intentional and willing acts is part of the human experience and reveals the spirit in man. In its orientation toward the infinite horizon of being the spirit in man enables him to be present to himself. The soul is defined by its openness to being, the intellect by its orientation to 'truth' and the will by its tending towards the 'good'. So in a desire or a particular good the will desires the ultimate good towards which it has a natural inclination, an apriori and necessary inclination.

---

[75] Cf. *S. Th.*, I, q.2. a.2. Also Cf. *De Veritate*, q.10, a.12, ad 3.

[76] Cf. Salatiello, *Il Soggetto Religioso*, 99-102.

[77] Cf. Salatiello, *Il Soggetto Religioso*, 103-105.

Hence concrete 'goods' cannot be willed unless they are part of the ultimate good which is willed because it is the end of man. "The highest good is desired… in its likeness, in which manner all things desire the highest good, for nothing is desirable except in so far as some likeness of the highest good is seen in it."[78] Truth and goodness are mutually immanent and convertible because the 'good' is contained in the 'truth' since the object of the will is the true 'good'. The truth is contained in the good because it is the end and good of the intellect. The 'good' is contained in the 'truth' because it is truly intended, and the true is contained in the good as the good that is desired. The truth has priority on the level of intelligibility, while the good has priority on the level of finality. Intelligibility and willing are mutually immanent and equally transcendent, and so are interdependent.

The dynamism of the human spirit toward the ultimate end comes from the will, while the form of the dynamism comes from the intellect. The immanence of the intellect in willing and in its acts gives these acts an 'intelligible inclination'. The will and its acts thus participate in the transcendental light of the intellect. There is a conscious tending towards the 'good'. The apriori tending towards the ultimate perfection of man, and the natural movement toward the good would not have been intelligible unless they were engraved on the spirit of man by the transcendent good. The spiritual dynamism of man is marked by an attraction to the 'ultimate good' and the 'final end'. Hence, in every intentional act and desire there is an implicit knowledge and desire for God.[79] The tending of the spirit toward the ultimate perfection makes the real ultimate the end of all thinking and willing evident:

> … Because God is the last end, He is sought in every end, just as, because He is in the first efficient cause, He acts in every agent. But his is what tending to God implicitly, means. For the efficacy of the first cause is in the second as the principles of reasoning are in the conclusions… All cognitive beings also know God implicitly in any object of knowledge. Just as nothing has the note of appetibility except by a likeness to the first goodness, so nothing is knowable except by a likeness to the first truth.[80]

Every person has an inclination to God, which is expressed in a natural desire for the beatitudes. In knowing his unlimited apriori aspirations man is able to grasp the ultimate real which is the goal of these aspirations, that is to say, God. In identifying God as this beatitude is to say that God is the unique and transcendent end of man. On a deeper level we can even say that this inclination toward God in engraved in the spirit within man. But this inclination has to pass through the formal transcendental of being, namely through the 'beatitudes'. Thomas Aquinas describes them as similar to the divine goodness. We are dealing here with a formal

---

[78] *De Veritate*, q.10. a.12, arg. 5.

[79] Cf. Salatiello, *Il Soggetto Religioso*, 115-124.

[80] *De Veritate*, q.22, a.2. in c. and ad 1.

similarity, that is to say, of a primordial participation of the Transcendent through which created realities concretely participate in the divine being. As beatitudes, the 'truth' and 'goodness' in man belong to the transcendental.[81]

It is in this sense that we can speak of man as the image of God. Man carries within him in his intellect an impression of the natural light for 'truth' and within his will he has a natural desire for 'goodness'. In short, man has an apriori orientation to being. It is in virtue of this orientation that the human spirit is present to itself in all its acts. It is conscious of its unlimited intending and willing and makes the 'complete return'. Through the reality of this world man receives a privileged participation of God and through the orientation towards 'truth' and 'goodness' man transcends his concrete acts of intending and willing, and in this transcending he aims at that one reality that is able to completely satisfy him, namely the transcendent beatitude that is called God. Man knows and desires God naturally inasmuch as he desires the beatitudes that are similar to the divine good. Alfaro says that this thomistic concept of man as the image of God is eminently dynamic. Man has the capacity for God, a radical inclination that triggers a search for God. Man is created by God, in his image, and he reaches his fullness only in God. In his finality there is the stamp of man who through the creative act of God is made in his image.[82]

7.2.6.3 The Sense of the Sacred

What takes place in experience is not sufficient to recognize transcendence. There is need for something more. The individual must be prepared for the encounter so that it can recognize transcendence. Man has this 'sense of the sacred' that makes the recognition of transcendence possible. This 'sense of the sacred' is inbuilt in the mental makeup of man and it gives him an inner conviction by which he is able to recognize transcendence. Transcendence cannot be described as merely that which is not normal, nor can it be said to be that which is beyond the 'powers' of nature. It belongs to a different order but is more than merely trans-empirical. We realize that there is a vast abyss between the immanent and the transcendent and yet they are closely connected. They are not simply two juxtaposed realities. Transcendence is beyond all that can be attained by merely human effort and hence is usually characterized by an element of mystery. But the 'sense of the sacred' is natural to man. It could be in certain events or experiences of his life, certain objects or persons, or just in the awe and wonder of life. Usually this sense of the sacred also gives rise to a particular behaviour which in a way is an acknowledgement of that which is sacred. Today in society this overwhelming sense of the sacred seems to have disappeared. Earlier it was all prevalent and nearly omnipresent. Today it is restricted to some individuals who perceive this presence or to certain events or

[81] Cf. Salatiello, *Il Soggetto Religioso*, 131-132.

[82] Cf. Salatiello, *Il Soggetto Religioso*, 132-134.

objects. The sense of the sacred has not disappeared altogether, but it is definitely less evident and much more hidden than before. This sometimes results in a wrong sense of the sacred, as a result of which, things, persons and events which are not sacred end up being considered as sacred, and this gives rise to questions and doubts about what exactly is sacred.

In every man there is the presence of the sacred, in his body and his spirit. Man is not made up only of matter. There is more to him than a mere empirical body. There are different aspects about man that indicate this presence of the sacred and the beyond. One unmistakeable sign of the sacred in man is his moral conscience. Within each person there is a principle that enables us to make a distinction between good and evil. This capacity to make the distinction is due to our conscience which has been described as a personal guide that we have and require in order to live a worthy life. The conscience always has a role to play in our life and is constantly active. It is our conscience that enables us to live up to our dignity as human beings. Following the dictates of our conscience is not motivated by the promise of a better condition in the after life, but rather it is based on the fact that living a moral life helps us to be better human beings in-this-world. Our conscience is a call to be true to ourselves.

Another aspect according to Henri de Lubac which bears testimony to the presence of the sacred within us, is our modesty, as a result of which we have a feeling of shame. When a person feels ashamed it is because that person feels estranged from himself. Modesty is not connected merely with the clothes we wear but it has to do with man's historical existence. If our liberty is false in the sense that if the exercise of our liberty leads to a separation from our true nature, then it leads to our being ashamed. We are created in the image of God who is love. Through immodesty we are excluded from intimacy with the Absolute. Immodesty breaks our rapport with the Absolute.[83] We also have to be wary of false conceptions of the sacred. Accepting as sacred that which is not sacred is equivalent to idolatry because a thing is given undue importance and value. As Henri de Lubac says, "The truly sacred is not far from any of us. It is not outside of us; it is enshrined in us by our moral conscience and our physical modesty. Anyone who makes himself ever more aware of their double and discreet testimony will find that his apprehension of God will revive in the same proportion and with the sense of the truly sacred."[84]

7.2.6.4 Openness to Being

The sense of the sacred that takes hold of man is not just because of the vast horizon of being within which man lives, but there is within man a dynamism that

---

[83] Cf. Henri de Lubac, *A Brief Catechesis on Nature and Grace*, trans. Richard Arnandez (San Francisco: Ignatius Press, 1984), 293-303.

[84] De Lubac, *A Brief Catechesis on Nature and Grace*, 308.

leaves him open to this horizon. The knowledge that man has of himself is based on what is referred to as a 'pre-apprehension' of being, whereby he is always aware of the infinite horizon of his existence. Some would experience this openness as an emptiness or nothingness, but usually it is hope and a movement towards freedom that makes this striving meaningful. It is man's openness to being in an absolute sense that makes his openness significant, or else it ends in the 'absurd'. This is not just man making meaning of his existence, but the beyond and the infinite horizon that is making itself present to the human being. It is in the presence of this absolute being that man is able to experience that original unity to which all existence tends. Transcendence then is this openness of the subject to being as such, an openness that aims for a presence before being.

When we speak about being we refer to being as such, and not merely to spatio-temporal being. In this sense the infinite horizon of being is not merely a unity of the horizon of the individual being, but it is the horizon of being as such that we refer to. This horizon is what does justice to the spirit within man because it allows for a dynamism toward being, a dynamism that cannot be controlled and satisfied by mere empirical reality. Besides, this infinite horizon of being which allows for the openness of the human being towards being as such also allows for openness to the transcendent. The openness of the human person to being as such is fundamental to the make up of the human being because it is this openness that enables transcendence to be a part of our world. This is the spirit in man, and it is what gives him his spiritual nature. An integral part of our humanness is this constant tending towards and reaching for the beyond, an openness toward the absolute that is always within reach and yet beyond our grasp. This tending toward the beyond is part of our being and it is what makes us unique and gives us our special identity and place in nature. It is man's openness that enables him to strive toward the beyond, a striving through which he attains the fullness of his humanity.[85]

In keeping with the human being as a person with intellect and emotions we also highlight that transcendence is not just a striving for the beyond as a mere principle. Such is the case for transcendence which is merely this worldly. But when we strive for transcendence it is so that we can attain oneness and union with a personal being that is the sum and summit of all being, so that we are freed of all human and earthly constraints and become part of that ultimate reality that unites all. "Man experiences his creatureliness and encounters God in it, not so much in nature, in its stolid and in feeling finiteness, but in himself and in the world… in the unlimited openness of his own spirit."[86]

[85] Cf. De Lubac, *The Discovery of God*, 52-54.

[86] Rahner, *Foundations of the Christian Faith*, 80-81.

7.2.6.5 Man's Openness and Dynamism Towards His End

In asking the ultimate questions about God, and about his essence and existence, man reveals his aspiration to the transcendent. This orientation to the end is part of the deeper level in man, and in which is found the 'image of God'. If God was not found apriori in man's spirit, man would not be able to meet him. His openness to being, through which he is open also to God, is the transcendental condition of every intellectual-willing activity of man and is a consequence of his categorical knowledge. From here we derive an important consequence. The understanding of the thomistic proofs of God demands that the transcendental perspective on which they are founded be taken into consideration. According to Thomas the discursive procedure that leads to the categorical affirmation of the transcendent presupposes the lived and apriori lived presence of God in the human subjectivity. It permits the knowledge of the transcendence that is immanent in the boundless drive of the spirit. Fundamentally it deals with the mental reflection that is guided by the principle of intelligibility, that is, by the transcendental light of being, and ultimately from the same Transcendent being. The thomistic metaphysical vision, on which the validity of the five ways is based, can finally be reduced to the necessity of the supremacy of the 'act' to understand the passage from 'potency to act'. The end, contingency, participation of real beings is not intelligible without the existence of pure Act, Fullness of Being and the Ultimate End. Precisely in the human spirit the passage from potency to act is made visible. All the thinking, willing and acting of man is passing from potency to act and for this it approaches the finite, contingent and the participated. Man carries the mark of his end. The tension between his end and his unlimited aspirations which man cannot fulfil by himself, is not intelligible or understood except as an apriori leaning toward the transcendent fullness, in which the being and essence are absolutely identified. The existence of man as finite spirit, that is to say, as oriented to the real fulfillment of his unlimited aspirations is not intelligible without the existence of God. The transcendent reality is the only one that can give ultimate sense to human existence.[87]

We need to philosophically reflect on God as the meaning and the future of history. Man and the human community in their action in the world, in their creating history, necessarily transcend every means in the act of realizing the act. A fullness that is immanent in history is therefore excluded in virtue of man's unlimited aspirations which constitute the transcendental condition of the possibility of history. The ultimate meaning of history must be transcendent. God is understood as the future that is anticipated in the present becoming of history. It is precisely this transcending of history, this constant attempt by man to attain his ultimate fullness, this 'something more' of the fundamental tendency of the human spirit, the natural desire to see God, which constitutes the radical

[87] Cf. Salatiello, *Il Soggetto Religioso,* 136-138.

capacity of a future fullness and the anticipation of this future fulfillment in the supernatural revelation of God in history. The transcendental and athematic presence of God in man renders him radically capable of grace as the self-revelation and self-gift of God.[88]

7.2.6.6 Transmediated Intuition

This dynamism is possible because of the 'transmediated intuition' which Le Senne speaks about in his book *La Découverte de Dieu.*[89] Transmediated intuition helps us to have a better understanding of the metaphysical sense of the passage from ideal-value to real Spirit value through a dialectic by which all values converge towards a 'one' that all are able to grasp. Man who has a sense of the sacred and is open to Being as such lives by values and all values appear to be oriented towards and converge towards the absolute Value. The solidarity of values leads from the beginning to the Absolute value as the source of all values. In all fields the value would be denied if each value was destined to fight the others. Hence, there is the need for the dialectic that is implied in the reality of the value, so that the values appear as various but are intimately united expressions of 'the' value before it had any determinations. The values therefore appear to us as expressions of the Absolute Value. We encounter them in some way in the intuition. We do not create the values, but we receive them, and so they always appear to us as given, as coming from an infinite source and presented to us as gift. The absolute is obtained through transmediated intuition in the encounter with particular values, as their infinite source or as the well-founded infinite presence. There is no ontological intuition of the absolute Value, but the particularized value that is immediately present in a situation, is seen as converging towards the Absolute from which it is inspired. The confirmation of the value manifests the nature of the value as revealing the gift of the union between us and the Absolute. We do not know the Absolute in itself but we know it only in its participation through values which we receive in proportion to our searching for it. The value is like a bridge between God and us. God is mediated through our intuition of his presence in values. Through the 'transmediated intuition' of values, the infinite becomes available to us finite beings and we can have a justified knowledge of transcendence.[90]

The Affirmation of God

Man's dynamism and openness, together with the sense of the sacred that he possesses, can only be fully satisfied when he is in union or encounters a being that could be an answer to all his striving to go beyond which motivates his entire

---

[88] Cf. Salatiello, *Il Soggetto Religioso,* 138.

[89] R. Le Senne, *La Découverte de Dieu* (Paris: Aubier Montaigne, 1955).

[90] Cf. Magnani, *Filosofia della Religione,* 108-109.

being. He needs to affirm a being that is transcendent. "The affirmation of God rises up from the very roots of being and thought, before all conscious acts before the formation of concepts, conferring upon consciousness its guarantee and upon the concept its universal validity."[91] It is always covered and not very evident, but at the same time is necessary and lies at the basis of all our judgements about being. It is this affirmation of God that gives our thinking and being coherence and consistency. We realize that looking for proof of God's existence is no easy task given the nature of the Absolute and the possibility of our knowledge of the Absolute. The notions and concepts of the Absolute, of the beyond as elaborated by our intelligence, requires a lot of intellectual purification and so runs the danger of ending up in nothingness, or in an affirmation that has no meaning. As we try to give this absolute being a form, being seems to evaporate since God who is pure being and pure existence is beyond all conceptual determinations and images. Thus in a way God is totally unknown to us. Yet when we say God 'is' we believe that this affirmation does justice to him. This affirmation can neither be denied, nor can it be questioned.

While we need to affirm a being that would make our existence and the existence of the beyond meaningful, it is not completely within our power to do so. The affirmation or capacity to make the affirmation must be given to us and hence we refer to it as 'gift'. Henri de Lubac calls this 'gift' the Gift of God. When looked at as a gift we take our endeavour on to another plane. This gives peace to the mind because of the spiritual content on this plane. Quite plainly it is of a different order. Together with Henri de Lubac we feel that, "By allowing us to participate in the Life of God himself, the life of charity furnishes our idea of God with a spiritual content. Instead of interrupting or discouraging the process of purification… this spiritual content helps us to pursue the work in peace; because, on another plane, it ensures at a single stroke the peaceful continuation of that work."[92] This Gift is the 'Spirit of God', the Spirit that makes all things new. This Spirit does not nullify the natural laws of intelligence, just that the increase of knowledge is not of the rational or philosophical order, but is knowledge related to experience. Still since this knowledge is beyond science, it is precarious and obscure because it cannot be possessed as something tangible. We cannot grasp what God is like because God is Charity and can only be grasped in Love. Only sanctity can help us understand him. From a logical point of view it is not a rational justification, but this is the affirmation of the believer.[93]

God is the wholly other, the mysterious infinite beyond and so we cannot pretend that we are capable of comprehending this mystery through rational knowledge alone. God is mystery and remains such and yet through our reason

---

[91] De Lubac, *The Discovery of God*, 107.

[92] De Lubac, *The Discovery of God*, 111.

[93] Cf. De Lubac, *The Discovery of God*, 107-116.

and beliefs we can affirm him even if reason cannot penetrate him. It is the spirit in man that gives man a dynamism toward the ultimate reality. Sometimes, the world that we live in together with the many sciences may distract or block this natural impulse, but deep within us this drive cannot be erased because it is part of our nature. The names by which we refer to God may differ, but that which is intended is the same beyond. "The idea of the Good, the Prime Mover, Necessary Being, the One superior to being, the Universal Principle, Nameless and Formless Deity; God of the Patriarchs, God of Moses... Between each of them [there is] an abyss—yet they are, or at least can be, the same God."[94]

In the apriori and necessary tending of the human spirit toward the final end, and in the desire for the 'beatitude', there is an affirmation of knowledge of God. In this primary intentionality and tendency toward the truth and goodness man is able to attain the transcendent reality which can be the only possible end of his searching. We do not refer to this end as merely an innate idea, neither merely as an immediate intuition of God. We refer to knowledge of God through a double mediation. That is to say through the mediation of the unlimited act of tending to the beyond, and also through the mediation of truth and goodness. Such knowledge of God is transcendental knowledge because it is a-categorical knowledge of God. Such knowledge does not allow us to make a reflexive distinction of God from that which is not God.[95] Only in the act of judgment which he expresses in a categorical proposition does man know the real in that which he has, and is able to distinguish it from every other reality. The transcendental knowledge of God in itself is not a reflexive affirmation of the existence of God. By transcendental knowledge of God alone man does not know that God exists. Man cannot have categorical knowledge of the existence of God without starting from a previous objective knowledge of finite reality, that is, through aposteriori knowledge. But he also has an apriori and transcendental knowledge of God through the formal mediation of goodness, truth and being. God is athematically present from the beginning in the same unlimited fundamental orientation of the spirit to being. The transcendental dimension of human knowledge of God is distinct from the categorical dimension of human knowledge of God. The transcendental dimension of his knowledge is the condition for the possibility of the categorical dimension. Man cannot know objectively, nor can he concretely will anything except in virtue of his unlimited intentionality to being and in the formal mediation of being, to God. The categorical dimension through reflection is the only means that allows a relation of the finite real to God and hence the same apriori orientation

[94] De Lubac, *The Discovery of God*, 116.

[95] For instance, I can know a person is coming walking towards me. But even if it is Matthew who is coming toward me, I may not know it is him. Because I know someone is coming to me, I need not know that it is *Matthew* coming to me.

of the spirit to the transcendent Reality. The transcendental and the categorical constitute two diverse aspects of the human knowledge of God.[96]

7.2.7 The Specific Presence of God in Mysticism

The presence of God is acknowledged by different individuals in different ways. After all that has been said, we are inclined towards the path followed by the Christian mystics which naturally follows a theistic form of mysticism wherein mystical knowledge and the mystical experience is the result of spiritual training that covers the areas of meditation, fasting, prayers, physical discipline and renunciation of the world and its pleasures. We have to remember that the mystical experience is ineffable because of the nature of the experience. It gives a sense of integration with a higher reality which can be attained only with a certain passivity. The mystic who has the experience of union is also aware at the same time of the sense of transcendence. The path that is chosen is the mysticism of love, a path that is dominated by a personal love of God, a love that involves the entire person and also the whole of creation. Hence in love the person is not restricted just to itself as image of God and a relation with God, but it is a relation and identity that involves other human beings and indeed the whole of creation. While stressing the role of humanity we cannot neglect God's presence 'within' creation rather than only 'beyond' creation. It is the immanence of transcendence that allows for a deeply human and earthly quality in Christian Love mysticism as we accept it. It is the mysticism of Ignatius of Loyola, Teresa of Avila, John of the Cross and many others, which includes a full involvement in human cares and worldly concerns. These saints led fully active lives, but were not attached to creaturely love. Their 'love without possessiveness' demands a mental and spiritual purity which is attained after going through a purifying process which can be very demanding and painful and which requires tremendous spiritual strength because it involves renouncing all that is superfluous and also the need of going against one's natural inclinations and desires. This path follows the way of Purgation, the way of Illumination and ultimately leads to Mystical Union, the supreme stage of the mystical experience in which the soul is united to the highest reality. All along the path, we are aware that while it is true that treading this path towards unity requires and demands personal effort, it cannot be achieved solely by one's efforts. It is received only in total openness as a gift that is bestowed from God to satisfy the thirst of the soul for God. This desire is satisfied because there is a mutual possession in which the soul is made divine and through participation is united to God in a gift of love. In this union lies the salvation of man, and ultimately it is this union with the transcendent, that is the goal of human existence.[97]

---

[96] Cf. Salatiello, *Il Soggetto Religioso*, 134-136.

[97] Cf. Louis Dupré, "Mysticism," in *The Encyclopedia of Religion*, Vol. 10 (1987), 245-261.

7.2.7.1 The Image of God

Man is seen by some as the 'image of God'. As Henri de Lubac says, "Man, made in the image of the incomprehensible God, is ultimately incomprehensible to himself."[98] The imprint of God is within us but we are not fully responsible for this image in the sense that we do not construct this image.[99] The image is given to us. It is our very selves. Yet, even though this presence of God is within us, it is not a presence that controls the activity of our mind. The presence is manifested in us, but does not control our thinking and willing faculties. It is not that the presence of God has no say at all because most of what we are and do is a response to this presence which has been described by philosophers[100] as the light that illuminates our reason.[101] It is this that can be described as the divine in man. As Henri de Lubac says of the soul:

> It possesses nevertheless a certain 'habitual knowledge' of itself, real in spite of being obscure and veiled, constant although forever fleeting—owing to the fact that it is always present to itself; the presence of the soul present to itself, in which it may learn, as in a mirror, the presence of God to the soul. In the same way that the reality of the divine image in the soul is at the centre and principle of all rational activity, which should lead it from knowledge of the world to the affirmation of God, so, in the same way the soul's habitual knowledge of itself can become the principle of an intimate process of reflection enabling it to recognise its reality as 'image'.[102]

Insofar as man is able to bear witness to the presence of transcendence within himself by leading a free and responsible life, he is able to attain the fullness of his existence, he is the image of God and reaches the fullness of his being man.[103] When we refer to man as the image of God, the individual has to be aware of this image within. That is to say the individual has to live in a continuous awareness of the presence of God. The more the person is aware of this image, the more he strives to conform to this image. This comes about because the awareness of the 'image of God' within results in a certain comprehension of the mystery of the transcendent that resides within. So it involves an inward turn through a process of mental and physical discipline, and contemplation on God who is present in

---

[98] De Lubac, *The Discovery of God*, 12.

[99] This idea of man as the 'image of God' is borrowed from Henri de Lubac. De Lubac also speaks of man as mystery and paradox besides being created in the image of God. His is a fascinating presentation but here we restrict ourselves to the concept of 'image of God.'

[100] St. Thomas, *Tertia*, q.v, a.4, ad 2 m; *De Veritate*, q. xvi, a.3, as quoted in De Lubac, *The Discovery of God*, 15.

[101] Cf. St. Augustine, *Soliloquies*, I, vi, 12 (PL, xxxii, 875) as quoted in De Lubac, *The Discovery of God*, 15.

[102] De Lubac, *The Discovery of God*, 16-17.

[103] Cf. De Lubac, *The Discovery of God*, 12-17.

the soul. As we proceed along the path of conversion into the image of God, it leads to a greater identity and finally ends in union.

7.2.8 Conclusion

We realize that our answer to the questions connected with transcendence are connected to two basic problems regarding experience and the possibility of knowledge of transcendence. The foundation of our explanation is based on Henri de Lubac's explanation of man who is a mystery, a paradox and an image of God. This is also the foundation of religious experience since it points towards the reality of the Ultimate Transcendent. De Lubac's contribution is significant because he speaks of the presence of God in man thus allowing for an experience of the transcendent. Besides by allowing for the immanence and transcendence of God he makes allowance for his presence in the world. But then being religious and the religious experience is not sufficient. Together with this we are aware of man's capacity for reflection. Man is a subject who is constantly reflecting on his experience. It is this capacity for reflection, especially '*riflessione totale*' that enables man to go deeper into himself and into the reality around him. This complete return is what makes for transcendence.

Still all this would be incomplete and end up in a blind alley if there was no God as the foundation of the religious experience. Man's reflection is also a reflection on a God who makes himself present. The God who reveals and man who is open to the transcendent enter into a dialectic that leads to transcendence. Naturally this movement of transcendence needs a gnoseological foundation and for this we have referred to Le Senne and Magnani's explanation of 'transmediated intuition' as an answer to immanentism. Man is a thinking and reflecting being who lives by certain values. These values are significant because there is an Absolute Value and this absolute is what gives meaning to man and his existence. The finite cannot think and be if there is no Absolute. Yet this absolute is still beyond, and this Absolute is not God. Through religion the Absolute is able to have a real presence and the individual can have a personal rapport with it. This is not a mere presence, but a known presence. The Absolute is thus known through its manifestations. Religious experience is an experience of the manifestation and presence of the Absolute which is a presence through participation, and thus we are able to enter into a personal relationship with the Absolute who is God. Thomas Aquinas would say that our knowledge of God is possible because he is implicit in all knowledge as the founding truth. From values to the perception of the absolute value, it is the transmediated intuition that indicates the absolute truth of values which then points towards the presence of God. The mystics are able through a path of reflection, discipline and prayer, to arrive at union with God, and the particular religions are various paths to salvation for man.

This journey is dependent in the first place on man who is able to reflect and who is open to the infinite horizon and a God who reveals. It is this that enables the discovery of the Presence that is there, a dynamic presence of the Absolute. This Absolute is not a fictional being but as the real absolute is the foundation of religion. Man naturally seeks relationships and so his ultimate seeking leads him to the Absolute and thus to transcendence. Transcendence is a way that is possible because the Absolute that is Being manifests himself, and man is capable of perceiving this presence because of his openness to the ultimate horizon. This he does following the path of transcendence.

General Conclusion

In conclusion we can say that Dupré has enabled us to have a fair understanding of the concept of transcendence. Through transcendence we have a better grasp of the self as a subject that is open to transcendence, the religious object as a self-manifestation that allows for transcendence, and of religion as dialectical and thus enabling a relationship between the immanent and transcendent dimension. This allows for a religious affirmation of transcendence which in turn is an affirmation that gives meaning to human existence. A practical aspect of this affirmation is a commitment to undertake the search for transcendence and to strive and attain transcendence by arriving at a synthesis that follows a three-fold path of Purgation, Illumination and ending in Union. And so about transcendence we say in Dupré's own words, "Transcendence is no longer found above creation but *in* creation. The creature is *in* God and God is *in* the creature. It is *as creature* and not only as uncreated essence that the creature manifests transcendence: God is the ultimate dimension of the finite reality."[1]

Dupré has described himself as a philosopher who reflects on religion. To do this, he critically reflects on the works of a number of philosophers, anthropologists, theologians, psychologists and spiritual writers down the ages. He approaches all of them with respect, while keeping a philosophical distance and is able to make his own synthesis. His synthesis is grounded in experience and so he follows a phenomenological method. He goes on to interpret the religious act and so sees the necessity of faith. But then since he is dealing with transcendence he also goes beyond phenomenology to examine religion and its various expressions. His goal is to arrive at a future in which spiritual men and women regard,

> Existence increasingly as an indivisible unity, wholly worldly and self-sufficient, yet at the same time they will be aware of a mysterious depth dimension that demands attention and that they allow to direct their basic attitude to their life. They may start from the negative experience of life lived in a secular environment, deprived of a transcendent meaning... Theirs will rather be a spirituality of world-affirmation, a mystique of creation

[1] Dupré, *The Other Dimension*, 525.

> that discovers a transcendent dimension in a fundamental engagement to a world and a human community perceived as totally autonomous and totally dependent.[2]

At the end of this study we can say that Louis Dupré is a person who makes a very serious and critical reflection on religion and the religious attitude. It is difficult to classify him solely as a philosopher who reflects on religion, but I find it more significant to refer to him as a thinker who makes significant reflections on fundamental questions. Dupré's reflection is largely phenomenological and so his study is usually based on the religious act and on religion as experience, but his style is not only phenomenological. The religious act is an awareness of God while the philosophical act is speaking about God. Since, he deals with both of them it is natural that one has an effect on the other.

As Dupré says the believer will generally not trust the efforts of philosophy to explain the religious attitude because philosophers generally look at God's existence and God's essence independently of the religious experience. Yet, the idea of God comes from the religious experience and so we have restricted our study to the experience and to an interpretation of this experience. Unfortunately, in the world today we "seldom encounter the sacred in an objectively given, universally attainable reality… Our way leads through private reflection and personal decision. Almost nothing appears directly sacred to us."[3] Where earlier nearly everything appeared to be sacred and had a trace of the sacred, we seem to have lost this sense of the sacred. Dupré holds that as a result of our culture we can no longer expect to experience the sacred 'out there', in reality, but rather we have to turn inward and aim to the rediscover the transcendent in the inner self. For Dupré this inward movement is imperative if we are to rediscover the transcendent. This movement inward to rediscover the transcendent would be the finding of a lost treasure for some, while for others especially in the modern culture it would be an entirely new discovery. But the aim of this journey inward and indeed of the whole of spiritual life would be to discover the image and to become the image through a greater unity with it. This is what Dupré aimed for in his synthesis because through interiority it would be possible to rediscover and revive the religious dimension of human life and man could once again discover the openness to transcendence.

In this book, we have restricted our study to transcendence in the religious sense. While for Dupré transcendence is not a univocal term and is used in different senses, in most cases he speaks of transcendence in connection with religion. As Dupré says, "The important thing to remember from this is that the term *transcendent*, so essential for religion, develops dialectically and takes various meanings in different contexts. It is always transcendent *in relation to* what

[2] Dupré, *Religious Mystery*, 143.

[3] Dupré, Transcendent Selfhood, 29.

surrounds it."[4] We have restricted ourselves to the religious aspect of transcendence because according to Dupré, "Faith alone can free the transcendent message from its immanent appearance... For the transcendent as such does not appear. What makes words and deeds surpass their intramundane appearance is the constitutive act of faith."[5] It is faith that enables the relationship with the transcendent. Faith does not have new data or new information, but what it does is that it gives a new attitude as a result of which the same data is seen in a different way. Dupré is clear that "the paradox of divine transcendence is that it can be consistently maintained only as long as God is conceived as fully immanent."[6] In this sense, he draws our attention to the immanence of transcendence, an immanence that is for us a presence. To be aware of this presence requires a perspective which he describes as "a divine perspective in which the finite and infinite remain united in God. In this perspective, transcendence, rather than constituting the opposition between finite and infinite, reveals the divine essence of the finite."[7] We agree with Dupré that what is needed is a new attitude and a new perspective. What we refer to may not be brand new, but is more of a different outlook that makes us open to the transcendent dimension of the real. It is this open outlook and attitude, especially embodied in religion that can help us perceive the presence of the transcendent in the immanent.

The path that Dupré traces out to rediscover transcendence and return to an awareness that earlier came naturally to the human being, is the path of Christian love. This is a path that proceeds through purgation and illumination, to finally arrive at union in love. The believer today in the face of "the practical atheism of his entire culture, is left no choice but to vitalize this negative experience and to confront his feeling of God's absence... Our age has created an emptiness that for the serious God-seeker attains a religious significance."[8] Dupré is well aware of the situation of modern man and the path that he suggests takes this situation of the loss of transcendence into consideration. Man today has to pass through the absence of God to arrive at the presence of transcendence. "Dread of the void around his contingent existence is the experience in which modern man is most poignantly confronted with the mystery of transcendence."[9] This is the mystical experience that through an inward turn is able to penetrate deeper into the source of selfhood, a way inward that leads upward.[10]

---

[4] Dupré, *The Other Dimension*, 16.

[5] Dupré, *The Other Dimension*, 294.

[6] Dupré, "Transcendence and Immanence as Theological Categories," 9.

[7] Dupré, *Religious Mystery*, 140.

[8] Dupré, *Religious Mystery*, 139.

[9] Dupré, *The Other Dimension*, 30.

[10] Cf. Dupré, *Transcendent Selfhood*, 93.

Having made a study of the writings of Louis Dupré we realize that we have undergone a journey. More than examining the writings of Louis Dupré we are aware that his writings have been a stimulus and have been the catalyst that has enabled us to undergo this journey. This study has led to a concept of transcendence as a journey that has to be undertaken, with the help of religion and the religious attitude, and it is through these that one is able to arrive at a synthesis that can be put together from the various fragments that are at our disposal in the universe. Dupré himself has not yet arrived at a synthesis, but his writings are the building blocks on which we can build up our own concept of transcendence.

The building blocks are available. The edifice of transcendence is ours to construct.

Bibliography

PRIMARY SOURCES

Books by Louis Dupré

and Don Saliers (Ed. and Intro.) *Christian Spirituality III: Post–Reformation and Modern*. World Spirituality: An Encyclopedic History of the Religious Quest, Vol. 18. New York: Crossroad, 1989.

The Common Life: The Origins of Trinitarian Mysticism and its Development by Jan Ruusbroec. New York: Crossroad, 1984.

Contraception and Catholics: A New Appraisal. Baltimore: Helicon Press, 1964.

The Deeper Life: An Introduction to Christian Mysticism. New York: Crossroad, 1981.

A Dubious Heritage: Studies in the Philosophy of Religion after Kant. New York: Paulist Press, A Newman Book, 1977.

The Enlightenment and the Intellectual Foundation of Modern Culture. New Haven and London: Yale University Press, 2004.

(Ed. and Intro.) *Faith and Reflection*, by Henry Duméry. trans. Stephen McNiernery and M. Benedict Murphy. New York: Herder and Herder, 1968.

Kierkegaard as Theologian: The Dialectic of Christian Existence. New York: Sheed and Ward, 1963.

and James Wiseman (Ed.) *Light from Light: An Anthology of Christian Mysticism.* New York: Paulist Press, 1988.

Marx's Social Critique of Culture. New Haven: Yale University Press, 1983.

Metaphysics and Culture. The Aquinas Lecture, 1994. Milwaukee: Marquette University Press, 1994.

The Other Dimension: A Search for the Meaning of Religious Attitudes. New York: Doubleday, 1972.

Passage to Modernity: An Essay in the Hermeneutics of Nature and Culture. New Haven: Yale University Press, 1993.

The Philosophical Foundations of Marxism. New York: Harcourt, Brace and World, 1966.

Religious Mystery and Rational Reflection. Grand Rapids: Eerdmans, 1997.

Symbols of the Sacred. Grand Rapids: Eerdmans, 2000.

Transcendent Selfhood: The Loss and Rediscovery of the Inner Life. New York: Seabury Press, A Crossroad Book, 1976.

Articles by Louis Dupré

"Aesthetic Perception and its Relation to Ordinary Perception." in *Aisthesis and Aesthetics.* Ed. Erwin Straus and Richard Griffith. Pittsburgh: Duquesne University Press, 1970, 171-177.

"Alienation and Redemption through Time and Memory: An Essay on Religious Time Consciousness." *Journal of the American Academy of Religion* 43 (December 1975): 671–679.

"Alternatives to the Cogito." *Review of Metaphysics* 40 (June 1987): 687–716.

"The Argument of Design Today." *The Journal of Religion* 54 (1974): 1–12.

"Ascent and Decline of a Self-Centered Culture." in *Individuality and Cooperative Action.* Ed. Joseph Earley. Washington, D.C.: Georgetown University Press, 1991, 137–147.

"Autonomy of Man and Religious Dependence in the Philosophy of Henry Duméry." in *Evolution in Perspective: Commentaries in Honour of Pierre Lecomte de Nouy.* Ed. George Shuster and Ralph Thorson. Notre Dame: University of Notre Dame Press, 1970, 161–169.

"A Basic Misunderstanding." *Humanist* 34 (January – February 1974): 10–11.

"Blondel, Maurice." in *The Catholic Encyclopedia for School and Home*. New York: McGraw-Hill, 1965, I: 734–735.

"The Broken Mirror. The Fragmentation of the Symbolic World." *Stanford Literature Review* 5 (Spring – Fall 1988): 7–24.

"Camus, Albert." in *The Catholic Encyclopedia for School and Home*. New York: McGraw-Hill, 1965, II: 211–212.

"Catholic Education and Predicament of Modern Culture." *The Living Light* 23 (June 1987): 295–306.

"Catholics and Birth Control After *Humanae Vitae*." in *Exploding Humanity*. Ed. Henry Regier and Bruce Falls. Toronto: Anansi, 1969, 57–64.

"The Challenge of Marxism." *Cross Currents* 12 (Summer 1962): 327–335.

"The Christian Experience of Mystical Union." *The Journal of Religion* 69 (January 1989): 1–13.

"Christian Philosophy: What is it? What could it be?" *American Catholic Philosophical Quarterly* 71 (Supp 1997): 25–29.

"Christian Spirituality Confronts the Modern World." *Communio: International Catholic Review* 12 (Fall 1985): 334–342.

"The Closed World of the Modern Mind." *Religion and Intellectual Life* 1 (Summer 1984): 19–29.

"The Common Good and the Open Society." *Review of Politics* 55 (Fall 1993): 687–712.

"The Concept of Truth in Husserl's Logical Investigations." *Philosophy and Phenomenological Research* 24 (March 1964): 345–354.

"The Constitution of the Self in Kierkegaard's Philosophy." *International Philosophical Quarterly* 3 (December 1963): 506–526.

"The Cosmological Argument after Kant." *International Journal for Philosophy of Religion* 3 (Fall 1972): 131–145.

"The Despair of Religion." *The Owl of Minerva* 16 (Fall 1984): 21–30.

"The Dialectic of the Mystical Experience." in *The Challenge of Religion: Contemporary Readings in Philosophy of Religion*. Ed. Frederick Ferre, Joseph Kockelmans, and John Smith. New York: Seabury Press, 1982, 247–255.

"Dialectical Philosophy before and after Marx." *The New Scholasticism* 46 (Autumn 1972): 488–511.

"The Enigma of Religious Art." *Review of Metaphysics* 29 (September 1975): 27–44.

"Evil – A Religious Mystery: A Plea for a More Inclusive Model of Theodicy." *Faith and Philosophy* 7 (July 1990): 261–280.

"Experience and Interpretation. A Philosophical Reflection on Schillebeeckx's Jesus and Christ." *Theological Studies* 43 (March 1982): 30–51.

"Faith and Reason." in *The Philosophy of Brand Blanshard*. The Library of Living Philosophers 15. Ed. Paul Schilpp. La Salle: Open Court, 1980, 996–1001.

"Feuerbach, Ludwig Andreas." in *The New Catholic Encyclopedia*. New York: McGraw-Hill, 1967, V: 904–905.

"Form and Transformation in the Modern Conception of Humanness." *Proceedings of the American Catholic Philosophical Association* 69 (1995): 47–55.

"From Augustine to Janssens." *Commonweal* 80 (June 5, 1964): 336–342.

"From Marx to Freud." *Philosophical Psychology* 1 (Summer 1980): 1–11.

"From Silence to Speech: Negative Theology and Trinitarian Spirituality." *Communio: International Catholic Review* 11 (Spring 1984): 28–34.

"The Glory of the Lord." in *Hans Urs von Balthasar*. Ed. David Schindler. San Francisco: Ignatius Press, 1991, 183–206.

"The Glory of the Lord: Hans Urs von Balthasar's Theological Aesthetic." *Communio: International Catholic Review* 16 (Fall 1989): 384–412.

"The God of History." *Commonweal* 85 (February 10, 1967): 516–522.

"Hans Urs von Balthasar's Theology of Aesthetic Form." *Theological Studies* 49 (June 1988): 299–318.

"Has the Secularist Crisis Come to an End?" *Catholic Council of Intellectual and Cultural Affairs Bulletin* 16 (Fall 1974): 60–68.

"Has the Secularist Crisis Come to an End?" *Listening* 9 (Autumn 1974): 7–19.

"Hegel and the Enlightenment." *The Owl of Minerva* 28 (1996): 13–26.

"Hegel Reflects on Remembering." *The Owl of Minerva* 25 (Spring 1994): 141–146.

"Hegel's Absolute Spirit: A Religious Justification of Secular Culture." *Revue de l'Universite d'Ottawa* 52 (October – December 1982): 554–565.

"Hegel's Concept of Alienation and Marx's Reinterpretation of it." *Hegel- Studien* 7 (1972): 217–236.

"Hegelianism and Neo-Hegelianism." in *The New Catholic Encyclopedia*. New York: McGraw-Hill, 1967, VI: 990–993.

"History as revelation." In *The Challenge of Religion: Contemporary Readings in Philosophy of Religion.* Ed. Frederick Ferre, Joseph Kockelmans, and John Smith. New York: Seabury Press, 1982, 269–277.

"Hope and Transcendence." in *The God Experience: Essays in Hope*. The Cardinal Bea Lectures 2. Ed. Joseph Whelan. New York: Newman Press, 1971, 217–225.

"Husserl's Notion of Truth – Via Media Between Idealism and Realism?" in *Teaching Thomism Today.* The Proceedings of the Workshop on Teaching Thomism Today conducted at the Catholic University of America, 1962. Ed. George McLean. Washington, D.C.: The Catholic University of America Press, 1963, 150–182.

"Husserl's Thought on God and Faith." *Philosophy and Phenomenological Research* 29 (1968): 201–215.

"The Idea of Historical Progress in Marx and Marxism." *Yale Review* 69 (Autumn 1979): 33–43.

"Idealism and Materialism in Marx's Dialectic." *Review of Metaphysics* 30 (June 1977): 649–685.

"Ignatian Humanism and its Mystical Origins." *Communio: International Catholic Review* 18 (Summer 1991): 164–182.

"Intimations of Immortality." in Filosofia e religione di fronte alla morte. Archivio di Filosofia 49 (1981): 259–277.

"Introduction, and the Major Philosophical and Theological Works of Nicholas of Cusa." in *Nicholas of Cusa. Special Issue: American Catholic Philosophical Quarterly* 64 (Winter 1990): 1–6.

"Is the History of Philosophy Philosophy?" *Review of Metaphysics* 42 (March 1989): 463–482.

"Kant's Theory of History and Progress." *Review of Metaphysics* 51 (4) (1998): 813–828.

"Kierkegaard on Man's Encounter with the Transcendent." in *Religion in Contemporary Thought*. Ed. George McLean, Staten Island: Alba House, 1973, 101–115.

"Kierkegaard, Soren." in *The Catholic Encyclopedia for School and Home*. New York: McGraw-Hill, 1965, VI: 146–148.

"The Life and Death of Religious Symbols." *The St. Luke's Journal of Theology* 14 (May 1971): 3–9.

"Marx and Religion: An Impossible Marriage." *Commonweal* 88 (April 26, 1968): 171–176.

"Marx and the Reintegration of Culture." in *Philosophy and Culture*. Proceedings of the 27th World Congress of Philosophy. Ed. Venant Cauchy. Montreal: Editions Montmorency, 1988, II: 311–315.

"Marx, Karl." in *The Encyclopedia of Religion*. Ed. Mircea Eliade. New York: Macmillan, 1987, IX: 238–240.

"Marx's Critique of Culture and its Interpretations." *Review of Metaphysics* 34 (September 1980): 91–121.

"Marx's Critique of Objectivism and the Rise of Cultural Alienation. " in *Intersoggettivita socialita religione*. Ed. Marco Olivetti. *Archivio di Filosofia* 54 (1986): 653–667.

"Marx's Idea of Alienation Revisited." *Man and World* 14 (1981): 387–410.

"Marx's Theory of Economics as Socio-Cultural Activity." *South African Journal of Philosophy* 2 (August 1983): 123–129.

"Marxism and Religion." in *Religion in Contemporary Thought*. Ed. George McLean. Staten Island: Alba House, 1973, 87–100.

"Meditations on Secular Theology." *The Christian Century* 85 (November 20, 1968): 1469–1472.

"Metaphysics and Religious Faith." in *The Future of Metaphysics*. Ed. Robert Wood. Chicago: Quadrangle Books, 1970, 263–273.

"The Modern Idea of Culture: Its Opposition to its Classical and Christian Roots." in *Modernity and Religion*. Ed. Ralph McInerny. Notre Dame: University of Notre Dame Press, 1994, 1–18.

"The Moral Argument, the Religious Experience and the Basic Meaning of the Ontological Argument." *Idealistic Studies* 3 (September 1973): 266–276.

"The Mystical Experience of the Self and its Philosophical Significance." *Proceedings of the American Catholic Philosophical Association* 48 (1974): 149–165.

"The Mystical Theology of Nicholas of Cusa's *De visione dei*." in *Nicholas of Cusa on Christ and the Church*. Ed. Gerald Christianson and Thomas Izbicki. Leiden: Bril, 1996, 205–220.

"Mysticism." in *The Encyclopedia of Religion*. Ed. Mircea Eliade. New York: Macmillan, 1987, X: 245-261.

"Nature and Grace in Nicholas of Cusa's Mystical Philosophy." *American Catholic Philosophical Quarterly* 64 (Winter 1990): 153–170.

"Nature and Grace: Fateful Separation and Attempted Reunion." in *Catholicism and Secularization in America: Essays on Nature, Grace, and Culture*. Ed. David Schindler. Notre Dame: Communio Books 1990, 52–73.

"Negative Theology and Affirmation of the Finite." in *Experience, Reason and God, Studies in Philosophy and the History of Philosophy*. Ed. Eugene Long. Washington, D.C.: The Catholic University of America Press, 1980, 149–157.

"A New Approach to the Abortion Problem." *Theological Studies* 34 (September 1973): 481–488.

"The New Humanist Manifesto." *Current* (December 1973): 22–27.

"New Publications in Phenomenology." *The New Scholasticism* 40 (April 1966): 199–216.

"Note on the idea of Religious Truth in the Christian Tradition." *Thomist* 52 (July 1988): 499–512.

"Of Time and Eternity in Kierkegaard's Concept of Anxiety." *Faith and Philosophy* 1 (April 1984): 160–176.

"On Being a Christian Teacher of Humanities." *The Christian Century* 109 (April 29, 1992): 452–455.

"On the Intellectual Sources of Modern Atheism." *International Journal for Philosophy of Religion* 45 (Fall 1999): 1–11.

"Phenomenology of Religion: Limits and Possibilities." *American Catholic Philosophical Quarterly* 66 (Spring 1992): 175–188.

"Phenomenology." in *Teaching Thomism Today*. The Proceedings of the Workshop on Teaching Thomism Today conducted at the Catholic University of America, 1962. Ed. George McLean. Washington, D.C.: The Catholic University of America Press, 1963, 371.

"Philosophical Analysis of the Catholic Moral Problem of Contraception." *Insight* 6 (Fall 1967): 57–59.

"The Philosophical stages of Self-Discovery." *Thought* 39 (September 1964): 411-428.

"Philosophy and its History." in *At the Nexus of Philosophy and History*. Ed. Bernard Dauenhauer. Athens: University of Georgia Press, 1987, 20–41.

"Philosophy and Religious Faith." in *The Human Person and Philosophy in the Contemporary World*. Proceedings of the Meeting of the World Union of Catholic Philosophical Societies, 1978. Ed. J. Zycinski. Cracow: The Pontifical Faculty of Theology, 1980, 352–384.

"Philosophy and the Natural desire for God: An Historical Reflection." *International Philosophical Quarterly* 40/2 (2000): 141–148.

"Philosophy and the Religious Perspective of Life." Presidential Address *Proceedings of the American Catholic Philosophical Association* 45 (1971): 1–8.

"Philosophy of Religion and Revelation: Autonomous Reflection vs. Theophany." *International Philosophical Quarterly* 4 (December 1964): 499–513.

"Philosophy's Uses and Abuses." *Commonweal* 75 (October 6, 1961): 36–38.

"Positivism." in *The Catholic Encyclopedia for School and Home*. New York: McGraw-Hill, 1965, VIII: 601–604.

"Postmodernity or Late Modernity? Ambiguities in Richard Rorty's Thought." *Review of Metaphysics* 47 (December 1993): 277–295.

"The Problem of Divine Transcendence in Secular Theology." in *The Spirit and Power of Christian Secularity*. Ed. Albert Schlitzer. Notre Dame: University of Notre Dame Press, 1969, 100–112.

"Rationality in Marx's Concept of History." *Tijdschrift voor Filosofie* 40 (September 1978): 418–451.

"Reflections on a Catholic/Humanist Dialogue." *The Humanist* 32 (July 1972): 36–40.

"Reflections on Blondel's Religious Philosophy." *The New Scholasticism* 40 (January 1966): 3–22.

"Reflections on the Truth of Religion." *Faith and Philosophy* 6 (July 1989): 260–274.

"Religion as Alienation, Ideology, and Utopia in Marx." *Logos* (USA) 5 (1984): 29–40.

"Religion as Representation." in *The Legacy of Hegel.* Proceedings of the Marquette Hegel Symposium 1970. Ed. J. O'Malley, K. Algozin, H Kainz, and L. Rice. The Hague: Martinus Nijhoff, 1973, 137–143.

"Religion in a Secular World." *Christianity and Crisis* 28 (April 15, 1968): 73–77.

"Religion, Ideology and Utopia in Marx." *New Scholasticism* 50 (Autumn 1976): 415–434.

"The Religious Crisis of our Culture." *Yale Review* 65 (Winter 1976): 203–217.

"The Religious Meaning of Secularity." in *Religion in Contemporary Thought.* Ed. George McLean. Staten Island, NY: Alba House, 1973, 311–322.

"Ritual, the Sacralization of Time." *Man and World* 19 (1986): 143–153.

"Ritual: The Divine Play of Time." In *Play, Literature, Religion: Essays in Cultural Intertextuality,* SUNY Series - The Margins of Literature. Ed. Virgil Nemoianu and Robert Royal. Albany: State University of New York Press, 1992, 199–212.

"Secular Man and His Religion." Proceedings of the American Catholic Philosophical Association 42 (1968): 78–92.

"Secular Philosphy and its origins at the Dawn of the Modern Age." in *The Question of Christian Philosophy Today.* Ed. Ambrosio Francis. New York: Fordham University Press, 1999, 61-79.

"Secularism and the Crisis of our Culture: A Hermeneutic Perspective." *Thought* 51 (September 1976): 271–281.

"Situation Ethics and Objective Morality." *Theological Studies* 28 (June 1967): 245–257.

"Spiritual life and the Survival of Christianity: Reflections at the End of the Millennium." *Cross Currents* 48 (Fall 1998): 381–390.

"Spiritual life in a Secular Age." *Daedalus* 111 (Winter 1982): 21–31.

"The Teleological Argument." in *The Challenge of Religion: Contemporary Readings in Philosophy of Religion.* Ed. Frederick Ferre, Joseph Kockelmans, and John Smith. New York: Seabury Press, 1982, 128–138.

"Theodicy: The Case for a Theologically inclusive Model of Philosophy." *Proceedings of the American Catholic Philosophical Association* 64 (1990): 24–39.

"Toward a Revaluation of Schleiermacher's Philosophy of Religion." *The Journal of Religion* 44 (April 1964): 97–112.

"Transcendence and Immanence as Theological Categories." *Catholic Theological Society of America Proceedings* 31 (June 9 – 12, 1976): 1–10.

"The Transcendent and the Sacred." in *The Challenge of Religion: Contemporary Readings in Philosophy of Religion.* Ed. Frederick Ferre, Joseph Kockelmans, and John Smith. New York: Seabury Press, 1982, 38–49.

"Transcendent Selfhood and Religious Community." *Listening* 13 (Winter 1978): 38–47.

"Transitions and Tensions in Hegel's treatment of Determinate Religion." *American Catholic Philosophical Quarterly* 64 (Autumn 1990): 429–439.

"Truth in Religion and Truth of Religion." in *Phenomenology of the Truth Proper to Religion.* SUNY Series in Philosophy. Ed. Daniel Guerriere. Albany: State University of New York Press, 1990, 19–42.

"The Truth of Religion." in *Morality Within the Life and Social World: Interdisciplinary Phenomenology of the Authentic Life in the "Moral Sense."* Analecta Huserliana 22. Papers of the 15th International Phenomenology Congress, 1985. Ed. Anna-Teresa Tymieniecka. Dordrecht: D. Reidel, 1987, 457–463.

"*Unio mystica*: The State and the Experience." in *Mystical Union and Monotheistic Faith: An Ecumenical Dialogue.* Ed. Moshe Idel and Bernard McGinn. New York: Macmillan; London: Macmillan, 1989, 3–23.

"Western Civilization: The Spiritual Crisis of our Culture." in *Minds Without Borders: Educational and Cultural Exchange in the Twenty-first Century.* The Fulbright 40th Anniversary Washington Conference Proceedings. Ed. Anne Rogers Devereux and George Seay. Washington, D.C.: USIA – Smithsonian Institution – Woodrow Wilson International Center, 1988, 32–39.

SECONDARY SOURCES

Boeve Lieven and John Ries. *The Presence of Transcendence: Thinking 'Sacrament' in a Postmodern Age.* Leuven: Peeters, 2001.

Caillois Roger. *Man and the Sacred.* Trans. Meyer Barash. New York: The Free Press of Glencoe, 1959.

CASARELLA Peter, and SCHNER George P. (Ed.) *Christian Spirituality and the Culture of Modernity: The Thought of Louis Dupré.* Grand Rapids: Eerdmans, 1998.

CASARELLA Peter. "On Dupré's Passage to Modernity." *Communio (US)* 21 (Fall 1994): 551–561.

DALY Gabriel. *Transcendence and Immanence: A Study in Catholic Modernism and Integralism.* Oxford: Clarendon Press, 1980.

DANIELOU Jean. *God and the Ways of Knowing.* Trans. Walter Roberts. New York: Meridian Books, 1965.

DESCARTES Rene. *Oeuvres.* Ed. Adam Tannery. Paris: Vrin, 1964.

DUMÉRY Henry. *La foi n'est pas un cri.* Paris, 1959.

________. *Le probleme de Dieu.* Paris-Bruges: Desclee de Brouwer, 1957.

ELIADE Mircea. *Patterns in Comparative Religion.* Trans. Rosemary Sheed. New York: Sheed and Ward, 1958.

________. *The Sacred and the Profane: The Nature of Religion.* Trans. Trask Willard. San Diego: Harcourt. Inc., 1957.

________ and Joseph KITAGAWA. Ed. *The History of Religions.* Chicago: Chicago University Press, 1959.

FARRELLY John. "Religious Reflection and Man's Transcendence." *Thomist* 37(1973): 1-68.

FAULCONER James E. Ed. *Transcendence in Philosophy and Religion.* Bloomington: Indiana University Press, 2003.

FREUD Sigmund. *Civilization and its Discontents.* Trans. James Strachey. New York: W. W. Norton, 1962.

FROMM Erich. *The Sane Society.* New York: Fawcett Publications, 1968.

GANDHI M.K. *Gandhi Selected Writings.* New York: Harper, 1972.

HAMANN Johann Georg. *Socratic Memorabilia.* Ed. and trans. James C. O'Flaherty. Baltimore: John Hopkins Press, 1967.

HEGEL Georg W. F. *Encyclopädie* (1831). Trans. William Wallace. Oxford: Clarendon Press, 1971.

________. *Lectures on the Philosophy of Religion.* Ed. Peter Hodgson. Berkeley: University of California Press, 1988.

________. *Phenomenology of Spirit,* Trans. A. V. Miller. Oxford: Oxford University Press, 1977.

________. Vorlesungen über die Philosophie der Religion. Ed. Georg Lasson. Hamburg, 1966.

HEIDEGGER Martin. *Being and Time.* Trans. Edward Robinson and John Macquarrie. New York: Harper and Row, 1962.

________. *Existence and Being.* Chicago: Henry Regnery, 1949.

HILL William. "The God of the Other Dimension." *New Scholasticism* 50 (1976): 212-222.

HOENEN Peter. *Reality and Judgement according to St. Thomas.* Trans. Henry Tiblier. Chicago: Henry Regnery, 1952.

HORKHEIMER Max. *The Eclipse of Reason.* New York, 1947.

HUBER Carlo. *Speaking of God.* Washington D. C.: The Council for Research in Values and Philosophy, 2000.

HUDSON Donald. "The Concept of Divine Transcendence." *Religious Studies* 15 (1979): 197-210.

HUME David. *Dialogues Concerning Natural Religion.* Buffalo: Prometheus Books, 1989.

JAMES William. *The Varieties of Religious Experience: A Study in Human Nature.* New York: Simon and Schuster, 1997.

JOHN OF THE CROSS. *Ascent of Mount Carmel.* Trans. Allison Peers. New York: Doubleday-Image, 1958.

JONAS Hans. *The Phenomenon of Life.* University of Chicago Press, 1982.

KANT Immanuel. *Religion Within the Limits of Reason Alone.* Trans. Theodore Greene and Hoyt Hudson. New York: Harper & Row, 1960.

________. *Opus Posthumum.* Ed. Erich Adickes. Berlin, 1920.

KAUFMAN Walter. Ed. *The Portable Nietzsche.* New York: Viking, 1954.

KIERKEGAARD Soren. *Either/Or.* Trans. David Swenson and Lillian Swenson. Princeton: Princeton University Press, 1944.

________. *Fear and Trembling.* Trans. Walter Lowrie. Princeton: Princeton University Press, 1941.

________. *Philosophical Fragments.* Princeton: Princeton University Press, 1962.

________. *Samlede Vaerker,* X. *Unscientific Postscript.* Trans. David Swenson and Walter Lowrie. Princeton: Princeton University Press, 1944.

KRINGS Herman. Ed. *Concetti Fondamentali di Filosofia.* Italian edition. Ed. Giorgio Penzo. Trans. Gerardo Cunico et al. Volume III. Brescia: Editrice Queriniana, 1982.

LEVESQUE Paul. Symbols of Transcendence: Religious Expression in the Thought of Louis Dupré. Louvain: Peeters, 1997.

LEVESQUE Paul. "A Symbolical Sacramental Methodology: An Application of the Thought of Louis Dupré." *Questions Liturgiques/Studies in Liturgy* 76 (1995): 161–181.

LONG Eugene. "Quest for Transcendence." *Review of Metaphysics* 52/1 (1998): 3-19.

LUTHER Martin. *Martin Luther, Selections from his Writings*. Ed. John Dillenberger. Trans. Karlfried Foelhlich. New York: Doubleday, 1961.

MAGNANI Giovanni. *Filosofia Della Religione*. Roma: Editrice Pontificia Università Gregoriana, 1993.

________. *Metodologia Fenomenologica Interdisciplinare delle Scienze della Religione*. Roma: Editrice Pontificia Università Gregoriana, 1996. (Ad uso degli studenti.)

________. *Religione e Religioni: Dalla Monolatria al Monoteismo Profetico.* Roma: Editrice Pontificia Università Gregoriana, 2001.

________. *Religione e Religioni: Il Monoteismo*. Roma: Editrice Pontificia Università Gregoriana, 2001.

________. Storia Comparata delle Religioni: Principi Fenomenologici. Assisi: Cittadella Editrice, 1999.

MARÉCHAL Joseph. *Studies in the Psychology of the Mystics*. Trans. Algar Thorold. New York : Magi Books, 1964.

MAGRIS Aldo. *Fenomenologia Della Trascendenza.* Milano: Guerini Studio, 1992.

NEVILLE Robert. *God the Creator: On the Transcendence and Presence of God.* Chicago: The University of Chicago Press, 1968.

________. Ed. *Ultimate Realities*. New York: State University of New York Press, 2001.

NEWMAN John Henry. *An Essay in Aid of a Grammar of Assent*. Oxford: Clarendon Press, 1985.

NIEBUHR Richard. *The Meaning of Revelation.* New York: Harper and Row, 1962.

OLSON Alan and Leroy ROUNER. Ed. *Transcendence and the Sacred.* Notre Dame: University of Notre Dame Press, 1981.

OTTO Rudolf. The Idea of the Holy: An Inquiry into the non-rational factor in the Idea of the Divine and its Relation to the Rational. Trans. John Harvey. London: Oxford University Press, 1923.

RAHNER Hugo. *Man at Play* . Trans. Brian Battershaw and Edward Quinn. New York: Herder and Herder, 1967.

RAHNER Karl. Hearer of the Word: Laying the Foundation for a Philosophy of Religion. Trans. Joseph Donceel. New York: Continuum, 1994.

________. *Spirit in the World.* Trans. William Dijch. New York: Herder and Herder, 1968.

Ruusbroec Jan. *The Adornment of the Spiritual Marriage.* Trans. Dom C. A. Wijnschenck. London, 1916.

Salatiello Giorgia. Ed. *Il Soggetto Religioso: Introduzione alla ricerca Fenomenologico-Filosofica.* Roma: Editrice Pontificia Università Gregoriana, 1999.

Scheler Max. *On the Eternal in Man.* Trans. Bernard Noble. New York: Harper and Brothers, 1960.

________. *The Christian Faith.* Trans. H. R. Mackintosh and J. S. Steward. Edinburgh, 1928.

Schleiermacher Friedrich. *On Religion: Speeches to its Cultured Despisers.* Trans. Richard Crouter. Cambridge: Cambridge University Press, 1988.

Tauler Johannes. *Signposts to Perfection: A Selection from the Sermons of Johannes Tauler.* Ed. and trans. Elizabeth Strakosch. St. Louis: B. Herder Book Co., 1958.

Torrance Robert. *The Spiritual Quest: Transcendence in Myth, Religion and Science.* Berkeley: University of California Press, 1994.

Van Der Leeuw Gerardus. *Religion in Essence and Manifestation.* Trans. J.E. Turner. Princeton : Princeton University Press, 1963.

Whitehead Alfred. *Symbolism: Its Meaning and Effect.* Cambridge: The Cambridge University Press, 1958.

Zdybicka Zofia. *Person and Religion: An Introduction to the Philosophy of Religion.* Trans. Theresa Sandok. New York: Peter Lang, 1991.